STUDIES IN THE EARLY HISTORY OF BRITAIN

General Editor: Nicholas Brooks

The West Midlands in the Early Middle Ages

The West Midlands

in the Early Middle Ages

Margaret Gelling

Leicester University Press   1992
Leicester, London and New York

Distributed in the United States and Canada
by St. Martin's Press, New York

First published in Great Britain in 1992 by
Leicester University Press (a division of Pinter Publishers Limited)

Trade and other enquiries
25 Floral Street, London WC2E 9DS, England

Editorial office
Fielding Johnson Building, University of Leicester,
University Road, Leicester LE1 7RH, England
and Room 400, 175 Fifth Avenue,
New York, NY 10010, USA

British Library Cataloguing in Publication Data

A CIP catalogue record for this book is available
from the British Library

Library of Congress Cataloging-in-Publication Data

A CIP catalog record for this book is available
from the Library of Congress

ISBN 0-7185-1170-0
     0-7185-1395-9 (pbk)

Typeset by Mayhew Typesetting, Rhayader, Powys
Printed and bound in Great Britain by Biddles Ltd., Guildford and King's Lynn

Contents

Foreword

The aim of the *Studies in the Early History of Britain* is to publish works of the highest scholarship which open up virgin fields of study or which surmount the barriers of traditional academic disciplines. As interest in the origins of our society and culture grows while scholarship yet becomes ever more specialized, interdisciplinary studies are needed more urgently not only by scholars, but also by students and laymen. The series will therefore include research monographs, works of synthesis and also collaborative studies of important themes by several scholars whose training and expertise has lain in different fields. Our knowledge of the early Middle Ages will always be limited and fragmentary, but progress can be made if the work of the historian embraces that of the philologist, the archaeologist, the geographer, the numismatist, the art historian and the liturgist - to name only the most obvious. The need to cross and remove academic frontiers also explains the extension of the geographical range from that of the previous *Studies in Early English History* to include the whole island of Britain. The change would have been welcomed by the editor of the earlier series, the late Professor H.P.R. Finberg, whose pioneering work helped to inspire, or to provoke, the interest of a new generation of early medievalists in the relations of Britons and Saxons. The approach of this series is therefore deliberately wide-ranging. Early medieval Britain can only be understood in the context of contemporary developments in Ireland and on the continent.

Margaret Gelling here continues the notable series of regional volumes which aim to provide brief, well-illustrated and up-to-date syntheses of the settlement and history of the principle regions of early medieval Britain. Her survey of five West Midland counties provides an instructive contrast with Pauline Stafford's companion volume on the East Midlands. In the west, though the English dominated the politics, the influence of the British element in the population was much greater; and the Anglo-Saxon and Danish transformation of the landscape were correspondingly less radical. Margaret Gelling brings to her analysis a unique understanding of the development of the place-names of the region, which enables her to pinpoint for the first time otherwise unrecorded developments and relationships. Once again a regional approach makes clear that our understanding of early English and British history can best be advanced through such detailed local study.

N.P. Brooks
University of Birmingham, June 1991

List of Figures

Acknowledgements

My greatest debt is to Harry Buglass, who has drawn or redrawn most of the illustrative material. His skill and experience in this type of drawing are invaluable, and it has been a great pleasure to work with him. Graham Norrie, also of the School of Antiquity at Birmingham University, has employed his consummate skill on the photographs. A constantly changing text was typed with patience and good humour by Valerie Howard, to whom also I am most grateful.

Professor Nicholas Brooks has taken a close interest in the project over many years. There have been times, in the agonies of successive rewritings, when I could have wished for a less conscientious General Editor; but the final version is much better for his insistence on clarity and precision.

Illustrations have been culled from many sources, and requests for permission to use them have been met with great courtesy. The sources of all illustrations other than those prepared for this book or taken from my own publications are acknowledged in the captions. I hope that the authors will be pleased with the use I have made of their work.

I am particularly indebted to Bill Ford for plans and brooch-drawings from the Warwickshire cemeteries of Alveston and Stretton on Fosse, and for information about these excavations in advance of publication.

It has been extremely convenient that Professor Brooks, Mr Buglass, Mr Norrie, Mrs Howard and myself are all based in the Arts Faculty of Birmingham University. I depend heavily on the University's facilities, particularly those provided by the library, where Dr B.S. Benedikz is a never-failing source of help.

Birmingham, 8 November 1991   Margaret Gelling

1 The Region

The area chosen for this study is that occupied by the pre-1974 counties of Cheshire, Staffordshire, Shropshire, Warwickshire and Herefordshire. Worcestershire is omitted, which leaves a gap in the southern half of what would otherwise be a rough rectangle. The survival of the monastic cartularies of Worcester and Evesham means that the documentation available for the pre-Conquest period in Worcestershire and Gloucestershire is on a totally different scale from that which survives for the five counties listed above. The Anglo-Saxon sub-kingdom of the Hwicce requires a different type of study, based on this rich archival material, some aspects of which have been explored in recent studies by Professor C. Dyer (1980), Dr Della Hooke (1985) and Dr P. Sims-Williams (1990). The south-western half of Warwickshire was also in the Hwiccan sub-kingdom, but surviving Anglo-Saxon charters are not so numerous for that area that it cannot be conveniently studied in the present volume. The significance of the eastern boundary of the area is that it divides our territory from the Danelaw. The five counties which are studied here constitute a large part of western Mercia as it crystallized briefly in the late ninth century.

In terms of the whole series, the area occupies the space between the East Midland counties covered by Dr Pauline Stafford's book (1985) and the whole country of Wales which is the subject of Professor Wendy Davies's volume (1982). It is remarkable how different it is from these neighbouring regions, both in its physical characteristics and in its history. It will be useful to consider the geography of the area in some detail, as this is likely to have been a factor of major importance in the developments of the post-Roman period.

Physical Geography: Elevation (fig. 1)

There is some mountainous country. The Pennines intrude into north Staffordshire and into the eastern edge of Cheshire. The Welsh mountains encroach on west Herefordshire and take up a large portion of south-west Shropshire and a much smaller one of the north-west of that county. In south-east Shropshire there are the two large massifs of the Clee Hills. Further east, in Staffordshire and Warwickshire, there is the modest elevation of the Birmingham Plateau, which occasionally, as in Cannock Chase, in the Clent and Lickey Hills, and at Barr Beacon, is too high for settlement. High ground is, however, the exception in the area as a whole. Much low ground is provided by the river-systems of the Trent, Severn and Avon, which surround the Birmingham Plateau; and in Herefordshire the broad plains of the Wye, Lugg and Frome occupy the major part of the county. Cheshire and north Shropshire constitute a single great plain which extends

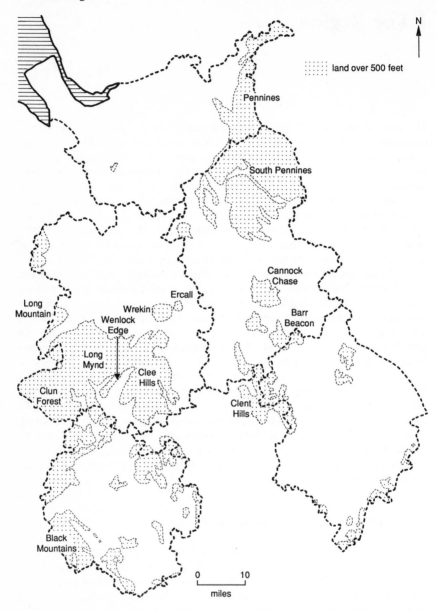

N

land over 500 feet

Pennines

South Pennines

Cannock
Chase

Ercall

Long
Mountain

Wrekin

Wenlock
Edge

Barr
Beacon

Long
Mynd

Clee
Hills

Clun
Forest

Clent
Hills

Black
Mountains

0   10

miles

Figure 1 High ground.

eastwards across the centre of Staffordshire; and in this large area only a
few small massifs, like that of the Wrekin and the Ercall south-east of
Shrewsbury, are too high for settlement except in Iron Age terms.

Physical Geography: River-systems (fig. 2)

The area contains two major watersheds: that which separates the rivers flowing through Cheshire to the Irish Sea from those which run either to the North Sea, via the Trent, or to the Bristol Channel, via the Severn; and the one which separates the feeders of the Trent from those of the Severn. Both watersheds coincide to a noteworthy degree with county boundaries.

To the north of the Staffordshire/Cheshire and the Shropshire/Cheshire boundary the drainage is to the north-west, to the Mersey and the Dee which flow into the Irish Sea on either side of the Wirral Peninsula. The county boundaries diverge from the watershed in places, but they follow its general direction. The watershed starts near the northern tip of Staffordshire and runs south west and then west till (at a point north of Oswestry) it runs between the Morlas Brook (which flows into the Dee) and the headwaters of the River Perry, which is a tributary of the Severn. The Staffordshire boundary is initially along the River Dane, to the north of the watershed; but it follows it fairly closely for about five miles to Mow Cop, after which it diverges to the north again, so that a number of settlements such as Talke, Balterley and Madeley lie in Staffordshire in spite of being on streams which are feeders of the River Weaver, a tributary of the Mersey. The projecting tongue of Shropshire which constitutes the parish of Woore has the watershed running down its spine. West of this, the Shropshire boundary follows the watershed with only minor divergences till it reaches the point north of Oswestry which is referred to above.

The dividing line between the streams which drain south-west to the Severn and those which drain north-east to the Trent runs close to the west side of Birmingham. Dudley Stamp (1946: 209) observed that 'Birmingham itself is an almost unique example of a large town situated nearly on a water parting.' The River Stour, rising in the Clent Hills near Romsley, flows west and then south to join the Severn at Stourport. The Bell Brook, a long tributary of the Stour, rises a short distance to the south, on the opposite side of Romsley Hill. The River Rea, however, rises near Gannow Green, a short distance to the east, and flows north-east through Birmingham to the Tame. This is close to the Worcestershire/Warwickshire boundary, but the watershed then cuts across Staffordshire for some distance before meeting the Shropshire boundary east of Albrighton and Donington. A narrow ridge separates the headstreams of the Stour from those of the Penk, then the watershed runs north, with the county boundary along it, for about five miles. After that the county boundary lies to the west of the watershed, which runs north with no major change of direction till it meets the valley of the River Sow, a major tributary of the River Trent. It curves west round the headwaters of the Sow, then east to Maer, where it meets the ridge beyond which the streams drain to the Irish Sea.

South of Birmingham, the Trent/Severn watershed is marked by the Lickey Hills, east of which it coincides with the Worcestershire/Warwickshire boundary for a short stretch before taking a meandering course north-eastwards across Warwickshire, eventually following a very narrow line between the headwaters of the Anker (flowing north) and those of the

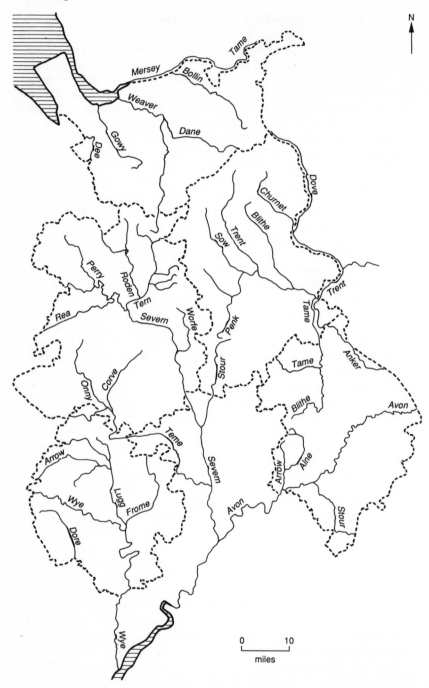

N

Figure 2   River-systems.

Sowe (flowing south). The artificial nature of Warwickshire as an administrative unit is emphasized by this division between the two major river-systems.

Physical Geography: Marsh and Heath

Just as the mountain areas are small by comparison with Wales, the marshes of the West Midland counties are insignificant compared with those of Lincolnshire and Huntingdonshire in the East Midlands. There is a large moss, roughly four miles long and two miles wide, on the boundary between Shropshire and the detached portion of Flintshire. This is called Fenn's Moss on the north of the county boundary (preserving the name – *the Fennys, the Fens* – by which it is called in sixteenth- and seventeenth-century references). On the Shropshire side it is named Whixall Moss and Wem Moss from the parishes in which it lies. It was never reclaimed for cultivation, though in the eighteenth century squatter hamlets grew up round its edges, some with expressive names like Cuckoo's Corner and World's End. It produces excellent peat. There are many smaller mosses in north Shropshire and in Cheshire.

Marshes more amenable to drainage and to agricultural and pastoral use are referred to by the place-name element *mōr*. A notable instance is the Weald Moors in Shropshire, with its settlements on raised patches for which the word *ēg* 'island' is used in place-names. The name Weald Moors, from Old English *wilde* 'waste', implies that the area had reverted to swamp when English colonists first saw it; but when the drainage was maintained the ground was valuable for dairy farming. Not all the 'moors' were amenable to this treatment in early times. Baggy Moor, also in Shropshire, on the course of the River Perry north of Ruyton-Eleven-Towns, was not brought under control until 1861, when an Act for its improvement was passed.

There is an interesting small marsh in Herefordshire in the basin which was formed by the collapse of the geological formation known as the Wigmore Dome. The picturesque ruin of Wigmore Castle overlooks this. It is fertile farmland, but is subject to the periodic eruption of blister bogs in different places, and it must have been this characteristic which caused the Anglo-Saxons to name it 'beetle marsh'.

There are a number of instances of the special type of flood-plain which the Anglo-Saxons designated *wæsse*, which are characterized by sudden flooding and equally sudden draining. These are referred to in the place-names Bolas and Buildwas (Shropshire), Rotherwas and Sugwas (Herefordshire), Alrewas and Hopwas (Staffordshire) and Broadwas (Worcestershire). The one at Buildwas is the most dramatic.

A distinctive feature of north Shropshire is a series of small lakes. The largest is the one which gives name to the town of Ellesmere. Hanmer, in the detached part of Flintshire, is named from a northern outlier. There is a smaller group to the south, between Baschurch and Myddle, and another to the north-east, the largest of which, Comber Mere, is in Cheshire. These lie in hollows in the glacial drift which covers the area. The meres of north

Cheshire, between Northwich and Altrincham, which are of comparable size, are in some instances formed by the subsidence of underlying rock-salt strata.

Areas of heath in the West Midland counties are mostly small. Dunsmore Heath in south Warwickshire is about four miles long and not much over a mile broad. Hine Heath in Shropshire is perhaps four miles square. Rudheath in Cheshire was quite large in medieval times, perhaps five miles by four. There are stretches of heathland in Cannock Chase. Many other patches of heathland in the five counties are, however, of a size to be contained within a parish, or shared by a small group of parishes.

Ancient Woodland

In the absence of large areas of mountain, marsh and heath, communications throughout the five counties would only be hampered by large areas of forest coverage. The extent of this coverage in post-Roman times can be estimated, probably with a high degree of accuracy, from the evidence of place-names.

It has been established beyond reasonable doubt that the place-name element *lēah* is a reliable indicator of the presence of ancient woodland at the date when English speech was gaining the ascendancy in the greater part of southern Britain. The word has gradations of meaning, from 'forest' through 'glade or clearing' to 'pasture' and 'meadow'. In settlement-names the sense 'clearing' is very much the commonest. Names in which this sense is appropriate frequently occur in clusters, and sometimes in belts as in north Warwickshire. An isolated *lēah* name (like Elmley Castle in Worcestershire and Willey in Warwickshire) is more likely to contain the word in its ancient sense 'wood' or its late Old English meaning 'meadow'. The period during which *lēah* was very productive as a place-name element is likely to have been c.750–c.950.

In the West Midland counties, the mapping of place-names containing this element provides convincing evidence for the extent of woodland in the middle Anglo-Saxon period. The reference will sometimes be to ancient, pre-English, settlements in a forest environment (as probably in north Warwickshire), sometimes to areas on the outer fringes of ancient forests which were being progressively cleared by the Anglo-Saxons when the names arose (as probably in the area north of the surviving part of Wyre Forest on the Worcestershire/Shropshire/Staffordshire border). Detailed study of each belt or cluster of -ley names is required in order to gauge the extent of settlement when the Anglo-Saxons formed these names, and also to distinguish between primeval forest and areas which had reverted after being cleared and settled in the Roman period. But the mapping of -ley names separates out the wooded areas of the early Anglo-Saxon period in a quick and effective manner, giving a good base for more refined studies.

In an article published in 1974 I presented a map for a large area centred on Birmingham which showed all names containing the elements *tūn* and *lēah* (Gelling 1974: 64; 1988: 127). There are a number of viable translations for *tūn*, ranging from 'farm' to 'estate'. The main reason for considering the

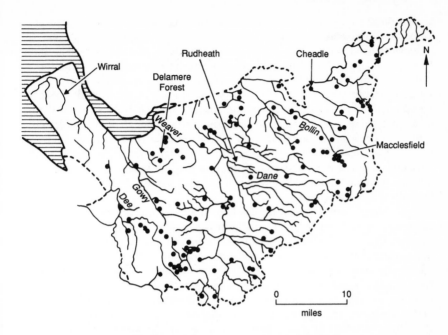

Figure 3 Cheshire: place-names containing *lēah*.

two elements together was that while they are overwhelmingly the commonest place-name terms in this large region, they are, to a considerable extent, complementary in their distribution, the use of *tūn* being restricted to areas which were not wooded. The map has proved very useful. Many conclusions can be drawn about the areas which are characterized by each type of name, and about the areas where neither are found. These last are either areas of very early English settlement, or areas of very late colonization. The comparison between the two words is not altogether sound, however, because *lēah* is frequently used in the naming of places of very minor status, and this is much rarer for *tūn*. So one is sometimes comparing late-recorded farm-names in *-lēah* with Domesday Book manors in *-tūn*, and some of the *lēah* names do not refer to settlements at all, but to actual woods. For the narrower purpose of estimating the extent of woodland in the post-Roman period it will be more useful to have maps of each of our five counties showing just the names containing *lēah*. These are provided in figs. 3-7. The criteria for inclusion are the appearance of the name on the 1″ Ordnance Survey map seventh series, and the existence of documentation from dates not later than the sixteenth century.

Woodland in Cheshire (fig. 3)

Cheshire has a few isolated *lēah* names. One of these is Lea-by-Backford, at the southern end of the Wirral Peninsula. This is surrounded by *tūn* names, which suggests that it refers to a wood, rather than a clearing.

Capenhurst, to the north west, confirms the impression of isolated areas of woodland, and Hargrave Hall, further up the peninsula, suggests careful management of such wood as was left, since 'grove' in place-names is likely to refer to coppiced woodland of special economic importance. There were birch trees on the headland of Birkenhead, and Woodchurch, near Birkenhead, probably means 'church by a wood' (rather than 'church made of wood'). It is clear, however, from the absence of *lēah* names in the Peninsula, that there was no ancient forest in Wirral, though it was declared a 'forest' in the legal sense by the Earl of Chester after the Norman Conquest. Morley Hall near Bridge Trafford is another isolated *lēah*. The name of the adjacent parish of Barrow derives from Old English *bearu*, which appears to be used in place-names of a wood of limited extent, perhaps less closely controlled than a 'grove'.

East of these isolated *lēah* names lies an area where the element is much more common. Here there are many village-names, like Alvanley, Manley, Bradley, Kingsley, Norley, and some farm-names, like Longley near Kelsall. There must have been a core of ancient woodland at the heart of the region which was later declared to be the Forest of Delamere. With some interruptions for the marshes along the River Mersey, the belt of *lēah* names straggles out towards the north-east corner of Cheshire, stopping abruptly just before the final line of settlements (running from Tintwistle to Glossop) on the fringe of the Pennines. Apart from areas by the Mersey, the main gap in this belt of -ley names is an arc of territory south of Cheadle. Cheadle, which is a tautologous hybrid compound of Primitive Welsh *cēto-* (Modern Welsh *coed*) 'forest' and Old English *lēah*, possibly denoted a forest where settlements were scarce till a relatively late date. Only Bramhall and Norbury are named in this area in Domesday Book.

The striking cluster of *lēah* names on the east boundary of Cheshire (which includes the settlements of Disley and Romiley), and the more scattered names like Shrigley, Butley, Alderley which run south-westwards from this cluster, may be settlements round the fringes of an ancient forest called Cheadle. The later royal 'forest' of Macclesfield included the eastern part of this hypothetical block of ancient woodland. There is a dense cluster of -ley names in the immediate vicinity of Macclesfield. In Cheadle, *lēah* probably means 'forest'. For all the other names the appropriate translation is '[settlement in] a forest clearing'. Macclesfield contains *feld* 'open land', probably referring to the edge of the ancient woodland.

South of Macclesfield, a cluster of -ley names which includes the Domesday Manor of Bosley bears witness to another area of settlement in forest clearings. West of these is North Rode, from *rod* 'clearing', probably a later settlement, named at a date when *lēah* had ceased to have this meaning, although North Rode also is recorded in Domesday Book.

There is a belt of rather scattered -ley names in the centre of the county, running from Brindley Green near Sandbach westwards to Cheveley by the River Dee. South of this, there is the densest cluster in the county, with Cholmondeley and Bickley on its western edge and Baddiley and Stoneley on the east. There was no medieval 'forest' in this area, however, whereas the 'forest' of Rudheath, in the centre of the county, occupied an area which place-name evidence shows to have been practically devoid of ancient woodland.

In Cheshire, place-name evidence has a rather slight relationship with areas where the medieval forest laws operated. There is a much closer correlation with the distribution of references to woodland in the Domesday Survey. Domesday Book bears out the place-name evidence for scarcity of wood in the Wirral, the only estate credited with this asset being Prenton, where there was woodland one league in breadth and width, presumably the wood from which Woodchurch was named. Elsewhere in the county there is a close correspondence between areas where there are -ley names and areas where the Domesday manors are stated to have woodland. Cheshire, apart from the Wirral, must have had a considerable amount of woodland throughout the Anglo-Saxon period, and a recent study (Yalden 1987) asserts that it was at least 25 per cent wooded in 1086; but none of the woods, or the areas of settlements in woodland clearings, was very extensive.

Woodland in Staffordshire (fig. 4)

Whilst a map of Cheshire place-names containing *lēah* could be compiled from the material in the English Place-Name Society survey, which is very detailed, for Staffordshire, the only volume yet published is for Cuttlestone Hundred in the south. Some additional names containing *lēah* which belong to hamlets, farms or woods will doubtless come to light when the rest of the survey is available. Fig. 4 probably gives a reliable overall impression, but it would be unwise to make firm statements for any area about the absence of *lēah*, such as can be confidently made for the Wirral Peninsula.

This caveat applies to the mountainous north-east of the county, where Throwley Hall near Grindon is the only -ley name for which early documentation is at present available. Woodland is also referred to in the Old Norse name Swinscoe ('swine wood'), and a few other relevant names will doubtless be documented in due course. But many of the major names of the area have generics (i.e. main elements) which refer to topographical features other than woodland, and the absence of references to wood in the Domesday Survey confirms the message of the place-names. Okeover ('oak-tree ridge') had a small area of woodland in 1086, Mayfield had an even smaller one, and Blore had a 'spinney'; otherwise no wood is mentioned in the north-east corner of the county. Throwley probably means 'wood in a trough-shaped hollow'.

To the south-west of this largely treeless upland, the Domesday returns show that there was woodland in 1086 further east than the -ley place-names. There is a substantial quantity entered for Leek, and a small area for Basford. Leek is probably a Norse name, and it is possible that settlement-names in this vicinity arose too late for the use of *lēah* in its woodland senses. West of Leek, and curving round to the south-east, there is an area between the Rivers Trent and Dove where -ley names are fairly common, with a marked cluster south of Abbot's Bromley. West of this

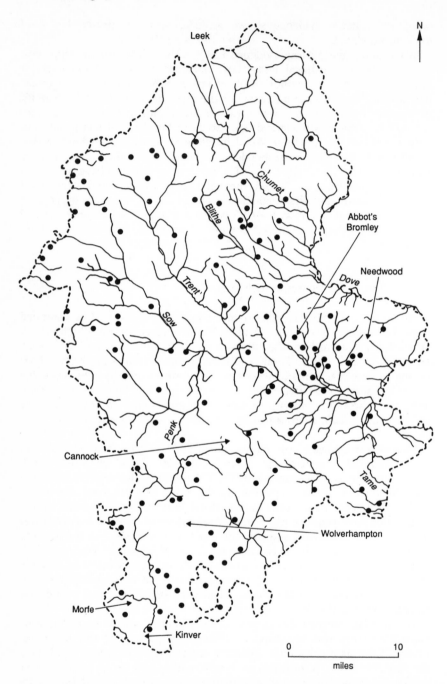

Figure 4   Staffordshire: place-names containing *lēah*.

again, there is a narrow belt in which such names are absent or rare, then another belt of -ley names, then another blank area extending to the middle stretch of the Staffordshire/Shropshire border. In the south of the county, also, there are bands of -ley names alternating with strips of territory from which they are absent. There were some large cleared areas, notably the one round Wolverhampton, but no part of the county can have been far from woodland resources.

The medieval 'forests' of Staffordshire were Kinver and Morfe, Cannock, and Needwood, all in the southern half of the county, and covering areas which the place-names show to have been particularly well-wooded.

Woodland in Warwickshire (fig. 5)

The line of *lēah* names which runs down the centre of the northern half of Warwickshire is remarkable not so much for the density of the names as for the high administrative status of most of the places to which they belong. Any suggested groupings will be to some extent arbitrary, but it is possible to see those names which run from Baddesley Ensor in the north to Stoneleigh in the south as having some cohesion. There are 22 relevant names in this narrow belt. Eight of the places (Baddesley, Bentley, Ansley, Arley, Astley, Fillongley, Corley and Stoneleigh) are Domesday manors, and 11 of them (Baxterley, Keresley and Allesley in addition to those in Domesday Book) are parishes. For Hurley, Kimberley and Whateley (in Kingsbury parish), Slowley (in Arley), Canley and Whoberley (in Stoneleigh) and Pinley and Whitley (in Coventry) the nature of the documentation leaves little doubt that they are pre-Conquest settlements, though not recorded till later. Only three of the names in this belt – Heanley in Kingsbury, Birchley Heath in Ansley and Birchley Wood in Brinklow – can be suitably classified as 'minor' names.

This is a most unusual proportion of 'major' to 'minor' for names containing *lēah*, and observation of this fact led to a suggestion in an earlier study (Gelling 1974) that in this part of Warwickshire *lēah* most commonly has the meaning 'settlement in a forest environment' rather than 'wood', 'glade' or 'newly made clearing'. Some of the settlements may be the result of pioneering by Anglo-Saxons, but it seems reasonable to suppose that some of them were already flourishing when the English arrived, and that they acquired in due course these new English names which recognize their forest setting. Arley is a special case. As late as the year 1001 it was still an appendage of Long Itchington, 18 miles south-east, and it may be presumed that the settlement evolved form a swine-pasture. Arley means 'eagle clearing', and this name, of which there are 10 examples in England, has been shown (Gelling 1987) to refer to the sea-eagle, which in inland situations builds a great nest on the tallest tree on the outskirts of a forest clearing. This bird would not survive for long in close proximity with farmers, so although some of the names in this belt may have been given by Anglo-Saxons to settlements established before their time, there was probably a good deal of relatively undisturbed woodland until the middle Saxon period. This observation applies also to Arley in Cheshire, one of the

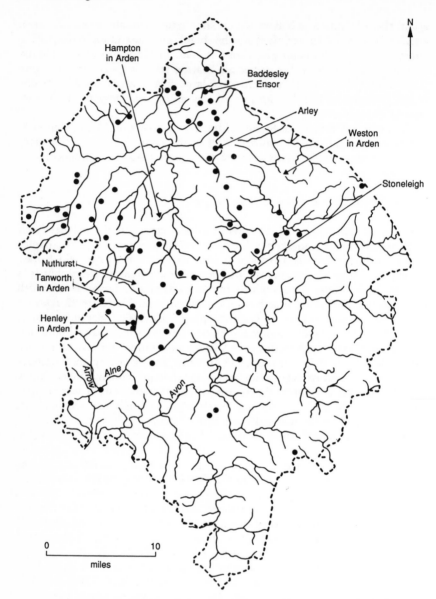

Figure 5 Warwickshire: place-names containing *lēah*.

-lēah names which straggle across the northern part of that county.

The frequency with which *lēah* refers to an ancient settlement in this region contrasts with situations elsewhere in which the word refers more frequently to minor settlements or to actual woods (as Heanley and the two Birchleys mentioned above may be suspected of doing). From this special aspect of the use of *lēah* in Warwickshire it follows that the place-name evidence cannot be expected to reveal the full extent of the ancient woodland which was visible to English settlers. What shows up on fig. 5 will be that part of the ancient woodland in which settlements were established in clearings a long time before the end of the Anglo-Saxon period. It is no surprise, therefore, on turning to the map which shows woodland recorded in Domesday Book (Darby and Terrett 1954: 292) to find that our belt of -ley names in the central part of north Warwickshire runs down the middle of a much broader area in which settlements are credited with woodland in 1086.

The woodland of north Warwickshire was, of course, the medieval Forest of Arden. In this case 'forest' is not a legal term, since Warwickshire (with the exception of a narrow strip between the Ridge Way and the River Arrow, on the west boundary of the county) escaped the imposition of the forest laws. Arden was a forest in the literal sense, and its extent is shown not only by the Domesday record but also by the occurrence of *-in-Arden* as an affix to place-names on its outskirts. Weston-in-Arden marks an eastern boundary, Henley-in-Arden a south-western one, and Hampton-in-Arden may also have been near the western edge. These boundaries accord well with the map showing Domesday woodland, and it may be suggested that there was much wooded territory in north Warwickshire which is not marked by *lēah* names because settlements were not established in it until the late Anglo-Saxon period, when *lēah* was no longer used in this way. The woodland area of north Warwickshire was probably the largest single block of such territory in the five counties under discussion, and the only one which offered opportunities for the practice of transhumance on a significant scale. Transhumance is the pasturing of animals on properties at a distance from the main estate, and the consequent driving of herds between the two areas. It was a seasonal practice when the animals were cattle, but in Warwickshire the outlying woodland was probably used for pigs, which would be brought to the main estate only when required for food. The connection between Long Itchington and Arley, discussed in Chapter 11, is a documented instance of this use of woodland by a south-Warwickshire estate. Another recorded example is the mention in a charter dating from the beginning of the eighth century of Nuthurst, near Tanworth-in-Arden, and *Hellerelege*, near King's Norton in the suburbs of Birmingham, as woodland properties attached to an estate at Shottery, near Stratford-upon-Avon. (S 64; Finberg 1972: 87; Sims-Williams 1990: 35 n.99). Links between other settlements and woodland pasture in Arden are revealed by post-Conquest evidence; they suggest systematic use by communities in the Avon valley of woodland in territory near the headwaters of the rivers Arrow and Alne (Ford 1976: 280-2).

A full analysis of the pattern of *lēah* names in Warwickshire would be disproportionate to the scale of the summary attempted in this chapter, but a few additional points should be made. The dichotomy between north and south Warwickshire shown on all maps recording woodland is a genuine one. The evidence of Domesday Book has been interpreted as indicating a large amount of woodland at Brailes, in the southern tip of the county, (Darby and Terrett 1954: fig. 100); but it has been shown that this was actually situated at Tanworth-in-Arden, about 25 miles to the north-west

(Ford 1976: 274). On the map published in 1974 which showed place-names in -tūn as well as those containing lēah, some of the areas adjacent to the Forest of Arden were indicated by clusters of tūn names. Weston-in-Arden is one of such a cluster. There is a negative relationship between tūn in place-names and ancient woodland, and the area between Weston-in-Arden and the county boundary (which runs along Watling Street) was certainly not wooded in the middle Saxon period. Willey is a single isolated lēah name on Watling Street, and Radley is another isolated specimen on the south-east boundary of the county. For isolated lēah names it is desirable to find a meaning other than 'clearing'. This will often be 'wood', which is the oldest meaning of the word. A particularly clear instance occurs in south Worcestershire, where Elmley Castle is an isolated lēah in the ring of -tūn names which surrounds Bredon Hill. This is obviously 'elm wood'. 'Red wood' seems a reasonable translation for Radley, and 'high wood' for Henley-in-Arden, which lay on the outskirts of the forest, not within it. For Willey there is another possibility. The latest Old English sense of lēah was 'meadow', and 'meadow with willow trees' perhaps suits Willey better than 'willow wood'.

Woodland in Shropshire (fig. 6)

The map which shows -ley names in Shropshire has a very dense concentration of symbols in the eastern half. Two groupings can be discerned, one running from Leegomery (south of the Weald Moors) to Meadowley (west of Bridgnorth), and another occupying the south-eastern corner of the county. The River Severn was here flowing through dense woodland, some of which survived to form the basis of the early industrial activity in Coalbrookdale, and some of which still survives in Wyre Forest, Worcestershire, which adjoins the Shropshire boundary.

Many of the symbols in both groups represent parish-names. Dawley, Stirchley, Madeley, Broseley, Willey, Linley, Astley Abbots and Tasley are contiguous parishes, and there is another such group to the south comprising Glazeley, Billingsley, Highley, Romsley and Claverley. There are other, non-contiguous, parishes in both groups, and several places which, though not parishes, are named in Domesday Book. This is a situation similar to that in north Warwickshire, but in Shropshire there is more frequent use of lēah in naming places of lesser status. Some of these latter names have first elements (such as 'cat' in Ketley, 'burdock' in Clotley, 'fern' in Farley, 'burnt' in Barnsley) which suggest a relatively underdeveloped landscape. It seems probable that in eastern Shropshire the -ley names give a fair impression of the whole extent of the Anglo-Saxon woodland, rather than just marking the core of it. If this woodland had been continuous it would have exceeded that of north Warwickshire in extent, but the place-names give evidence of an open belt running from Upton Cresset to Eardington separating the northern group of -ley names from those which adjoin Wyre Forest. At the south-west edge of the southern cluster there is a minor place-name Hoopits (in the parish of Greete), which is recorded as Wulfputtes in the thirteenth century.

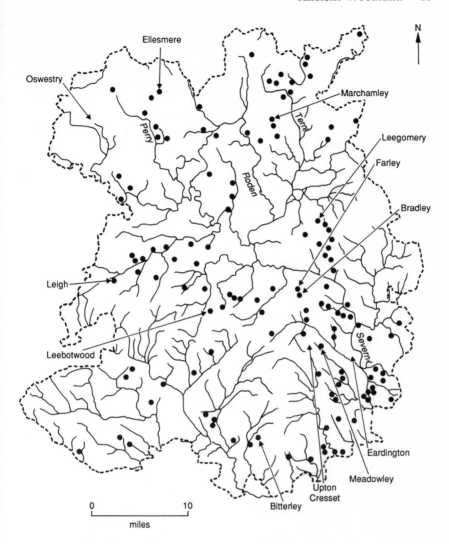

Figure 6 Shropshire: place-names containng *lēah*.

There is another belt of -ley names running east/west across the centre of Shropshire. Two outliers, Bradley and Farley, at the eastern end of the belt are minor names in Much Wenlock parish. West of these are Harley, Hughley, Kenley, Langley, Ruckley, Frodesley, Lydley Heys and Leebotwood. These are all 'major' names, the last two referring to places in Botwood where Haughmond Abbey was making assarts (the technical term for woodland clearings) in the second half of the twelfth century. Since *lēah* is not likely to have been used in the sense 'forest clearing' as late as that it is likely that some small settlements here had the name *Lege* from an earlier date, and that these provided bases from which the abbey developed more land. West of Leebotwood the -*lēah* names testify to the presence of ancient woodland extending as far as Leigh near Worthen, but stopping four miles short of the county boundary.

No other groups of -ley names in Shropshire are as extensive as these belts in the east and centre, and there are large areas in which the word does not occur at all. There was some ancient woodland north of Shrewsbury (referred to in Pimley, Albrightlee, Astley), and Lee Brockhurst, Marchamley and some minor names attest to another patch further north, between the Roden and the Tern. In some names in the north-east angle of the county, however, in the marshy ground along the River Perry south of Ellesmere, and in a few names south of Wem it may be suspected that the word is used in its late Old English sense of 'pasture'. This is appropriate also for Bitterley ('butter-producing pasture') in the south of the county. The main areas of ancient woodland in Shropshire can be detected from the *lēah* names, but it is possible that a fair number of settlements acquired their English names as late as the tenth century, when the word was beginning to lose its senses of 'wood' and 'forest clearing'.

The conjecture about English names being coined in some areas of Shropshire too late for *lēah* to have its 'wood/clearing' meanings receives some support from the map which shows records of woodland in Domesday Book. The central and eastern belts of *lēah* names accord well enough with the Domesday distribution, but otherwise the correspondence is not good. Domesday records a good deal of wood in the north-west, round Oswestry, where *lēah* does not occur at all; and conversely the *lēah* names curving south from Ellesmere are in an area shown blank on the Domesday map. There are other similar discrepancies.

The medieval royal forests of Shropshire were contiguous areas in the central part of the county (except for a tiny forest of Haughmond, which was detached from the main block). Morfe and Kinver spilled over from Staffordshire and adjoined Shirlet. The larger Long Forest adjoined Shirlet to the west. The Wrekin Forest was north of the Severn, opposite to Shirlet. Clee Forest, which became a chase in the mid-twelfth century, may originally have been contiguous with the Long Forest and with Shirlet. Long Forest included the upland area of the Long Mynd, and most of it was certainly treeless, as were the Clee Hills. The Wrekin and Shirlet, however, took advantage of the heavy woodland of the middle Severn.

Woodland in Herefordshire (fig. 7)

As will be seen from fig. 7, *lēah* occurs in Herefordshire much less frequently than in the other four counties under consideration. This may indicate that Herefordshire had less woodland. The *Domesday Geography of Midland England* (Darby and Terrett 1954), commenting on the records of woodland in 1086, says 'it is clear that there was far less wood in Herefordshire than in the other border shires of Cheshire, Shropshire and Gloucestershire – we can only suppose that extensive clearing had taken place since Saxon days.' But if the crude test of frequency of *lēah* in place-names be indeed a fair indication of middle-Saxon woodland, the Domesday record may be consistent with a much earlier situation.

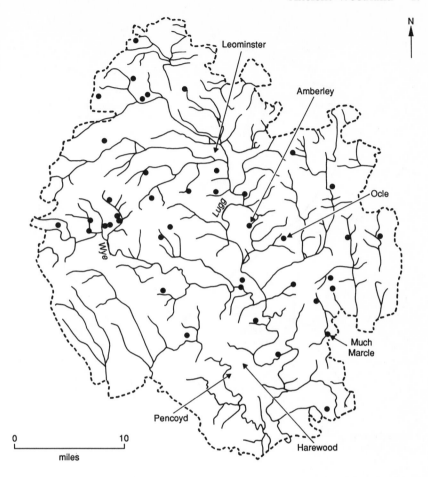

Figure 7 Herefordshire: place-names containing *lēah*.

The only closely spaced cluster of -ley names in Herefordshire lies on the River Wye, 12–15 miles north-west of Hereford. Of the seven names in this cluster, three – Almeley, Eardisley and Kinnersley – are parishes, and, in addition to these, Willersley and Ailey are Domesday manors. The remaining two – Kinley and Hurstley – refer to places of lesser status, but there can be little doubt that in this area settlements were either newly established or renamed by English-speaking people for whom *lēah* still had its clear association with ancient woodland. The more widely-spaced *lēah* names to the west and east of this group suggest a belt of woodland running from the county boundary to the River Lugg. South of this, numerous names in -*tūn* suggest an open landscape, and the two -ley names which do occur here, Amberley and Ocle, may be using the word in the sense 'wood', which is particularly appropriate for Ocle ('oak wood').

In the south of the county the widely-spaced *lēah* names are found round the edges of the medieval royal forest of Archenfield. In the heart of this

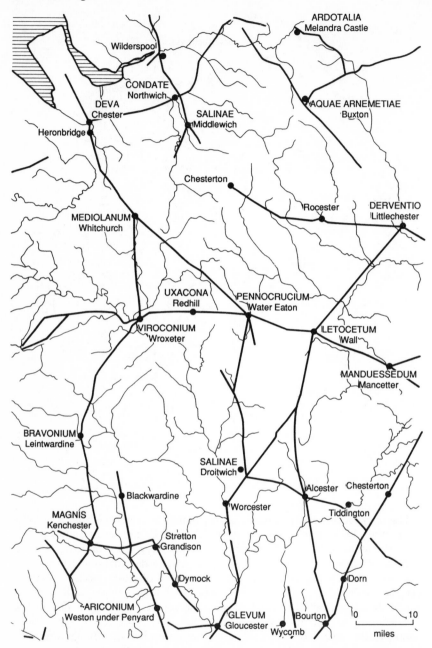

Figure 8 Known Roman roads, urban settlements and road-stations.

forest the absence of *lēah* may be due to the fact that many of the place-names are either Welsh, or English translations from Welsh like Bridstow, Marstow, Peterstow. Two names, Harewood and the Welsh name Pencoyd ('place at the end of the wood'), refer to the woodland here.

The place-names also suggest patches of woodland east of the River Wye, where Marcle, Putley, Pixley and Munsley are adjoining parishes, and in the north-west of the county. The large quantity of wood with which Domesday Book credits Leominster must have lain in the outlying parts of this enormous manor, since Leominster itself stands in a large belt of territory from which -ley names are absent.

The only densely populated area in these five counties which did not have access to woodland locally is the southern half of Warwickshire, and estates here had outlying properties in Arden. There were probably similar arrangements, on a small scale, in the other counties. For the most part, however, woodland seems likely to have been dispersed over the West Midland landscape in a manner which made its resources available to most settlements without forming barriers to communication. There would be progressive clearing for arable as economic priorities changed, but it is probable that the woodland of the area was considered an asset rather than a hindrance in the Roman and post-Roman periods. Place-names containing *lēah* and *tūn* are not likely to have arisen in the immediate post-Roman period, but the conditions of settlement indicated by these words can reasonably be assumed to have prevailed for several centuries before the terms became fashionable.

Roman Roads (fig. 8)

It may seem perverse to include the major Roman roads with the physical geography and natural vegetation of the region, but it is likely that English administrators and settlers regarded them as a fixed and ancient component in the landscape. They were laid out in the early part of the period of Roman rule as part of a network of military installations. Many of them remained in use throughout the Anglo-Saxon and post-Conquest periods, and in the country as a whole they have continued to be important into modern times. In our five counties, however, the known Roman roads are sparse; and probably the only one which had much significance in post-Roman times was Watling Street, which offered an obvious route from central Mercia to the west. The southward continuation of Watling Street, which runs from Wroxeter to Leintwardine and Kenchester, uses the Church Stretton valley which would have conditioned the route of any road in that area. Roman-road junctions were not particularly favoured sites for settlement growth in the Anglo-Saxon period. Chester remained a place of great importance, but this was due as much to its position in relation to sea-routes as to the road system.

2 The End of the Roman Period

Information about the Roman period in the five counties under discussion is considerably less than is available for most counties to the east and south. Our five counties lie outside the area where Roman villas are frequent. The number of villas south-east of a line from Exeter to York is estimated at the best part of a thousand (Esmonde Cleary 1989: 40) but in the territory of the Cornovii, which included most of our region, Dr G. Webster (1975: 83) lists only eight buildings 'which could be described as villas'. The Ordnance Survey map of Roman Britain shows them to be scarce, also, in Warwickshire, which lies outside the area of Dr Webster's book. There is a good deal of information available about the military installations of the early Roman period, but this is of little relevance to our purpose. Knowledge of Romano-British life in the West Midlands comes mainly from excavation of Roman towns, such as Chester, Wroxeter, Kenchester and Alcester. Apart from this there is little to draw on for most of the period except the testimony of chance finds of Romano-British objects.

The West Midland people know as *Cornovii* are recorded in several classical sources (listed in Rivet and Smith 1979). A magnificent inscription from Wroxeter identifies this central-Shropshire site as their capital. Ptolemy attributes *Deva* (Chester) to them, and in Webster 1975, fig. 4, this is shown as the northern limit of their territory. Their precise boundaries are not recoverable. It seems probable that the area which became Warwickshire lay mostly in the territory of the neighbouring tribe to the east, who used to be referred to as the *Coritani*, but who are now, on the basis of an inscribed tile, believed to have been called *Corieltauvi*. Their capital was at Leicester. The two peoples to the south were the *Silures* and the *Dobunni*, on either side of the lower Severn. Most of Herefordshire may have been in Silurian territory, but a case has been presented for the presence here of another tribe called *Decangi* (Stanford 1980: 121-2).

Iron Age peoples of the sort represented by the *Cornovii* were formed into administrative units called *civitates* by the Romans, and *civitas* capitals were built for them. The only town of this status known in our area of study was that at Wroxeter, the Roman *Viroconium Cornoviorum*. Wroxeter was not occupied after its sub-Roman phase came to an end, and most of its area is therefore available for excavation. Discussion of the immediate post-Roman period in the West Midlands must draw heavily on information derived from excavations at Wroxeter, and an account of this is given below. First, however, it should be noted that in the virtual absence of Roman villas very little can be said about the life of the countryside. The West Midlands are not atypical as regards the difficulty of identifying farmsteads of the period other than the heavily Romanized villas. This is a problem which affects the study of the whole of Roman Britain, and lack of knowledge about such sites may be the main reason for the failure of archaeology to bridge the gap between the late fourth and the mid-fifth centuries.

Dr Simon Esmonde Cleary's recent book *The Ending of Roman Britain* demonstrates that the search for Roman/Anglo-Saxon continuity on known Roman sites has for the most part been doomed to failure because towns are not the likely places for it (Esmonde Cleary 1989). The life of the towns depended on the tax system, and once that had collapsed, residence in, or regular resort to, such centres would be pointless. The specifically Roman way of life had been extinct for two generations before the earliest Anglo-Saxon settlers came, and archaeologists cannot obtain firm dating for occupation of any site after c.430 because no Roman-style objects were being produced by that time. Continuity must have occurred at a large number of sites which have not yet been identified, and many of these will be the farmsteads of the people who worked the land from about 410 to about 450.

It will be demonstrated in the next chapter that in most of the area under consideration there is no likelihood of any early Anglo-Saxon presence, but Dr Esmonde Cleary's thesis is nevertheless relevant, as it demonstrates that we have no criteria for identifying non-military, non-urban sites of the late Roman and post-Roman periods. This means that Roman archaeology is of limited relevance to the study of the Dark Ages.

That said, however, attention must be focused on the remarkable results of Philip Barker's excavations at Wroxeter, which constitute the most extensive and painstaking of all attempts yet undertaken to demonstrate continuity of occupation into the Dark Ages on a Roman site. The story of Wroxeter has been carried forward to c.500, and the nature of the post-Roman evidence enables conjectures to be made about the political situation in a wide area round the town.

One of the major public buildings at Wroxeter was the basilica – an aisled exercise hall – which formed part of the baths complex. This was demolished in late Roman times, probably c.380, only the south aisle wall being left standing. Philip Barker's excavations have revealed that the site was subsequently occupied by a range of timber buildings, placed on carefully laid rubble platforms, eventually fronting a street which was made by the deposition of carefully-sieved silt. The principal building was a winged corridor house of a Romano-British type. The latest find was a skeleton, dated by scientific methods to the seventh century, probably the first half. The estimated lapse of time from the abandonment of the post-Roman buildings to the deposition of this burial leads the excavators to date the abandonment to about A.D.500.

Evidence of the sort drawn upon by Mr Barker in his reconstruction of fifth-century developments on the baths basilica site could only have been detected in a Roman town where wide areas are available for excavation. Similar evidence would be likely to go unnoticed in towns where excavation is limited to modern development areas, even if it had survived medieval disturbances. The plan of the Wroxeter evidence is not obviously impressive, and the almost universal acceptance of Mr Barker's interpretation and reconstruction (fig. 9) owes a great deal to his reputation as an outstandingly skilled excavator. Some of the verdicts of leading authorities

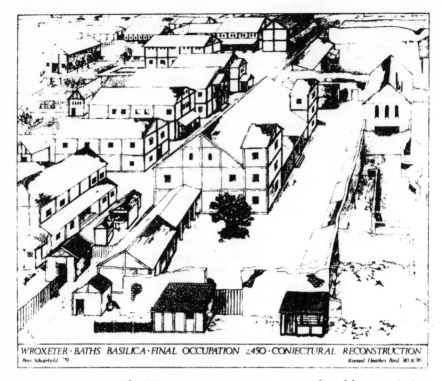

WROXETER · BATHS BASILICA · FINAL OCCUPATION ⊂450 · CONJECTURAL RECONSTRUCTION
Peter Scholefield '79   *Revised Heather Bird '80 & '85*

Figure 9   The Wroxeter reconstruction (reproduced by permission of P. Barker). A revised version of this is in preparation.

on Roman Britain are worth quoting.

Dr Graham Webster (1975: 117-18) writes:

> Thus we have a powerful character, building himself a kind of country mansion in the middle of the city, surrounded with small buildings ... A vigorous force is in command and from whatever source it came, there was a wish to have some semblance of the classical past from which authority could have been tenuously extended.

Three works published in 1981 contain similar opinions. Professor Peter Salway says 'Wroxeter, where meticulous excavation of the topmost layers by the latest techniques has revealed large fifth-century timber buildings constructed after the demolition of what had previously been thought to be the latest Roman structures' (Salway 1981: 245). Professor Malcolm Todd says

> ... and Wroxeter, where the site of the baths basilica was carefully replanned and covered by a series of timber buildings at the beginning of the fifth century. The impression conveyed ... is of sizeable communities able to act effectively in concert and still possessing an elementary internal structure. (Todd 1981: 245)

Professor Charles Thomas says 'Philip Barker's lengthy campaign at Wroxeter ... shows ... a town-centre reconstruction appropriate to some sub-Roman *tyrannus*, using timber framed buildings on rubble foundations and moreover using, when appropriate, essentially classical models' (Thomas 1981: 145). The most recent discussion echoes these verdicts: 'Philip Barker's long, meticulous and brilliantly-conducted excavations have revealed a long sequence of late- to post-Roman use on the site of the baths-basilica' (Esmonde Cleary 1989: 152).

To set against these well-qualified testimonies, only two scholars have registered doubts that the emperor's clothes may be imaginary (Stanford 1980: 170; Myres 1986: 22n.). We must allow that Mr Barker's meticulous excavations have indeed established the fifth-century date and the plan and form of the timber buildings on the baths basilica site at Wroxeter. As regards the 'powerful character' or 'sub-Roman *tyrannus*' whose presence there was conjectured by the authors quoted above following Mr Barker himself (Barker 1981: 19), he is unfortunately an insubstantial entity. The excavations provided no material context for him beyond the actual buildings, since there were so few datable finds of the fifth century. But negative evidence should be considered. There is no sign of either Christianity or a Germanic presence in the latest period of occupation, and this is important.

As regards Christianity, there is a single hint of it from the city at an earlier date in the 'Wroxeter letter', a text inscribed on a thin lead tablet which was found at Bath in 1880 (Thomas 1981: 126-7). It is written from *Viroconium*, and it contains what may be an allusion to a follower of an Eastern heretical sect. On p. 192 of his book Professor Thomas cites Wroxeter as a place where a Christian church might be expected, and on p. 154 he notes that a small timber church might have been missed if its site had been excavated by techniques less advanced than those used by Mr Barker. The fact remains, however, that nothing of a specifically Christian nature has been found in Roman levels at Wroxeter. The place-name-forming term *ecles*, by which English speakers acknowledged the survival of Romano-British Christianity, is not found in Shropshire, though there are names containing it in the surrounding counties of Herefordshire, Staffordshire and Cheshire (see Chapter 4). Some of the finds from the baths basilica site suggest pagan cults. There is the strange and unique phenomenon of the 50 or 60 wall-plaster roundels with eyes painted on them (fig. 10). There have also been finds of one Samian eye, a bronze one, and a pair of eyes made of gold. These are not certain to be contemporary with the timber buildings, as they (and other finds) are from the rubble and mortar foundations, so could have been brought in with the rubble and be evidence for activities at an earlier period in a different part of the city.

The characteristic metalwork - buckles, belt-stiffeners, and strap-ends - issued from imperial equipment factories in the late fourth century is barely represented in finds from all the sites excavated in Wroxeter. Salway (1981: 388) notes that 'There is ... evidence for one (but perhaps only one) late Roman soldier in the city of Wroxeter, which has also produced a piece of the metalwork we have been considering.' The metalwork in question was once considered to be evidence of soldiers of Germanic race; but

Figure 10   Wall-plaster eyes from Wroxeter (photograph R. White).

this theory has now been discarded, and Professor Salway notes that the presence of a small quantity of it does not necessarily indicate a military presence, as an individual soldier or a small detachment might be employed on official business of a non-military character. Dr Esmonde Cleary (1989: 55) suggests that these objects may have been issued to civilian administrators. Whatever their significance, belt-fittings of this type are much better represented at Caerwent than they are at Wroxeter.

There are other items in the sparse finds from the baths basilica site which reveal traces of the Germanic fashions prevalent at the end of the Roman period, but nothing which constitutes evidence for the presence of people of Germanic race. It is particularly noteworthy that there are no sunken-floored buildings.

It is tempting to try to fit the fifth-century development of the baths basilica site at Wroxeter into the political situation which can be deduced from the writings of the sixth-century British monk, Gildas, whose text has been described as the foundation of all enquiry into the events of this period (Stenton 1943: 2). Gildas addresses his exhortations to five British kings/tyrants, one of whom is Aurelius Caninus (perhaps a descendant of Ambrosius Aurelianus), who has been considered to be the ruler of a kingdom in the Gloucester region. Professor Thomas has suggested that 'Alternatively, the Aureliani may have been the rulers of Wroxeter, with its grandiose fifth-century town centre and half-timbered classical palace' (Thomas 1981: 251-2). But he also ventured another suggestion: 'one might toy with placing the *superbus tyrannus* and his circle no further north than

Wroxeter, the Aureliani then being at Gloucester and the lower Severn' (*ibid.*: 249).

Before being carried away by the tempting thought that Philip Barker might have excavated the foundations of the building from which Vortigern issued his fateful invitation to Hengest and Horsa, we should consider whether the fifth-century site at Wroxeter is an appropriate one for a tyrant's headquarters. Professor John Wacher (1975: 412) implies that it is. He says 'A civitas was still centred on a town, even if it no longer entirely controlled its surrounding area, and was ruled by a "tyrant" instead of by elected magistrates and a council'; and the reference to a 'powerful character' and a 'vigorous force' in Dr Webster's account of fifth-century Wroxeter suggests that he would agree with this. Professor Wendy Davies, on the other hand, expresses a different view of the type of site likely to have been occupied by one of Gildas's tyrants and their descendants. She emphasizes the evidence from written sources and from archaeology for the association of forts and fortified places with the holders of political power in the Dark Ages (Davies 1982: 22-4). Whatever else fifth-century Wroxeter may have been, it was not a citadel, and this is a likely reason for its eventual desertion.

There is general agreement that whatever the identity of the place which succeeded *Viroconium* as the centre of government for this part of the Marches, it must have been in a more easily defended position. The Wrekin hill-fort has yielded no trace of post-Roman occupation; and common sense seems to rule out this inconvenient place as a political centre for people who had long ceased to think in the extravagant terms of Iron Age society. The strongly fortified archaeological site called the Berth north of Shrewsbury is frequently mentioned in this connection. Another possibility is Shrewsbury itself, with its promontory-site in a bend of the River Severn. The transfer of political power to Shrewsbury certainly took place at some date between the fifth and ninth centuries, but there is room for several moves in that long period.

The general lack of closely datable finds from post-Roman Wroxeter is relieved by a single, enigmatic, fascinating object. This is the famous tombstone which was turned up by the plough in 1967, outside the walls, on the outer edge of the counterscarp of the defences in the north-eastern area of the city (fig. 11). This bears the inscription

CUNORIX

MACUS MA

QVI COLINE

The date suggested on linguistic grounds by Professor Kenneth Jackson is A.D.460-75 (Wright and Jackson 1968). The stone commemorates a person named Cunorix who was, to judge by the term *Macus* 'son of' which precedes his father's name, an Irishman. The father's name is thought to mean 'son of the holly'. Some conjectures about this tombstone envisage Cunorix as the leader of a band of mercenaries hired by the ruler whose capital was Viroconium for protection against barbarian raiders. Professor L. Alcock (1971: 268) envisaged him as the furthest-inland manifestation of the Irish immigration for which there is evidence, in the form of Latin and

Figure 11 Tombstone from Wroxeter (photograph S. Esmonde Cleary).

Ogham inscriptions, in parts of Wales, particularly Dyfed, Brycheiniog and the upper Usk valley. But the Wroxeter tombstone is surely too far removed and too isolated to be seen as part of that corpus of material.

I find it easiest to think of Cunorix as a guest, a high-ranking visitor to a British court, whose hosts had sufficient courtesy and just sufficient literacy to give him a memorial in the style appropriate to his nationality. This stone seems to me a strong piece of evidence for the maintenance of a high-status sub-Roman lifestyle at Wroxeter far into the fifth century, probably in peaceful conditions. Mr Barker (1981: 18) speaks of the tombstone as 'probably Christian', and says that it 'implies the presence of a Latin-speaking community in the city at that time'. This is pressing the evidence too far. The stone offered an obvious opportunity for overt Christian symbolism if the people commissioning it had wished this; and the Latin is minimal. Lack of evidence for Christianity seems to me a salient characteristic of the archaeological material from fifth-century Wroxeter. The absence of casual finds, like the metal bowls with chi-ro signs embossed or scratched on them from Wall (a Roman site on Watling Street, south of Lichfield, fig. 8) and Caerwent, is surprising.

The Welsh kingdom of Powys which emerged in the region of the Cornovii is generally considered to be the successor to the Roman *civitas*, as Gwent was to that of the Silures. But while Gwent preserved the name (*Venta*) of the administrative centre of the Silures, there is no such continuity between the names of Powys and *Viroconium*. J. Lloyd Jones suggested in 1927 that Powys was derived from a Latin name based on the word *pagus*. This last is a term in Roman administration for a unit in which the inhabitants of an area were grouped below the level of the *civitas*. If the Latin collective suffix *-enses*, 'people of', were added to the root of *pagus*, the resulting name *Pagenses* would be philologically acceptable as the origin of the Welsh Powys; and derivation from *Pagenses* was in fact assumed without question in Jackson 1953. The suggestion has been treated more critically by Professor Gwynedd Pierce in a discussion of the name Dinas Powys in Glamorgan (where Powys is another occurrence of the kingdom-name). He is not convinced that derivation from a Latin term for an administrative district is appropriate there (Pierce 1968: 216ff). It could also be objected that while the Cornovii may fairly be supposed to have been the people of a number of *pagi*, it is not clear how this label would distinguish them from their neighbours in Roman Britain.

If it were certain that Powys was the name of a kingdom which evolved from the canton of the Cornovii, whose *civitas* was Wroxeter, it would be tempting to conjecture a name in which 'people of a *pagus*' means 'pagans', i.e. people who reject Christianity. The recorded Latin term for this is, of course, *pagani*; but if an alternative formation *pagenses* had been used in the same sense, it would not seem impossible that such a term could reappear at Dinas Powys in Glamorgan. The Latin derivation is probably not definitive, however. A similar name near the Scottish border has been derived from Old Welsh *poues* 'rest, repose' (Watson 1926: 382-3).

The early history of the Welsh kingdom of Powys is very vague, and any connection between it and Wroxeter rests on a series of inferences. The most recent discussion of the emergence of the Welsh kingdoms is that of Professor Wendy Davies. She deals quite firmly with Gwynedd, Dyfed and Gwent, but considers that 'Powys ... is more problematic since the term itself is not used in association with kings or kingdoms in sixth-century sources and does not certainly so occur until the ninth century' (Davies

1982: 94). The earliest firm evidence for a kingdom in north-east Wales seems to be the references in seventh- and eighth-century sources to princes (Brochfael, and Selyf son of Cynan) who were on the losing side at the battle of Chester in 613–616. These princes reappear in genealogies of the kings of Powys, and it is clear that in the ninth century they were believed to have belonged to the Cadelling family from which these kings were drawn. In the ninth century this family traced its descent from Vortigern, who was represented as the son-in-law of Magnus Maximus, the unsuccessful claimant in the late fourth century to the throne of the western Roman empire. This emerges from the pedigree of Cyngen, a king of Powys who died in 855, as it was recorded on the cross-shaft popularly known as the pillar of Eliseg, which still stands in the vale of Llangollen. The long inscription is mostly illegible now, but the content is known from a facsimile copy made by the antiquary Edward Llwyd in 1696 (Nash-Williams 1950: 123–5).

Dr Webster (1975: 111) says that this inscription 'places Vortigern in direct contact with the Cornovii', a statement which assumes that the kingdom of Powys arose directly from the Roman *civitas*. But without a name-link, such as there is between Gwent and *Venta Silurum*, or between Ergyng and *Ariconium*, or between Dyfed and the tribal name *Demetae*, a direct connection cannot be regarded as susceptible of proof. Also, in the light of present-day thinking about royal genealogies (on which see Chapter 5), the references on the pillar to Vortigern and Magnus Maximus should probably no longer be treated as literal historical statements.

The most which can be said is that princes of a state probably to be identified with the ninth-century kingdom of Powys were active in the vicinity of Chester in the early seventh century – in what capacity will be considered in a later chapter. They, or their immediate predecessors, could have carved out a kingdom which was at several removes from the earlier Roman cantonal arrangements, and Wroxeter may have been of no administrative significance after the end of the fifth century.

The story of Wroxeter cannot be fitted into what is known or conjectured of the history of the region in post-Roman times. The archaeological evidence must be allowed to stand clear of theories about Vortigern or the origins of Powys. The main thing which seems apparent about the man who held court in the timber mansion at Wroxeter is that he was not anticipating trouble. The Anglo-Saxons must have seemed far away to the east, and any Irish immigrants or raiders comfortably distant to the west. There is no evidence to suggest that the people of Wroxeter had any contacts with people close to the Irish Sea or the Bristol Channel, since none of the imported pottery which is diagnostic of such relations has been found in the city. The rulers of the area in the century between A.D.400 and A.D.500 cannot have felt so threatened by insurrection or invasion that they were moved to abandon the Roman city for a more typical Dark Age defensive site. But the evidence of Wroxeter only takes us to c.500, and the history of this part of our region is a total blank for a long time after that. The obscurity of the sixth century in Shropshire and Cheshire is impenetrable. What is known about the seventh century will be considered in a later chapter, but first it is necessary to look at the pagan Anglo-Saxon archaeology of Staffordshire and Warwickshire.

3 Anglo-Saxon Archaeology

Staffordshire

In Cheshire, Shropshire and Herefordshire there have been no Anglo-Saxon finds of the pagan period. There are a few pagan cemeteries in Staffordshire (Smith, R.A. 1908). A large settlement-site at Cat Holme near Alrewas has been excavated in more recent times, but this does not alter the impression conveyed by Smith's account, which is that it is only by virtue of lying adjacent to Derbyshire that Staffordshire scrapes into the category of counties which have pagan Anglo-Saxon remains. Finds made within the Staffordshire boundary are overflows or strays from the cemeteries of the East Midlands or from the barrow burials of north Derbyshire. They are very sparse, and none of them has a distinctive character which would suggest a different cultural background from that of the East Midland and Derbyshire material.

Burials which can be attributed to the early part of the sixth century extend down the River Trent as far as Wychnor, a parish on the east Staffordshire boundary. The settlement-site at Cat Holme is in a loop of the Trent within Wychnor parish, to the east of the village (fig. 12). The two sites are clearly associated, and dating evidence is provided by pottery from the cemetery. The settlement-site produced virtually no objects, only the plans of buildings, which numbered about a hundred (Losco-Bradley 1977). A cemetery discovered in 1881 at Stapenhill in Burton-on-Trent is also on the east boundary of the county. This was a mixed inhumation/cremation cemetery, with one particularly well-furnished female inhumation which yielded a typical assemblage of Anglian ornaments. Stapenhill was indeed included as an East Midland cemetery in Dr Stafford's volume (Stafford 1985: fig. 30), and Wychnor could well have been shown there also. These are the most westerly manifestations of the pagan Anglian archaeology of the East Midlands; they do not provide evidence for the English penetration of the *West* Midlands.

There is a small group of burial-sites in the north-east angle of Staffordshire, two of them – Steep Low near Alstonfield and Readon Hill north of Ramshorn – in tumuli. The Alstonfield burials are secondary ones in an earlier tumulus, and this is a phenomenon which may occur anywhere, but it seems probable that any manifestation of Anglian barrow-burial in this area is to be seen as outlying from the major concentration of such burials in north Derbyshire. A Roman coin-pendant mounted in a setting of gold cell-work with garnet and blue glass fillings was found at Forsbrook in central north Staffordshire, and this is probably to be interpreted as a stray from the corpus of cell-work jewellery found in the Derbyshire barrows. At Barlaston, south-west of Forsbrook, an isolated burial was accompanied by a knife, a sword and a hanging bowl; and the bowl had escutcheons

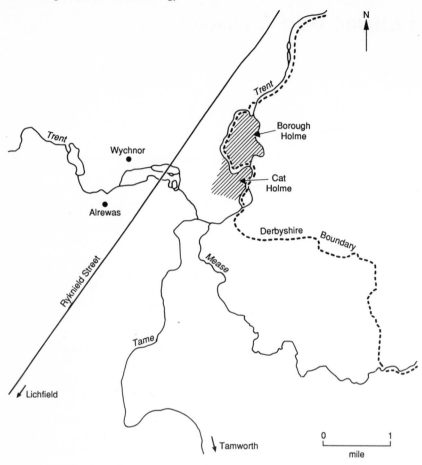

Figure 12   The sites of Wychnor and Cat Holme.

decorated with red enamel and millefiori glass. This, also, looks like a stray from the Derbyshire concentration, where a barrow on Middleton Moor, near Youlgreave, produced enamelled hanging-bowl escutcheons.

The Avon Valley (fig. 13)

By contrast with the sparse, peripheral Anglo-Saxon archaeology of Stafford-shire, that of Warwickshire shows the valley of the Avon in the southern half of the county to have been an important focus of pagan burial prac-tices. A re-examination of the material from the cemeteries of this area is a major requirement of present-day Anglo-Saxon studies. Mr W.F. Ford's long-awaited publication of excavations at Stretton-on-Fosse and Alveston will do much to fill this gap. With these and other modern excavation reports still in preparation generalizations about this important corpus of

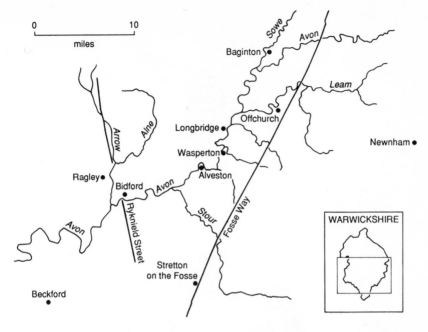

Figure 13   Pagan Anglo-Saxon cemeteries in the Avon Valley.

material are difficult, but something can be offered on the basis of Mr Ford's brief published discussion (1976) and, most importantly, a privileged pre-publication sight of the Stretton report.

The cemeteries of the Avon Valley were not large. Only four of them, at Bidford, Alveston, Baginton and Wasperton, are known to have contained over a hundred burials. At Wasperton there were 137 graves which were certainly Anglo-Saxon, but others were either unfurnished or provided with artefacts which were not ethnically diagnostic, and some had Romano-British characteristics. Anglo-Saxon brooches from the Wasperton cemetery are shown in fig. 14.[1] Stretton-on-Fosse was one of the larger cemeteries in the group, but it contained fewer than 100 burials, and most of the others contained fewer than 10. It must be remembered that Stretton-on-Fosse and Wasperton are the only two of which the limits are definitely known, but it is considered that most are likely to have been small (Ford 1976: 274). Mr Ford considers that a cemetery with 60 or fewer burials is unlikely to represent more than a single household in occupation at any one time, and that this suggests little more than an aristocratic element imposed upon existing native peasant settlement. The point to note is that there is no evidence here for a dense reservoir of Anglo-Saxon settlers which could have supplied a population for Staffordshire and Shropshire. The Avon burials are moreover in the area which was to become the sub-kingdom of the Hwicce, and there is no reason to suppose that they have a direct bearing on the English settlement of the Mercian heartland, which lay round Tamworth and Lichfield in south Staffordshire.

The distinctive nature of the corpus of grave goods found in the Avon

Figure 14 Wasperton brooches (photograph Warwick Museum).

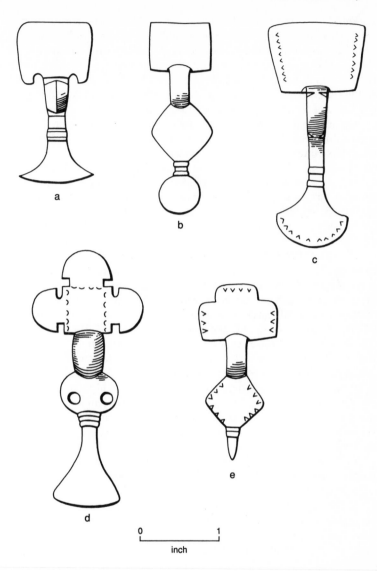

Figure 15 Small-long brooches from (a) Baginton, (b) Bidford-on-Avon, (c, d and e) Watling Street, Leicestershire or Warwickshire (from Leeds 1945, by permission of the Society of Antiquaries of London).

valley emerges from the distribution maps of certain types of brooches published in 1945 by E.T. Leeds, the pioneer of modern study of pagan Anglo-Saxon jewellery. The distribution patterns established in this early study still have some validity, though a great deal of material from excavations of the last 50 years is obviously not represented there.

The Avon valley is shown by these maps to be a region with a remarkable diversity of brooch types, including some which are characteristic of southern England in addition to the Midland types which might be expected. Leeds showed the distribution (according to the evidence available before the second world war) of the type of brooch known as 'small-long' (Leeds 1945: figs 7, 8, 9, 12, 17, 19, 24). Warwickshire examples are reproduced here in fig. 15. The types of small-long brooch which Leeds classified as 'trefoil-headed', 'cross pattee', 'square-head plain' and 'square-head with lozenge foot' are well-represented in south Warwickshire. Small-long brooches have a predominantly Midland and East Anglian distribution, and are rare south of the Thames.

Fig. 16 shows the distribution of penannular brooches known in 1945. They are not very common in Anglo-Saxon graves, and it is significant that there were six examples known from the Avon valley. Annular brooches (Leeds 1945: fig. 29) are a more numerous and widespread category, and these are well-represented in the Avon cemeteries, as are disc brooches (*ibid.*: fig. 30). 'Swastika and openwork' brooches, on the other hand, have a much more limited general distribution, and the pattern shown on Leeds's fig. 31 (here fig. 17) links the Avon valley in this respect with the regions around Cambridge and Peterborough, and with an area on the borders of Lincolnshire and Kesteven. Mr Ford tells me that 'the central core of graves at Alveston and to a lesser extent at Stretton were burials with disc (8), annular (4) and penannular (7) brooches'. He believes these to be the commonest brooch-types in the Avon cemeteries.

Three of Leeds's distribution maps which are here reproduced as figs 18–20 bring out clearly the exceptional nature of the Avon valley grave-goods. Figs 18 and 19 show the distribution of cruciform brooches excluding the latest ('florid') type. The cruciform is the typical Anglian brooch, and it might have been expected to be numerous in south Warwickshire, but in fact Leeds recorded only seven specimens, a meagre quantity compared with those found in the East Midlands and in Yorkshire. The small cemeteries on the Staffordshire and Derbyshire border produced four cruciform brooches, and this emphasizes the purely Anglian character of the Wychnor and Stapenhill grave goods. Fig. 20 shows the distribution in 1945 of the typically Saxon saucer brooch, which has a particularly heavy concentration in the upper Thames valley. These brooches are rare in East Anglia, and not very numerous in the East Midlands, so it is a noteworthy feature of the distribution that they are very well-represented in south Warwickshire. There will, of course, be new distribution patterns when the post-war excavations are published, but it seems likely to remain the case that saucer brooches are commoner in the Avon cemeteries than cruciform ones.

In the commentary on the distribution maps Leeds had little to say about the Avon valley; it is clear that his attention was focused on other areas. He does not comment on the Anglian/Saxon mixture in the brooches. This matter has been considered by Mr Ford in lectures, and will be fully discussed in the forthcoming reports. His conclusion is that the saucer brooches are imports, and constitute evidence for trade with the Thames valley rather than for Saxon people moving north from there. They are relatively late in date. In all the Avon cemeteries the earliest elements are

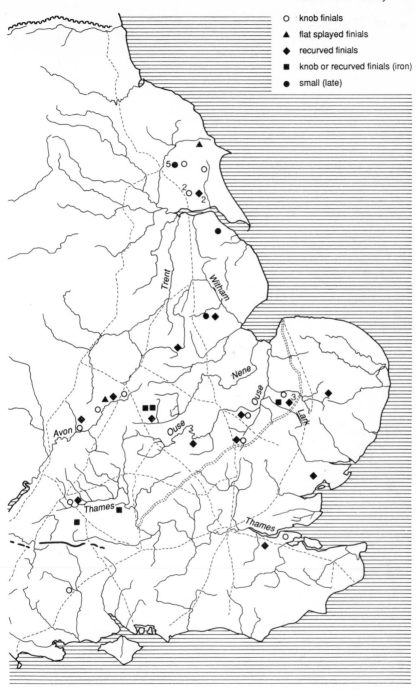

○ ·knob finials

▲ flat splayed finials

◆ recurved finials

■ knob or recurved finials (iron)

● small (late)

Figure 16 The distribution of Anglo-Saxon pennanular brooches (from Leeds, 1945, by permission of the Society of Antiquaries, London).

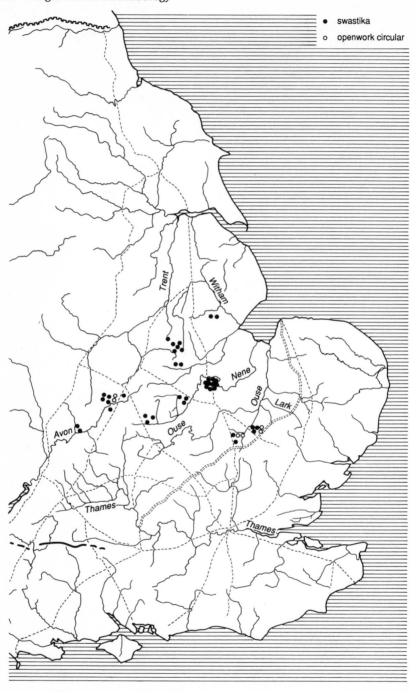

Figure 17 The distribution of Anglo-Saxon swastika and cognate openwork brooches (from Leeds, 1945, by permission of the Society of Antiquaries, London).

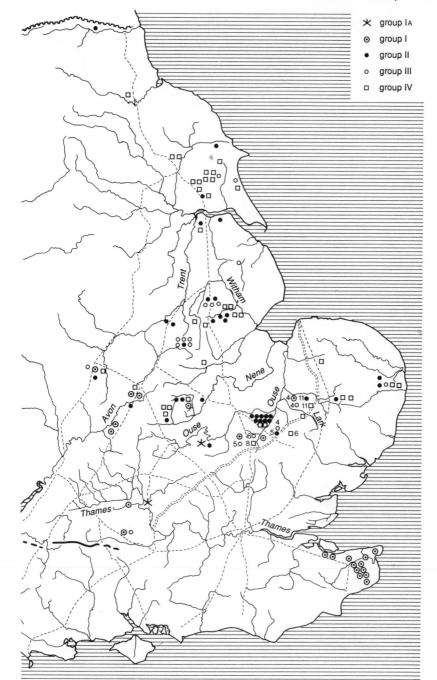

Figure 18 The distribution of Anglo-Saxon cruciform brooches, groups I–IV, with simple knobs (from Leeds 1945, by permission of the Society of Antiquaries, London).

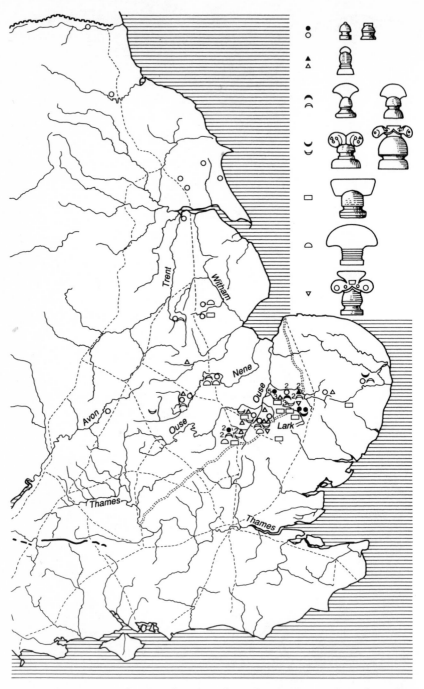

Figure 19 The distribution of Anglo-Saxon cruciform brooches, groups III and IV, with decorated knobs (from Leeds 1945, by permission of the Society of Antiquaries, London).

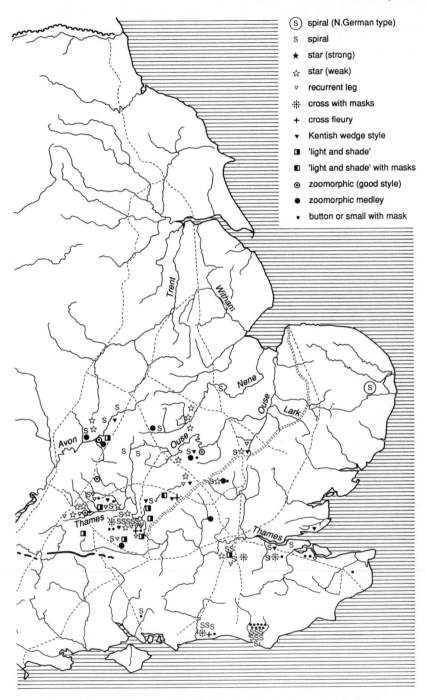

Legend:

- Ⓢ spiral (N.German type)
- s spiral
- ★ star (strong)
- ☆ star (weak)
- ▽ recurrent leg
- ✳ cross with masks
- + cross fleury
- ▼ Kentish wedge style
- ◻ 'light and shade'
- ◨ 'light and shade' with masks
- ◉ zoomorphic (good style)
- ● zoomorphic medley
- • button or small with mask

Figure 20 The distribution of Anglo-Saxon saucer brooches (from Leeds 1945, by permission of the Society of Antiquaries, London).

STRETTON – ON – FOSSE 1968 –1971

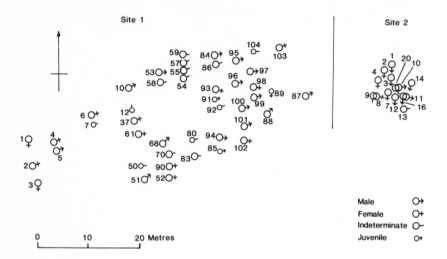

Figure 21   The Stretton-on-Fosse cemetery (by permission of W.J. Ford).

Anglian in character, and these early grave goods indicate colonization from the north-east, beginning in the late fifth century.

The Stretton-on-Fosse cemetery (fig. 21) was smaller than that at Alveston (figs 22, 23) (Stretton and Wasperton are the only ones of the Avon valley cemeteries whose limits are definitely known). At Stretton there were between 50 and 60 inhumations, most of them grouped in six recognizable rows. There was a group of five graves in the western sector, the goods from which had a date-range of A.D.475–525. These probably represent the early nucleus, and one male burial may be the 'founder' grave. One of the two females in the group had a cross-potent small-long brooch with shovel foot. The other had a pair of disc brooches, but a single-brooch style of dress was predominant in the earlier graves.

Saucer brooches were only found in the eastern sector of the cemetery, where the burials were of later date. Six such brooches occurred in pairs. Some of them are very large, so likely to belong to the late sixth century. Most of the paired brooches in the cemetery were accompanied by beads. Mr Ford considers that (as for Alveston) the earliest settlers had contacts with the East Midlands, especially the Cambridge region, and that the saucer-brooch phase marks a later period of trading contacts with Wessex.

The maximum date-span of the cemetery is A.D.475–625, and for this number of burials to have taken place in that time suggests a normal population of 10–12 inhabitants. This small community was relatively prosperous. The proportion of weapon burials is surprisingly high, comprising 88 per cent of adult males, with shield and spear the commonest combination.

One female burial had been decapitated, with the head placed between the feet. There were hob nails around the toes, and Mr Ford says that this burial could be described in all its aspects as typically Romano-British. Both decapitations and the presence of footwear are recognized features of Romano-British inhumations.

For much of the period during which grave-goods were deposited with the dead, the grandest female personal ornament which could be aspired to by wealthy people in most of central England was probably the great square-headed brooch. We do not have in our area of study aristocratic burials like the barrows in Derbyshire, which contained a certain amount of gold and garnet jewellery, but there are bronze brooches of the type known as square-headed from the Avon valley (Leeds 1949). Such a brooch would be used to fasten a cloak at the neck, whereas smaller brooches, such as the earlier cruciform, the small-long and the saucer types, were worn in pairs to fasten a tunic on the shoulders, often with a string of gaudy beads between.

The merit of the great square-headed brooch to the Anglo-Saxon artist (and to his contemporaries in northern Europe) was the large area of flat surface which it offered for deployment of the type of ornament known to archaeologists as Animal Style I (Salin 1904). The rectangular headplate, curved bow and lozenge-shaped footplate are all used for this purpose, and there are animal heads or whole animals at the junction of the bow and the footplate. The Anglo-Saxons delighted in this ornament, and it probably had symbolic meanings for them. The whole brooch may have been thought of as roughly representing an animal. Modern students require some training in order to recognize the component parts of the designs, and only the specialist is likely to recover the full pleasure which this art would give to the people for whom the brooches were made; but at their best they are objects of great beauty which repay detailed examination. The ornament is in fairly high relief, and in wear human and animal masks must have emerged dramatically from the background of jumbled animal limbs as the light caught them.

Two great square-headed brooches from the Alveston cemetery are illustrated here, one from grave 89, the other from grave 5 (figs 24, 25). The cemetery appears to have been used by two communities, with burial progressing generally in an easterly direction from the two earliest inter-ment groups focused on graves 45 and 70. As can be seen from fig. 23 there was a linear space extending between graves 49 and 100, and above this the burials were mixed inhumation and cremation, whereas below it inhuma-tion predominated. These brooches are from either part.

The brooch from grave 5 is an exceptionally ornate specimen. Leeds described it as the largest of all the known great square-headed brooches (Leeds 1949: 70 and no.116). There is a great deal of animal ornament on its surface, including a border of moustached face-masks round the headplate, two drooping heads with curly jaws at the top of the footplate, and contorted animals on the bow and in the central portion of the footplate. There is spiral and linear ornament also, and a number of raised settings in which coloured glass and white shell were inserted. A setting at the centre of the footplate holds a Roman intaglio of cornelian engraved

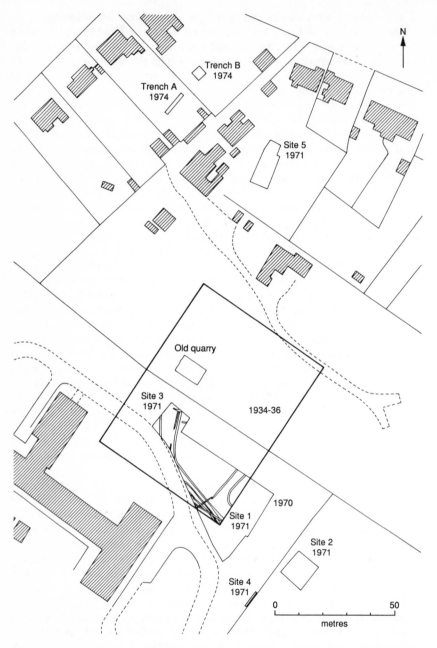

Figure 22   The Alveston cemetery, location plan (by permission of W.J. Ford).

ALVESTON MANOR 1933-1974

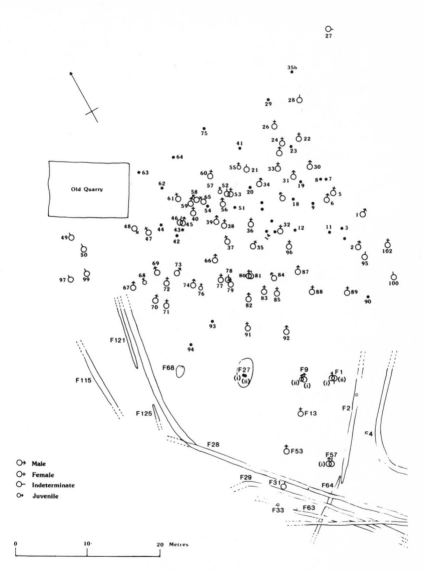

Figure 23 The Alveston cemetery, plan of burials (by permission of W.J. Ford).

with a Cupid milking a goat.

A particularly interesting feature of the Alveston 5 brooch is the material used to make the fastening mechanism on the back (*ibid*.: no.116). The pin-catch is welded to a plate in the shape of a fish, and the hinge-plate has the

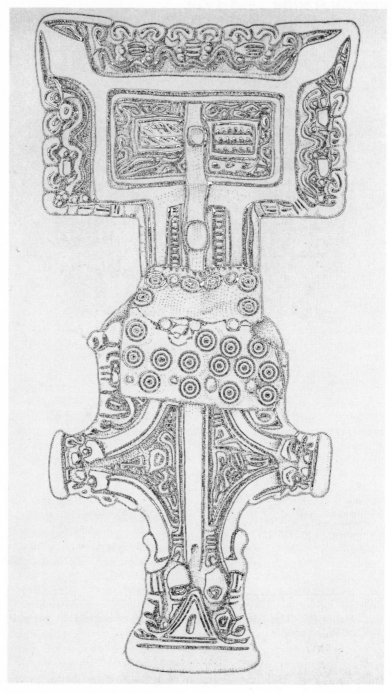

Figure 24   Square-headed brooch from Alveston grave 89 (by permission of W.J. Ford).

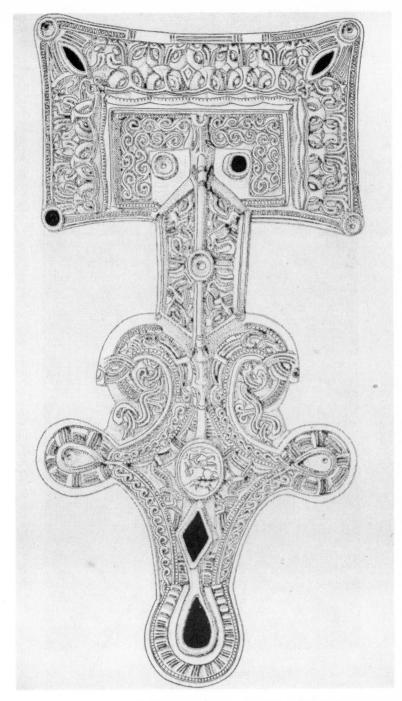

Figure 25 Square-headed brooch from Alveston grave 5 (by permission of W.J. Ford).

Figure 26 Ragley park brooch (from Leeds 1949, by permission of Oxford University Press). This brooch has been stolen from Ragley Park.

form of a curvilinear cross. These components are believed to have belonged to another, cannibalized, object, which may have been a cross-headed brooch. They clearly have Christian associations, and seem to indicate that the square-headed brooch (which has had some wear) was still in use at a time when pagan and Christian practices overlapped.

The woman who wore this great square-headed brooch was buried with many other adornments. She also had two saucer brooches with Kentish button brooches mounted on them, a penannular brooch, a rock-crystal ornament and an iron buckle; and 20 amber beads were suspended between her saucer brooches. Her grave was adjacent to the richest male burial in the Alveston cemetery, and both are at the eastern side, where (as at Stretton) the latest burials are found. Mr Ford considers the early seventh century the likely date for this burial.

A brooch from Ragley Park, Warwickshire (fig. 26) is perhaps the most pleasing of all English square-headed brooches to the modern eye. Some of its surface is left undecorated, affording a rare relief from the *horror vacui* which caused most of the more pretentious Anglo-Saxon jewels to be entirely encrusted with ornament. The animal motifs included two delightful crouching animals on either side of the headplate, human masks looking in opposite directions (up and down) at the top and bottom of the bow, and very clearly delineated downward-biting heads at the top of the footplate. The most remarkable feature, however, is a pair of coherent animals on either side of the bar which divides the footplate. They have their heads turned over their backs, and they look like deer. They are not in the 'meccano' style usual on these brooches but are reminiscent in their naturalism of Anglo-Saxon animals executed in the round, like the boar on the helmet from Benty Grange in Derbyshire, and the stag and the fish from the sceptre and the hanging bowl at Sutton Hoo. There are two other brooches of similar design (though not so well-executed) from Linton Heath and Quy in Cambridgeshire, and a fragment of one from Girton, Cambridge. Leeds considered that 'The members of this group may fairly be regarded as an interesting Cambridgeshire creation in which inventive originality has been combined with a ready adaptation of features taken from a Kentish model' (1949: 61). A more recent study of square-headed brooches accepts Leeds's classification (Hines 1984: 162-3).

Neither the Alveston brooches nor the beautiful Ragley Park one could be claimed as Warwickshire productions. Leeds did, however, recognize a 'South Midland group' containing five brooches, four of them from Warwickshire; and he suggested that in these 'a semblance of a regional style seems to be in process of development' (Leeds 1949: 47ff.). This group, which includes two brooches from Baginton, one from Bidford-on-Avon and one from Offchurch, can be augmented by a more recently found example from Beckford, Glos. They are particularly homogeneous, and it is agreed that the Bidford-on-Avon one (*ibid*.: 71) is the earliest. In addition to homogeneity of style, the group is linked by the relatively compact Western Midland distribution, the only outlier being from the Ock valley in north Berkshire. These brooches, it has recently been claimed, were probably buried in the central decades of the sixth century, having been manufactured in the period from c.510-50 (Hines 1984: 181, 197). The absolute chronology of square-headed brooches is, of course, open to debate, but it is instructive to have a local group attributed to the early sixth century.

The Anglo-Saxons of the Avon valley clearly appreciated the great square-headed brooch. They appear, on the other hand, to have largely eschewed the least attractive of all the jewellery styles of this period, the brooch known as the florid cruciform. This unlovely creation results from modification of the cruciform brooch in order to obtain areas of flat surface for animal ornament similar to those offered by the square-headed type. To this end, the three knobs which projected from the headplate to make the 'cross' shape in the original design were replaced with three flat plates, the animal head at the bottom end sprouted a triangular excrescence, and 'lappets' appeared at the base of the bow, all these areas being covered with ornament. Some of the ornament is good, but the overall effect is hideous. One of the Northamptonshire specimens is from Newnham, south of Daventry, near the Warwickshire border, and Leeds instanced one from Longbridge near Warwick as the nadir of the style (1936: 83), so they were not unknown in our area of study. But florid cruciforms are not typical of the Avon valley burials, as they are of Eastern Midland and East Anglian cemeteries.

As noted above, a detailed study of the grave goods from the Avon valley cemeteries is greatly to be desired. The findings from such a study will eventually combine with full accounts of cemeteries excavated by modern methods to give a firm basis for evaluation of the origins and social status of the earliest English settlers in the West Midlands, and of their relationship to the British population. From the information available at present, it seems likely that they came from the Cambridge region, and that they constituted a small population scattered among the earlier inhabitants of the fertile lands bordering the Avon in south Warwickshire and the adjacent part of Worcestershire. They were hardly sufficiently numerous to have replaced the native British people of this area, certainly not numerous enough to have formed a reservoir for the colonization of the rest of the West Midlands. In the later sixth century they established trading links with the people of the Thames valley. In the seventh century their territory formed part of the sub-kingdom of the Hwicce. There is no reason to suppose that they played a significant part in the establishment of the kingdom of Mercia.

Place-names Which Refer to Tumuli

Among the most exalted members of Anglo-Saxon society the deposition of grave goods continued far into the seventh century, perhaps even into the eighth, and there was a substantial overlap with Christianity. Some of the finds from Derbyshire barrows belong to this late phase, but, as already stated, none of these late aristocratic burials is known from our five counties. There is, however, a tantalizing class of place-names in which Old English *hlāw* 'tumulus' is combined with a personal name, and these deserve mention here, though it is unprofitable to spend too much time considering archaeological 'might-have-beens'.

There have been several painstaking studies of place-names and boundary marks which refer to burial mounds, and attention has recently focused upon the West Midlands (Hooke 1980-1). Dr Hooke's paper discusses occurrences of the Old English words *beorg, byrgels, byrgen, hlǣw* or *hlāw*, and the Welsh word *crug*, in the counties of Warwickshire, Worcestershire and Gloucestershire. *Byrgels* and *byrgen* mean 'burial place'; the other words can mean 'tumulus' but are also used of natural hills. It has long been considered that there is circumstantial evidence for connecting the word *hlāw, hlǣw* with Anglo-Saxon barrow burials in some of its occurrences in place-names (Gelling 1978: 154). Dr Hooke elaborates this theme (1980-1: 15-28), but firm evidence for the connection remains obstinately slight. A recent excavation of a tumulus in Wiltshire which is called *posses hlǣwe* in an Old English charter boundary has revealed a splendid burial of an Anglo-Saxon woman of aristocratic status; but it is a secondary insertion in a Bronze Age barrow. The only proven instance of a *-hlāw* place-name which definitely dates from the pre-Conquest period and which refers to an aristocratic Anglo-Saxon burial in a tumulus built for the purpose still appears to be Taplow, Bucks.

The place-name Taplow probably means 'Tæppa's tumulus', and it seems reasonable to assume that Tæppa was the prince for whom the mound was built. It would be most gratifying if a similar burial were to be discovered in a mound at another place with this type of name. The Wiltshire name *posses hlǣwe* is not strictly comparable, as it only occurs in a boundary survey, and personal names used in boundary marks are often those of the owners of neighbouring estates. Also if *posses hlǣwe* is to be interpreted as Poss's burial-mound, then it needs to be remembered that *posses* is a masculine genitive, while the burial is that of a woman. The seven ancient settlement-names in Shropshire which consist of *hlāw* and a personal name are, however, strictly comparable to Taplow in being place-names rather than once-recorded boundary marks; and Winslow and Wolferlow in north Herefordshire are also examples. The Shropshire names are Beslow, Longslow, Munslow, Onslow, Purslow, Walkerslow and Whittingslow. (Walkerslow was accidentally omitted from the version of this list in Gelling 1978: 156, but this addition is balanced by the deletion of Peplow, where subsequent inspection of the site found the soil to be unusually pebbly, making it seem perverse to reject the etymology 'pebble tumulus'.)

These names are shown on fig. 27. They are widely distributed in the county, and if there were tumuli at any of the places, and if Anglo-Saxon grave-goods were found there, they would fit splendidly with the view now held by archaeologists that late barrow burials are political statements of territorial claims. But, alas, there is no certain visible sign, and no record, of a tumulus at these places. On the other hand, at some of them, notably Beslow and Purslow in Shropshire and Wolferlow in Herefordshire, there is no natural hill, and nothing the name could possibly refer to except a vanished tumulus. Others, notably Walkerslow and Whittingslow, are in commanding situations, eminently suitable for tumuli. At Onslow, a stately home west of Shrewsbury, there is a feature in the park in front of the house which the eye of faith might see as a demolished tumulus.

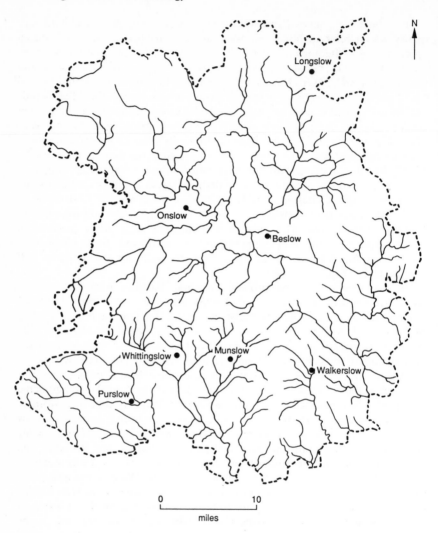

Figure 27   'x's tumulus' names in Shropshire.

The hypothesis that -low in Shropshire place-names is likely to commemorate an unrecorded burial mound has led to a number of fruitless 'hunt the tumulus' expeditions to places where the name can be pinpointed with precision by the aid of Tithe Award maps. One such is Shirlow in High Ercall parish, where the fields shown by the Tithe Award to make up the area called *Sherlow* are on a smooth, flat-topped ridge, and there is nothing in the topography for which *hlāw* could be appropriate. Burial mounds of probably Bronze Age date seem to have been exceptionally liable to obliteration in Shropshire. There are records of such demolitions at Farlow and at Ludlow, and it is just worth while offering the hypothesis that when a place-name in *-hlāw* has as first element an Old English

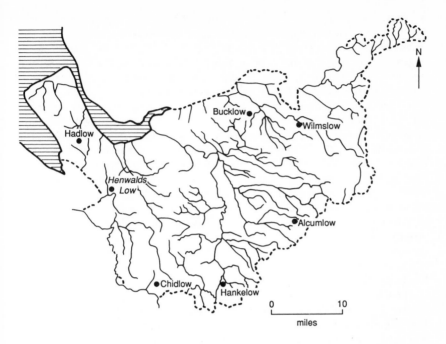

Figure 28 'x's tumulus' names in Cheshire.

personal name, the reference might have been to a late Anglo-Saxon barrow burial, which has shared the recorded fate of tumuli from earlier periods.

Cheshire also has seven names of this type which are sufficiently well-recorded to be certainly of pre-Conquest origin; these are Alcumlow, Bucklow, Chidlow, Hadlow, Hankelow, Wilmslow and a lost *Henwalds Lowe* in the city of Chester. Some other names placed in this category by Professor Dodgson (1981: 226) are too late-recorded to be considered for this purpose, and Shutlingsloe has been omitted as it may contain *hlāw* in its north-country sense of 'mountain'. The seven names are plotted on fig. 28. It would be possible to see the three examples near the southern boundary of Cheshire as marking a territorial divide from the Wreocensæte of north Shropshire (for whom v. Chapter 5). There are no extant tumuli to go with these names, but some of them, notably Alcumlow and Hadlow, are in country where no natural feature deserves the term *hlāw*.

Two of the five hundreds of Staffordshire have names which consist of *hlāw* and an Old English personal name; these are Offlow in the south and Totmonslow in the north of the county, and the names refer to the meeting-places of the hundredal assemblies, discussed in Chapter 8. In 1978 I described Offlow as 'the most notable instance in the West Midlands of a -low place-name which may refer to an Anglian burial' (Gelling 1978: 155). Offlow is the name of a mound which was sufficiently well-preserved to be drawn on the nineteenth-century Ordnance Survey map, but which has now been reduced by ploughing to a diffuse spread. There is no settlement, and recent Ordnance Survey maps do not print the name. The position, two miles south-south-west of Lichfield, and the incorporation of the personal name Offa have suggested to many commentators that this might be the burial place of a member of the Mercian royal family in the pagan period. In the light of a recent discovery in Buckinghamshire, however, caution must now be exercised in considering the nature of mounds which marked Anglo-Saxon meeting-places.

It now appears that the Anglo-Saxons were accustomed to construct artificial mounds which would serve as markers for meeting-places. This conclusion arises from the excavation of the mound (now incorporated in Milton Keynes) which marked the meeting-place of the Buckinghamshire hundred of Secklow. This was not sepulchral, and could have had no other purpose but to serve as a marker for the court of the hundred (Adkins and Petchey 1984). R.A. Adkins and M.R. Petchey list 11 examples of meeting-place mounds which have been excavated and found to be probably or certainly not sepulchral; seven of these have names in -low. They also draw attention to Oswaldslow Hundred in Worcestershire, an administrative unit created in A.D.964 and named in honour of the contemporary Bishop of Worcester; this seems very likely to have had as its meeting-place a mound constructed at that date.

The Cheshire and Shropshire names discussed above include three which belong to hundreds, as well as to settlements which grew up at the meeting-places. Munslow and Purslow in Shropshire, and Bucklow in Cheshire, are hundreds, and the mounds which the names commemorate may never have been used for burial, and so may be of no relevance in the forlorn search for possible archaeological traces of early Anglian settlers in those counties. The same may fairly be suspected with regard to Totmonslow in the high moorlands of north Staffordshire, and, alas, to Offlow.

4 The British People of the West Midlands

Authors dealing with British place-names in England have sometimes done so under the heading *The Celtic Survival* (e.g. Gelling 1978: ch.4), but that title would be inappropriate in this regional study. Chapter 3 of the present book has set out the limited evidence which exists for the presence of pagan Anglo-Saxons in the area. That there is no physical evidence at all for their presence in most of it cannot be ascribed to lack of archaeological interest. Since the end of the second world war archaeologists based in Shropshire, Herefordshire and Cheshire have looked assiduously for this material, and it should now be accepted that it is unlikely to be forthcoming, at any rate in significant quantities. If this be accepted, then it follows that we must consider the British population of the area not as 'surviving' (which implies a struggle against adverse circumstances or superior numbers) but as continuing to be there and as forming the main stock of the population.

The failure of the British farmers of the sixth and seventh centuries to manifest themselves to archaeologists constitutes no objection to this hypothesis, as this invisibility is everywhere characteristic of the British people who would have been equivalent in social and economic terms to the Anglo-Saxons of the Avon valley. In Wales, south-western England and southern Scotland there are high-status sites (the 'citadels' of Davies 1982: 22–4), and discoveries are made of objects which must have belonged to exalted people. In the West Midlands, however, especially in Staffordshire, historical sources leave no room for doubt that the political hierarchy was Anglo-Saxon by the seventh century, so sites comparable to Dinas Powys (Glamorgan), South Cadbury (Somerset) and Dunadd (Argyll) would, if they had existed, have had relatively short lives.

If the British people cannot be expected to manifest themselves archaeologically, what traces ought there to be of them? One of the signs is, of course, linguistic. We should have relatively large numbers of British place-names, and this chapter is concerned with the names in our five counties which are either in the British language or which contain references to British people and pre-English institutions. Such items are not as numerous as could be wished. A possible reason for this is that many of them were eventually superseded by English names of an 'administrative' type, which may have originated as convenient labels for Welsh settlements in the speech of the Mercian governing class. The exceptionally high incidence of these administrative names in the West Midlands, particularly in Shropshire, will be demonstrated in a later chapter. Meanwhile our task is to examine in each of our five counties those names which may fairly be considered to provide evidence for the continuance of British speech and

British institutions into the period when the area was incorporated into the enlarged Mercian kingdom, that is in the later seventh and early eighth century.

Figs 25 to 30 display a corpus of place-names which are relevant to our theme because, in one way or another, they demonstrate linguistic contact between speakers of Primitive Welsh and speakers of Old English. (These are the terms used by philologists for the Celtic and Germanic languages which were spoken in England from the fifth century onwards.) This is a very important body of evidence, since Dark Age linguistic contact which results in the adoption or formation of names still in use today must be supposed to have taken place in a context of peaceful coexistence, even if the speakers of one language were forced into a position of social inferiority.

The material shown on the maps can be divided into the following categories:

(i) Items which preserve or incorporate recorded Romano-British toponyms. The administrators of Roman Britain used native British place-names supplemented by only a handful of new Latin ones. They were able to pronounce British names without difficulty owing to the close kinship between the sound-systems of the two languages. There is a good deal of later corruption in the texts in which these names are recorded, particularly in that of the Ravenna Cosmography; but in spite of this it is clear that the Romans were able to spell British names with great precision. After the Roman period British names developed as part of the evolving Welsh language, and when encountered by Anglo-Saxons in the West Midlands they were in Primitive Welsh, not in the British speech of Roman times.

(ii) Names of rivers. These are universally recognized as having the highest survival rate among all classes of toponyms when one language is superseded by another.

(iii) Names of mountains and conspicuous hills. The relatively high survival rate here (as for major rivers) is due to the use of such names by all the communities to whom a feature like Barr Beacon or the Malvern Hills forms a conspicuous landmark. The greater the number of people using a name, the better will be its chances of survival.

(iv) Names of forests. Here again, such toponyms would be in use by widespread communities living round the fringes.

(v) Names which do not fit into any of the above categories but which are easily explicable in Welsh and meaningless in English.

(vi) Hybrids, the term used for names with one element in Welsh and one in English. (Most of the recorded Romano-British names which survive – category (i) in this list – do so in hybrid formations, but they should be treated as a separate category because documentation proves their origin in a manner which cannot be expected for any other names shown on these maps.) Some of the hybrids are tautological, like Cheadle and Bredon. These may sometimes have arisen by a process of imperfect understanding, whereby English speakers heard Welsh speakers referring to '*the* wood' or '*the* hill', and concluded incorrectly that *cēd* and *bre* were the names of those features. It is perhaps more likely, however, that the Anglo-Saxons were using their own terms *lēah* and *dūn* to define the precise type of wood and hill referred to by the Welsh terms.

(vii) English names which refer to Welshmen, using either the term *cumbre* (the Old English adaptation of Welsh *Cymro* 'Welshman') or the term *walh*. The significance of *walh* has occasioned much discussion, culminating in Professor K. Cameron's definitive study (1980). The word originally meant 'foreigner', then came to mean 'Welshman'. Hence modern English Wales from the plural *walas*, and Welsh from the derived adjective *welisc*. *Walh* also developed a meaning 'serf', but Dr Margaret Faull (1975) has demonstrated from a study of laws and other literary sources that this use did not cause the ethnic meaning to become subordinate until the late Anglo-Saxon period. *Walh* was used as an element in Old English personal names, including those of rulers of kingdoms, and the term cannot have been derogatory in this context. Professor Cameron's study of the corpus of place-names containing *walh* establishes that the people referred to are most likely to be Welshmen, who were probably distinguished from the people of neighbouring settlements mainly by their continued use of Welsh speech. The distribution of the names, and the frequent recurrence of compounds with *tūn*, *cot* and *worth*, indicates that most of them arose after A.D.700.

(viii) Names containing *ecles* 'church' or 'Christian community'. This is believed to be an Old English borrowing from Primitive Welsh (ultimately from Latin *ecclesia*), adopted when the pagan Anglo-Saxons needed a word for a Celtic Christian centre. The definitive study of *ecles* is Cameron 1968.

(ix) Names containing Old English loan-words from Latin. These occur mainly in southern and eastern England (Gelling 1978: ch.3; Gelling 1988: 245–50), but barely impinge on the present area of study; Chadshunt Warws. is the only example.

Warwickshire (fig. 29)

While the incidence of all these categories of names is disappointingly low over most of the region, it is at least encouraging to note that the evidence is sparsest in Warwickshire. This is the only one of our five counties in which there is archaeological evidence for a community of Anglo-Saxon farmers, and this may have been a factor which encouraged the almost total replacement of the pre-English name stock.

In category (i), Warwickshire has Mancetter, which consists of the Romano-British name *Manduessedum* with the addition of Old English *ceaster*, the regular term applied by the Anglo-Saxons to a Roman site where the ruins were impressive. *Manduessedum* is an unusual British name meaning 'horse-chariot', perhaps a reference to sporting activities. This is the first item in a line of names along Watling Street (fig. 8) which were adopted and perpetuated by English speakers. Lichfield and Penkridge,

Figure 29   Warwickshire: ancient Celtic names, and names which refer to British people.

Staffordshire, and Wroxeter, Shropshire, are the examples to the west, and there is a stark contrast between the survival of these four names and the disappearance of the seven which belonged to stations on Watling Street to the east, between Mancetter and London. The names are known because they occur in the document known as the Antonine Itinerary, which gives a list of stopping-places on the main roads of the Roman Empire. Their situations are also known, as the Itinerary notes distances; and it is certain that between London and Mancetter none of them is commemorated in a later place-name, whereas between Mancetter and Wroxeter *Uxacona* is the only station whose name was lost. In this respect, at least, the place-name evidence supports a more vigorous British survival in the West Midlands than in the East and South Midlands.

Pre-English river-names in Warwickshire number eight which are generally accepted as being of Celtic origin, and some possibles. Alne ('very white'), Anker ('winding'), Arrow (?'surging'), Avon ('river'), Cole ('hazels'), Itchen (?'powerful'), Leam ('elms') and Tame (?'dark') are the more or less unequivocal items. Avon, here and elsewhere, may have been mistaken for a name by Anglo-Saxons who heard Welsh people using it as a noun. In addition to these, there is a stream-name *Leonte* in an Old English boundary survey near King's Norton, south of Birmingham, which is likely to be of similar origin to Leint- which survives in two names shown on the Herefordshire map. Avon in the village-name Avon Dassett is probably a stream-name. Sow, of which there is another example in Staffordshire, has been given a tentative Celtic etymology (Ekwall 1928: 375-6), but this is now regarded as very doubtful (Jackson 1953: 373, 519). Coundon near Coventry, *Condelm* in DB, is ingeniously derived in Ekwall 1960 from Old English *wielm* 'river-source' and the Celtic river-name Cound, which occurs also in Shropshire. This suits the spellings well, but the name would have to be allocated to a tiny tributary of the River Sherbourne, which is not the type of watercourse expected to keep its ancient name in this county. The same caveat applies to Humber Brook in the south-west of the county, and in addition to this reason for hesitation, the origin of the widespread river-name Humber has not been satisfactorily elucidated. The *Leonte* in King's Norton is also a very small stream.

Worcestershire is not included in the present study, but it may be noted that there is a marked contrast between the two counties as regards the size of streams with Celtic names. Examples like *Leonte* and Cound in Coundon would certainly be acceptable in Worcestershire, where some tiny feeders of the Avon and Severn have unequivocal Celtic names, like *Trent* and *Parret* (Avon), and Lem and Dowles (Severn).

The only hill-name shown on fig. 29 is Meon, which is a spur crowned by a hill-fort projecting from the Cotswolds. (This, and the little Humber Brook, were actually in Gloucestershire till modern times, but they fall within the outline of the county which is used for this set of figures.) No satisfactory etymology has as yet been proposed for Meon, but it is not explicable in English, and the hill is the sort of feature which might be expected to keep an ancient name. The name occurs again in Meon, Hampshire. Ekwall 1960 explains it as a British river-name, but this is not established with certainty. There, also, it could be a hill-name, though it was transferred to a district.

Arden is the only district name in Warwickshire which may be suspected of being pre-English, and if derivation from Celtic *ardu-* 'high' be accepted, it is both hill-name and forest-name, like the Ardennes in France. The Warwickshire Arden is not, however, certain to be exactly the same name as the French one. Doubts arise because from 1174 to 1547 there are spellings with a second -r-, *Erderna*, *Ardern(e)*, alongside the spellings with *-dene* which precede them and which eventually prevailed. The earliest form is *Eardene* in 1088, in the surname of Turchil *de Eardene*, who was called Turchil *de Warwic* in DB, but whose descendants used the Arden surname.

He was an English magnate, not a Norman, and this lends authority to the spelling *Eardene*. The name subsequently appears as *Ardena*, *Ardene* from 1130 to 1166, and as *Arden* from 1220 onwards; but from 1174 to 1547 many references to the family and the region have *-ern-*, not *-en-*. This phenomenon led to the derivation in Ekwall 1960 from an unrecorded Old English *eardærn*, which would mean 'dwelling-house', and Ekwall states that the *-r-* of *-rn* has been lost in the *Arden(e)* series of spellings by dissimilation, because of the *-r-* in the first syllable. This is not the place to argue the matter in detail, but it should be noted that neither the loss of *-r-* postulated by Ekwall nor the hypothetical addition of an inorganic *-r-* required for the association of the name with Ardennes can be paralleled in other place-names. Until a satisfactory explanation of the *-ern* spellings is found, the Celtic derivation of Arden cannot be regarded as wholly secure. This is a pity, because a name parallel to that of the Ardennes would suit the circumstances admirably. The east side of the Birmingham plateau, from which there is an abrupt descent to the Avon valley, would be fittingly described as 'high, wooded place', which is the meaning postulated for the Continental name.

Categories (v) and (vi) of the above classification are not represented in Warwickshire, but there are two instances of the name Walcot ('cottages of the Welshmen'), which is one of the items in category (vii). A caveat must be offered against the assumption that all modern instances of Walcot and Walton refer to Welshmen. If a place-name contains the genitive plural of *walh*, which is *wala*, then the Middle English spellings will mostly have a medial *e*, as in *Walecote*, which occurs in 1235 and 1279 for Walcot in Haselor, and from 1086 to 1366 for the lost *Walcote End* in Grandborough. The spellings for the two Warwickshire Waltons, in Wellesbourne Hastings and Monks Kirby, do not have this characteristic, so those names are believed to be of different origin. The Old English words *wald* 'upland forest', *weall* 'wall', and *wælle*, the West Midland form of *well* 'spring', can all yield modern forms such as Walcot and Walton. The names shown on figs 29–31, 33–4 are all vouched for by early documentation.

Professor Cameron's study of *walh* 'Welshman' in English place-names establishes the probability that such names arose in the eighth century to denote settlements where Welsh speech could still be heard, though at that date this would have been exceptional, as the change to English must have been far advanced (Cameron 1980). An earlier date must be ascribed to names containing *ecles*, since these refer to the contrast between the Christian worship which survived from Roman Britain and the pagan practices of the first generation of English settlers. Exhall, of which Warwickshire has two examples, is a shortened version of Eccleshall in Staffordshire and Yorkshire. No firm decision has been reached about the significance of the triple occurrence of this compound in the West Midlands. The second element is Old English *halh*, which has numerous meanings, some topographical and some administrative (Gelling 1988: 100ff.). The topographical sense, 'slight hollow', is common in the vicinity of all three place-names, and it may be no more than a coincidence that three such sites are referred to in conjunction with the term *ecles*. Certainly Exhall near Coventry and Eccleshall, Staffordshire are in typical *halh* country, where the contours do not produce well-defined valleys of the types which the Anglo-Saxons called *cumb* and *denu.*

The only remaining name on fig. 29 is Chadshunt. The Old English form of Chadshunt is recorded, and it is *Ceadeles funtan,* which shows that this is one of a corpus of perhaps 20 names in which the Anglo-Saxons used a term borrowed from Latin *fons, fontis* in preference to their own word *well.* It has been demonstrated that springs at these places are particularly copious (Cole 1985). It is a reasonable hypothesis that Roman stonework was visible when the Anglo-Saxons first saw them, and that this was why they used the Latin-derived word. The spring at Chadshunt may later have been associated with St Chad, of whose name *Ceadel* would be an affectionate diminutive.

Staffordshire (fig. 30)

Fig. 30 shows all the place-names in Staffordshire which can be considered as evidence for coexistence between Welsh- and English-speaking people. They are more numerous than in Warwickshire, though not dramatically so. A more important difference than the quantitative one is the status of some of the settlements to which they refer. Only Mancetter and Chadshunt in the Warwickshire corpus are names of parishes, whereas nine of the Staffordshire names have this status, some of them denoting major administrative centres of the Anglo-Saxon period.

Staffordshire has two names which preserve recorded Romano-British toponyms; these are Penkridge and Lichfield. Penkridge has recently become a very special item in place-name studies. It was always of interest as one of the rare instances in which a dithematic Romano-British name survived with both its elements and without the addition of an English word. The Roman station on Watling Street, two miles south of Penkridge, was called *Pennocrucium* (fig. 8), and the recorded Old English spelling for Penkridge, *Pencric* (985, S 667), faithfully reproduces the Primitive Welsh form of the earlier British name. *Pennocrucium* is a compound of *penn* 'head', frequently used of hills and headlands, with *crug,* a word sometimes used for a tumulus. The obvious meaning is 'tumulus on a headland', and it is shaming to note that commentators, including the present author, failed to pursue this archaeological clue. Mr J. Gould has pointed out to us, however, that there are records of a tumulus at Rowley Hill Farm, 1,200 yards north of Watling Street at GR SJ 90251180. It has been virtually ploughed out, but the site can still be evaluated, and it can be seen that it would have been a striking visual feature in the low relief of the landscape. This is a welcome object lesson in the essential simplicity and trustworthiness of place-names. Even the most ancient names may refer to something which is still there. Penkridge is a large parish and was a great composite estate in 1086. It is possible that a large area had this name in Romano-British times also.

For Lichfield, as for Penkridge, the Old English documentation is exceptionally good. The Romano-British name of the station at Wall, two miles south of Lichfield, was *Letocetum,* a British name meaning 'grey wood',

Figure 30   Staffordshire: ancient Celtic names, and names which refer to British People.

which occurs several times in England, Cornwall and Wales. The Primitive Welsh form of this is faithfully represented by the first part of the spellings for Lichfield in the earliest manuscripts of Bede's *Ecclesiastical History*, which are *Lyccidfelth, Lyccitfeld, Licidfelth, Liccitfeld*. It seems likely that *Letocetum* was the name of a wood which, in Romano-British times, extended some distance north of Watling Street, and that Lichfield was the 'open land' on the north side of it.

British river-name survival in Staffordshire is mainly confined to some of the larger watercourses. Trent ('trespasser'), Dove ('black'), Hamps ('summer dry'), Churnet ('winding'), Tean (obscure) are all major rivers or large tributaries. Ilam, although the name of a settlement, has been considered to preserve a pre-English name of the River Manifold, but it has recently been explained, more satisfactorily, as a Norse name meaning 'at the pools' (see Chapter 8). The only small stream noted in Staffordshire with a pre-English name is the one at Leamonsley near Lichfield. The first part of Leamonsley is the river-name which has become Leam in Warwickshire.

Penn and Barr, in the south of the county, are the two obvious Staffordshire examples of British hill-names. Great Barr is a large parish (though not as large as Penkridge), and there were three DB manors using the name Barr. It is reasonable to assume that when the English came there were settlements here which were using the name of the hill (now called Barr Beacon), and that there is a deeper level of continuity than would be implied by the simple passing on of the hill-name; but in the nature of the case this cannot be proved. Penn is not a parish, but there were two estates using this name in 1086. Talke in the north-west of the county is probably also a British hill-name, from Welsh *talcen* 'forehead, brow, gable-end', with loss of -*n* in an unstressed syllable (Coates 1988: 33).

The Staffordshire forests believed to have pre-English names are Morfe and Kinver. Neither has been satisfactorily explained, though it seems clear that Kinver has *bre* 'hill' as second element. The district-name Lyme, which impinges on the north-west fringe of the county, is discussed below.

Among the British names in Staffordshire which are not those of great features of the landscape is Hints. The settlement is on Watling Street, and the name seems virtually certain to be formed from the Welsh word *hynt* 'road'. This perhaps indicates that the settlement performed a special function in relation to the Roman road. It may be the Welsh equivalent of the English name Stretton.

The category of hybrid Welsh/English names is well-represented in Staffordshire. The only tautological hybrid is Cheadle, in which Old English *lēah* 'wood' has been added to the word which is the second element of *Letocetum*. Chatterley is 'wood by the hill called *Cader*', and Creighton is 'settlement by the rock called *Creic*'. Penkhull is 'hill by *Pencet*', and *Pencet* is a recurrent Primitive Welsh name which means '(place at) the end of the wood'. Ridware, though now attached to four settlements, must originally have been the name of a group of people, formed with Old English *ware* 'dwellers'. The *Ridware* were the dwellers near a feature called *Rhyd*, from the Welsh word which means 'ford'. The settlements are in wet country between the Rivers Blithe and Trent, an area where river-crossings may well have been particularly important. In Brewood the English word *wudu* has been added to British *bre* 'hill'. The hill is a prominent one, and *bre* may have been an appellative which the English heard, rather than its ancient name.

Under the heading 'English names which refer to Welshmen', there are two points to be made about the Staffordshire map. One is that in addition to *walh*, found in the genitive plural in the three Waltons, we have the alternative term, *cumbre*, in Comberford. This is perhaps a politer way of referring to Britons than *walh*, since it is the Old English version of *Cymro* (plural *Cymry*), the Welsh name for themselves. The other point concerns Walsall. Here the term *walh* occurs in the genitive singular, and could be a personal name. In fact both *Walh* and the adjective *Welisc* occur among the names of witnesses to Anglo-Saxon charters. It is, however, reasonable to suppose that such names were either given to boys by parents who were proud of their Welsh blood, or (perhaps more likely) acquired as nicknames by men who were known to have Welsh connections. It is most unlikely that *Walh* ('foreigner, Welshman, serf') could ever have been considered a colourless term to be used randomly in personal names. The same consideration applies to *Cumbre*, which occurs as a personal name in Comberton Worcestershire, as well as appearing in the genitive plural in such names as Comberford.

With regard to Eccleshall, it should be noted that this is an exceptionally large parish (bigger than Penkridge), and the centre of a composite estate described in the Domesday Survey. The name indicates Anglo-Saxon cognisance of British institutions, and the administrative unit may also predate the coming of the English.

Cheshire (fig. 31)

The incidence of place-names which result from the use of Welsh speech in the Anglo-Saxon period is lower in Cheshire than it is in Staffordshire, but the high administrative status of some of the places concerned is even more noteworthy. This may be a clue to continuity of land-units from pre-English times. In Cheshire (as generally in northern England) the township is a unit comparable to the parish in more southerly counties. Of the names shown on fig. 31, five (Cheadle, Eccleston, Ince, Tarvin and Wallasey) belong to parishes, and seven (Comberbatch, both instances of Crewe, Liscard, Walton and Werneth) to townships.

This is not, however, a county in which small streams kept their pre-English names. The British names Dane ('trickle'), Dee ('goddess'), Gowy (?'bend'), Peover ('bright'), Tame (?'dark'), Wheelock ('winding') all belong to substantial rivers. There are four names which preserve pre-English terms for hills. In Barhill the English word has been added to Primitive Welsh *barr* 'top, summit', this being a better-documented name than the Bar Hill shown with a query on the Staffordshire map. Bryn near Weaverham appears to be Primitive Welsh *brinn* 'hill', though the site is only modestly elevated. Minn, which occurs in Bosley Minn and Wincle Minn, is Primitive Welsh *minith*, Welsh *mynydd*, used here of a ridge of moorland on the boundary between several townships. In Pensby, the Norse word for a settlement has been added to the genitive of a hill-name *Penn* at a date when this would have been meaningless; the *penn* is Heswall Hill a prominent feature whose Welsh name must have been adopted by English speakers before it was used to make the Norse name.

None of the officially designated forests of medieval Cheshire had a pre-

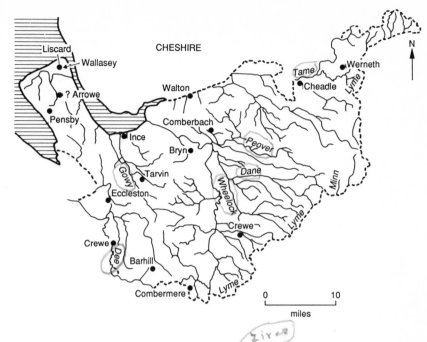

Figure 31 Cheshire: ancient Celtic names and names which refer to British people.

English name, but under the heading 'Names of forests' it is necessary to insert a discussion of the district-name The Lyme.

It is not certain to what extent Lyme should be regarded as referring originally to a wood, though there are frequent references in thirteenth- and fourteenth-century sources to *boscus de Lyme.* (Ekwall 1922: 23-6; Dodgson 1970: 2-6.) Ekwall regarded Lyme as a wood-name, but Dodgson suggests that the association with a forest 'is a secondary development, the original application being to the region above the 400-foot contour from south Lancashire to north Shropshire, and from east Cheshire to north and perhaps east Derbyshire'. This would mean that Lyme was originally the name of the southern part of the Pennine Chain.

The evidence for the extent of the region consists of the use of such phrases as *subtus Lime, iuxta Lyme* as affixes to settlement-names, supplemented by occasional minor names like Lyme Wood, Lyme Park and the use of Lyme as a second element in Audlem and Burslem (fig. 32). There are only two relevant minor names on the east side of the Pennines, Morley Lime, north-east of Derby, and Limb Hill in Dore, south of Sheffield. Dodgson considers that the much greater frequency of references on the west side of the Pennines is due to the more dramatic nature of the escarpment there.

In spite of the tenuous nature of the evidence for it on the east side of the Pennines, Dodgson's suggestion that Lyme was originally the name of the whole southern part of the massif is convincing. In the post-Conquest

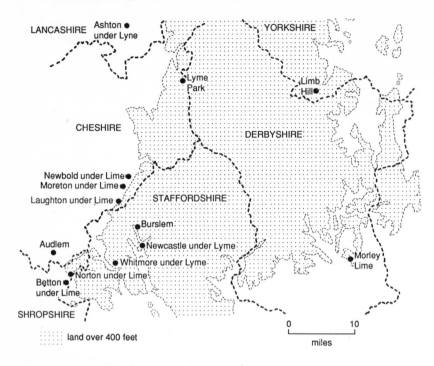

Figure 32   Place-names containing Lyme.

period a great deal of this area was included in the royal forests of Macclesfield and Peak, and Dodgson suggests that it is because of this that Lyme came to be considered as the name of a wood. The 'wood' application was current well to the south of Macclesfield, however. The earliest recorded use of the name Lyme is in a document of 1121-6 concerning Norton-in-Hales in the north-east corner of Shropshire, which includes the phrase 'Nortona que sita est iuxta nemus quod lima dicitur' ('Norton which lies next to the wood called Lyme') (Rees 1975: 2). But the place-name evidence mapped on fig. 32 shows that Lyme was a long, narrow strip rather than a wood of normal dimensions, so perhaps it can be considered as primarily the name of the escarpment. In that capacity it could well be a restricted application of an earlier name for the whole massif.

There is general agreement that the district-name Lyme is likely to be of pre-English origin, and it has frequently been regarded together with a number of other names in Britain and on the Continent, as a Celtic name derived from a British stem *lemo-* meaning 'elm'. But this view has recently been challenged (Rivet and Smith 1979: 385ff.).

There is a group of toponyms (comprising the Rivers Lymn, Lincolnshire and Lympne, Kent, the Lemon and Loman, Devon, the Leam, Warwickshire, several instances of River Leven in Scotland and a number of names on the Continent) in which a base such as *lemo-* has been adapted for use as a place-name (in most instances a river-name) by the addition of an *-n* suffix. This is explained as a Celtic adjectival suffix, which would give a meaning 'elmy river' or 'elmy place'. It is not certain that the Pennine district-name had this suffix. There are no Old English spellings, but Dodgson argues that the alternative form *Lyne* indicates that the suffix was present in the Old English form. The earliest instance of *Lyne* which he cites, however, is 1319, and it is easily explained as a late corruption.

Lyme Regis in Dorset, which is recorded as *Lim, Lym* in charters of A.D.774 and A.D.938 (so certainly without an -*n* suffix) is named from a River Lyme. The 'elm' derivation is not adduced by philologists for this name, a root *lim- connected with modern Welsh *llif* 'flood' being preferred (cf. e.g. Jackson 1953: 486). Rivet and Smith (1979: 385-6) suggest that this word is a better base than *lemo-, 'elm' for all the Lymn, Lympne, Lemon names as well as for the Pennine district-name and the Dorset river, and they clearly see no objection to the phenomenon of the adjectival suffix appearing in some names and not others. The use of a suffix is, however, more obviously required when a tree-name is used as base for a river-name than it is when the base is a word meaning 'wet'. Perhaps the Dorset river and the Pennine district should be associated with each other on the grounds that neither has the suffix, and the 'elm' derivation should continue to be regarded as appropriate for all the other names.

It is difficult for the modern observer to evaluate the rival claims of 'elmy place' and 'marsh' as applied to the southern end of the Pennines. That there was woodland on the western slopes is attested by the references noted above to *nemus* and *boscus de Lyme*. It is a reasonable hypothesis that this woodland once extended much higher up the massif, but is it likely to have been characterized by elm-trees? A sprinkling of elms among other, perhaps commoner, trees could account for a name with this meaning. On the other hand, a word meaning 'flood' or 'marsh' could well have been applied to an upland region in addition to being used of lowland marshes. This is paralleled by the use of Old English *mōr*, modern *moor*, in place-names.

If this whole group of names were reconsidered by an expert in the Celtic languages, it might be seen that other roots deserve consideration besides those meaning 'elm' and 'wet'.

In our category (v) (names explicable in Welsh, not so in English), Cheshire has Ince, Liscard, Tarvin, Werneth, and two instances of Crewe. Ince derives from the word which has become modern Welsh *ynys* 'island', used here, in a manner comparable to the place-name function of Old English *ēg*, for raised ground in a marshy place. Liscard is 'hall of the rock', and early spellings, such as *Lisnecark* 1260, show that it is a name derived from a phrase, with the definite article as middle element. This, and the use of the habitative term, *llys*, mark it as a name formed in the post-Roman period. Tarvin is Welsh *terfyn* 'boundary', a loan-word from Latin *terminus*. Dodgson (1970: 26, and 1971: 281), regarded this as an alternative name of the River Gowy. It certainly was the name of the river in the thirteenth century, but it is recorded in DB as the name of the settlement, and it seems possible that its original application was to a boundary zone. Werneth is a well-evidenced British and Gaulish name meaning 'alder place'. The names Ince and Werneth occur in Lancashire as well as in Cheshire.

Crewe has been frequently said to mean 'ford' or 'stepping-stones', but this old definition has been revised and the meaning is now said to be 'weir'. The basic sense of Welsh *cryw* is probably 'basket', from which it was extended to a wickerwork fence placed across a river to catch fish. A meaning 'stepping stones' probably developed from the use of a row of stones to reinforce such a structure, and this may have become a crossing-place, hence 'ford' (Dodgson 1971: 10).

Barhill (noted above as a hill-name) and Cheadle (identical with the Staffordshire example) are the only Welsh/English hybrids noted in Cheshire. Names referring to Britons are Comberbach and Combermere ('river valley' and 'lake of the Cymry') and Walton. Wallasey was *Walea* in DB *Waleie* c.1150, *Walleye* 1259. This means 'island of the Welshmen', but in view of the situation it could perhaps refer to immigrants from Wales rather than to descendants of Romano-Britons. It is possible that Liscard and Wallasey, together with Landican (further south in the Wirral, not shown in fig. 31) should be ascribed to Dark Age influence from Wales.

Cheshire has a single *ecles* name, Eccleston, a parish south of Chester.

Shropshire (fig. 33)

In Shropshire, survival of known Romano-British names is represented by Wroxeter and the Wrekin. Non-surviving names of recorded Romano-British stations are *Mediolanum* (a doublet of Milan) at Whitchurch and *Rutunium* near Stanton upon Hine Heath (fig. 8).

The Roman name of the Cornovian cantonal capital was *Viroconium Cornoviorum*. In Wroxeter, Old English *ceaster* has been added to the British place-name, and the compound has been much reduced by late Old English shortening and the dropping of the second *s* sound in *-cester*. Wrekin, the name of a large massif four miles east of the Roman town, preserves the British name without any addition. There is a large hill-fort on the Wrekin which may have been the tribal 'capital' in pre-Roman times. It is likely that when the Cornovii accepted Roman rule and were provided with a capital city by the River Severn they transferred the name of their ancient capital to the new site. The name probably means 'place associated with a man named *Virico*'.

Among the larger rivers of Shropshire there are four – Clun, Cound, Roden and Tern – which have pre-English names, and one – Perry – which is partly pre-English. Clun is a name of uncertain meaning which is well-evidenced elsewhere in England in the forms Clowne and Colne. The same can be said of Cound, which elsewhere takes the modern forms Kent and Kennet. The British form of Roden ('swift river') was used by the Romans to name the station of *Rutunium*, but the survival of the river-name probably owes little to this. Tern ('powerful river') was remembered in Welsh tradition as marking the eastern boundary of Powys before Mercian rule was established over Shropshire. It is possible that Cantern, the name of a brook near Bridgnorth, contains the same element. Perry consists of the British river-name *Pefer* ('radiant') with the addition of Old English *ēa* 'river'. Onny has hitherto been regarded as a British name, but the full

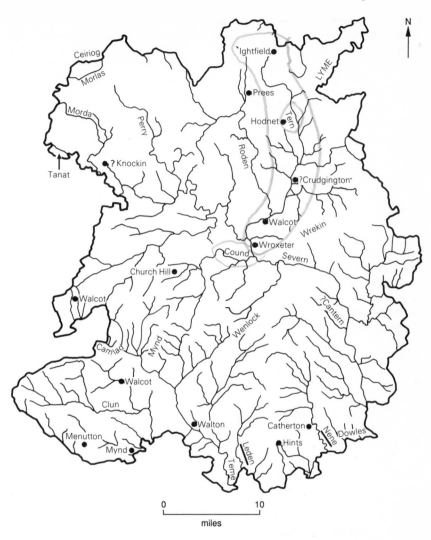

Figure 33 Shropshire: ancient Celtic names, and names which refer to British people.

collection of spellings now available makes an English origin more probable (Gelling 1990: 227-8).

Whether the settlements called Cound and Clun existed with those names during the Roman period and continuously to the time when the Mercians took control, or whether the English named them from the rivers, is a problem comparable to that raised by the Staffordshire names Penn and Barr, discussed above.

Apart from these rivers, and those like Teme and Severn which are not specific to Shropshire, British stream-names only survive in significant numbers on the west and south boundaries. On the north-west boundary

are Morlas, Morda, Tanat, and Ceiriog, from which last the town of Chirk
is named; and further south is the Camlad. These are best seen as an extension of Welsh river-nomenclature. More significant for our purpose are
some names on the south-eastern boundary. Dowles Brook forms the boundary between Shropshire and Worcestershire for part of its course. This
name, which means 'black stream', recurs frequently throughout the British
Isles. The settlements called Neen Solers and Neen Savage preserve the pre-
English name of the River Rea. The etymology of Neen is obscure; it recurs
in the East Midlands in the form Nen(e). Lower and Upper Ledwyche
preserve in their first element the river-name *Lede(n)* ('broad'), which has
become Leadon in Herefordshire. These south-east Shropshire names,
together with the minor settlement-names Catherton and Hints, form part
of a significant cluster of pre-English names mainly lying in north-west
Worcestershire.

The surprising scarcity of pre-English names in Shropshire is particularly
apparent in the matter of hill-names. Wrekin could be seen as an instance,
but as suggested above it is more likely to have originated as the name of
the fort than as that of the hill. The first part of Wenlock could be the
remnant of a British name for the limestone escarpment; the *Win-* of the
obscure early name *Wininicas* and the *Wen-* of the Old English *Wenlocan*
probably represent Welsh *gwyn* 'white'. The only unequivocal item,
however, is Mynd. A large area of high ground in the south-west of the
county is called Long Mynd. This may result from a misunderstanding
which caused Welsh references to 'the mountain' to be taken by English
speakers for a proper name. Mynd occurs again as a minor settlement-name
near the southern border of the county, and this preserves the Welsh term
for Bucknell Hill, as Menutton (DB *Munetune*) a few miles to the west
preserves it as a term for the massif of Clun Hill. Another Welsh hill-term,
crug, 'tumulus, pointed hill', which was borrowed by the English in the
forms *crūc* and *crӯc*, is probably found in Church Hill near Pontesbury; and
the first part of the settlement-name Crudginton is probably *crӯc-hyll*.
Crickheath near Oswestry, which appears to be the same name as Criccieth
in Caernarvonshire, has not been included on fig. 33 because the order of
elements, with the generic placed first, indicates a post-Roman date.

The hill-names adopted from Welsh speakers in this county are a pathetic
clutch. None of the peaks on the east side of the Church Stretton valley
has an ancient British name, and the several massifs of the Clee Hills,
which dominate the south-east, have a collective name which is much
more likely to be Germanic than Celtic (Gelling 1990: 82ff.). Intensive
exploitation of the upland pasture by English-speaking overlords may have
contributed to this great renaming. It is possible that *mynydd* was
perceived as a term denoting such pasture.

The most impressive items of Celtic survival which do occur in the
nomenclature of this county are the parish-names Prees and Hodnet, in the
north-east. Hodnet means 'pleasant valley', and there are other instances of
the name in Wales and Cornwall. Prees means 'brushwood' or perhaps
'grove', and other instances occur in Lancashire and Cornwall. These are
likely to be pre-English names for ancient estates, or perhaps for
complementary halves of a single great estate. The only other wholly Celtic

Figure 34 Herefordshire: ancient Celtic names, and names which refer to British people.

settlement-name which is not that of a river is Hints, in the south-east, which is assumed to be identical with Hints in Staffordshire. It is a minor settlement.

Hybrid names not already discussed are Ightfield (containing a river-name *Giht*, unexplained but assumed to be pre-English) and Catherton, which is probably identical with Chadderton and Chatterton in Lancashire, containing Welsh *cadeir* 'chair', used in place-names for a prominent hill.

There are four Shropshire names which contain *walh* 'Welshman': these are three instances of Walcot and one Walton.

Herefordshire (fig. 34)

In Herefordshire, pre-English place-name survival occurs on a scale which renders the name-by-name analysis offered for our other four counties inappropriate. Fig. 34 shows the items which can fairly be claimed as dating from Roman times, but in this county such a map seriously underestimates the likely extent to which Welsh speech continued in use. Parish-names in south Herefordshire include items such as Treville, Kilpeck and Hentland which are of types not found in the other counties except on the extreme western edge of Shropshire. Treville is 'mill settlement', Kilpeck is Welsh *cil* 'retreat' with an unexplained qualifier, Hentland is 'old church'. Because of the order of elements (generic followed by qualifier) in the first two and the Christian reference in the third, these must be assigned to the post-Roman period, but they arise from the 'modernizing' tendency which caused so many names in Wales to be either remodelled or replaced in the early Middle Ages. Llangarren and Llanwarne are obvious Welsh medieval formations of a type which was once widespread in south Herefordshire. A number of parishes now bearing only a saint's name, such as Foy, St Weonard, Sellack and Cloddock, are *Lanntiuoi, Lann Santguainerth, Lann Suluc, Merthirclitauc* and the like in the charters preserved in the Book of Llandaff. In Kentchurch, Dewchurch, Kenderchurch and Michael-church, English -church has clearly replaced Welsh Llan-, and this is true also of -stow in Marstow, Peterstow and Bridstow. Neither *cirice* nor *stōw* is used with this sort of frequency in areas where there was an early change to English speech.

Some English parish-names, like Craswall and Knill, occur even on the western boundary of Herefordshire, but large areas of the country must have been wholly or partly Welsh-speaking up to and beyond the Norman Conquest. There is only one name containing *walh*, and the significant situation of this is discussed in Chapter 7. In the greater part of Hereford-shire, Welsh speech cannot have been exceptional.

Conclusion

In most of the West Midlands Welsh speech must have disappeared by the end of the ninth century. There are tenth-century charters with detailed boundary clauses for estates in Warwickshire, Staffordshire, north Herefordshire and east Shropshire, and these indicate that with very few exceptions the smallest features of the landscape had English names by that time.

Another indication of complete change to English speech is the rarity in most of our area of place-names referring to churches. This is significant because the jettisoning of ancient names for new ones which referred to churches or their dedications happened on a massive scale in Wales and Cornwall: its occurrence in a significant number of instances in the Archenfield district of Herefordshire is evidence for the continuance of Welsh speech there throughout the Anglo-Saxon period. Shropshire has some of these names – St Martin's, Llanyblodwel, Llanymynech, Bettws-y-Crwyn, Llanfair Waterdine; but these are on the west boundary, and other-wise Shropshire resembles other English counties in only having two names – Baschurch and Whitchurch – with *cirice* as generic. There are two references to minster churches – Emstrey and Minsterley – but most of the known minster sites in Shropshire, like Morville, Shifnal and Stottesdon, have English topographical names. Warwickshire, Cheshire and Stafford-shire have only a few -church names.

There is no conclusive evidence which tells against the possibility that some Welsh speech continued into the ninth century, and places where this happened may be referred to in names containing the terms *walh* and *cumbre*. The document known as the Testament of St Mildburg (Finberg 1972: 197–216) would, if it were accepted at its face value, indicate the predominance of English place-names at a much earlier date, but this docu-ment cannot be called in evidence without qualification. It was put together in the late eleventh century by a hagiographer using documents preserved at Wenlock Abbey. These included a number of late seventh-century grants of land to Mildburg, the foundress. The estate-names are *Homtun, Magana* (Maund, Herefordshire), *Kenbecleag, Cheilmers* (Chelmarsh, Shropshire), *Peandan Wrye, Lingen* or *Liya* (?Lingen, Hereford-shire), *Magdalee*. Other estates are said to be by the river called *Munube* (Monnow, Herefordshire), in the district called *Lydas* (Lyde, Herefordshire or Lydham, Shropshire), around the hill called *Clie* (Clee, Shropshire) and by the river called *Corf* (Corve, Shropshire). *Homtun, Kenbecleag,* Chelmarsh, *Magdalee,* Lyde (or Lydham), Clee and Corve are English, and if this document were wholly trustworthy it would be evidence that there were more hills, rivers and settlements with English names than with Welsh ones by c.685. But some of the names appear in post-1066 forms. Chelmarsh and Clee would not be spelt with *-ei-, -ie-* before 1066, let alone before 700, and Lyde and Lydham would both have had initial *H-*. The occurrence of one name in *-tūn* and two in *-lēah* is suspicious, since both these generics are rare in genuine sources before A.D.730 (Cox 1976). It is legitimate to suspect that the documents available to St Mildburg's biographer were recopied, perhaps several times, with substitution of some estate-names which had come into use later than the grants.

5 The Reign of Penda in Welsh Literature and English History

The first point to be made about the two kinds of evidence denoted in the title to this chapter is that they are in flat contradiction with each other concerning the manner in which a large area of the western part of our region was absorbed into the English kingdom of Mercia. There is no doubt that the area passed from Welsh to English control some time during the seventh century, but there are no English accounts of how this was accomplished. There is, however, early authority in Bede's Ecclesiastical History for alliances between Mercia and the northern Welsh kings. From the Welsh side there are laments in medieval Welsh poetry which assume that the rulers of Powys lost this territory to the English in a devastating war; which is difficult to reconcile with the English-Welsh alliances recorded by Bede. Some historians have laboured to achieve such a reconciliation, others have rejected the poetry as fiction concocted on the basis of English and Welsh relations in the ninth to eleventh centuries. The latter course seems to the present writer to offer the more satisfactory solution.

The Welsh Tradition

Welsh traditions concerning the loss of eastern Powys to the English are enshrined in poetry of great literary merit, which celebrates the deeds of a prince of Powys named Cynddylan, whose devoted sister was named Heledd. There is a cycle of poems known as *Canu Heledd* ('The Heledd Song'), and a single poem known as *Marwnad Cynddylan* ('The Cynddylan Elegy'). Consideration of these and other Welsh poetic sources has recently been greatly facilitated by the publication of Dr Jenny Rowland's book *Early Welsh Saga Poetry* (Rowland 1990).

The date of composition of *Canu Heledd* has been the subject of much discussion. Sir Ifor Williams, in a number of works dating from the 1930s to the 1970s, favoured the mid-ninth century. David Dumville (1977) has argued that the composition could be as late as c.1100. Dr Rowland (1990: 388) concludes that 'a late ninth or early tenth-century date would fit better with other indications of date and would not be inappropriate historically.' The traditions incorporated in the poems are linked to an event of A.D.642 because a poem associated with the *Canu Heledd* cycle refers to the battle of *Maes Cogwy*, the name given in Welsh sources to the battle which Bede calls *Maserfelth* (Rowland 1990: 445). This battle is called *Bellum Cocboy* in other Welsh sources (HB, AC). The poet states that Heledd's brother Cynddylan was an ally there. The poems have therefore to be considered in the context of what is known about the Midlands in the seventh century, but there are sound reasons for believing that they do not represent a reliable historical tradition of the events of that era. The dominant factor in the political life of central England in the middle decades of the seventh century was the violent hostility between the Anglian kingdoms of Mercia and Northumbria. The northern Welsh kingdoms of Gwynedd and Powys were caught up in this warfare, but they took part in it not as enemies of the English (as the poetry suggests) but as allies of Mercia. The seventh-century battles which were remembered in Welsh tradition were between Mercia and Northumbria. This warfare provided the context in which lands in Shropshire which had once been the eastern part of Powys became part of Penda's Mercia, but the Welsh poets were mistaken in their belief that the Mercians obtained them by a bloody conquest.

The encounter at *Maserfelth* or *Maes Cogwy* was the battle in which King Penda of Mercia defeated and killed King Oswald of Northumbria, and Cynddylan's role there could only have been as an ally of Penda. Historians have perceived that this makes it impossible to accept as historical record the message of *Canu Heledd*, which is a lament for the loss of Cynddylan's kingdom to English enemies who could only be Mercians. Ifor Williams put forward this view (1932: 269-303), and his opinion was taken up by H.P.R. Finberg (1964: 66-73); but it is necessary to continue to stress the unhistorical nature of the poet's view of Cynddylan's relationship with the Mercians, as the powerful poetry of the verses can still seduce scholars into accepting their message.[1] The new discussion of the poems by Dr J. Rowland finally releases historians from the need to make sense of *Canu Heledd*, and, in addition to giving emphatic support to earlier suggestions that the author of this cycle had no sound knowledge of seventh-century events in Shropshire, Dr Rowland offers a new interpretation of the *Marwnad Cynddylan*, which she regards as an earlier poem. The *Marwnad* contains references to a great Welsh victory at *Caer Luitcoed*. *Luitcoed* is *Letocetum*. The capture of cattle and horses at this battle is mentioned, and the presence of 'book-clutching monks' who failed to protect them from capture. Because the location is near Lichfield (*v.* p. 59) it has been assumed that Cynddylan's army was invading Mercia; but as Dr Rowland points out (p. 133) Cynddylan could have been there as an ally of Penda, helping him to defend his kingdom against an invasion from Northumbria, in which case the captured animals would be spoil from the Northumbrian army's train. Attempts have been made to explain the monks as members of an ancient Celtic church surviving in Mercian territory, but Dr Rowland thinks it more likely that they were serving the religious needs of a Northumbrian army (p. 134). She suggests that the battle of the Winwæd, at which Penda and his Welsh allies were at last defeated by the Northumbrians, was the occasion of Cynddylan's death, and that this battle was the disaster lamented in the poem.

The occurrence in *Canu Heledd* of a number of Shropshire place-names shows that when these poems were composed, in the ninth century or perhaps later, the people of Powys knew that their kingdom had once extended over that county. It seems clear that the River Tern, in eastern Shropshire (fig. 33) was remembered as their ancient boundary. The river is frequently named in *Canu Heledd*, and *Marwnad Cynddylan* uses the phrase *tra Thren* ('beyond Tern'), which Dr Rowland (p. 132) regards as a conventional way of saying 'beyond the borders of Powys'. Before discussing the Shropshire names which occur in *Canu Heledd* it is desirable to consider the evidence concerning the site of the battle of *Cogwy/Maserfelth*, and the almost universally accepted identification with Oswestry.

Oswestry is an Old English name meaning 'Oswald's tree'. It is not recorded till c.1180, when it appears in Shrewsbury Abbey Cartulary as the name of the site of a Norman Castle, but it is a type of name which can confidently be ascribed to the pre-Conquest period. In the Domesday Survey the castle had a French name, *Luvre*, and the manor in which it stood was called *Meresberie*. This last survives as modern Maesbury, the name of a hamlet two miles south of Oswestry, and it means 'manor of the boundary'. The estate later acquired a French name, *Blancmuster*, and a Latin one, *Album Monasterium*, both meaning 'white collegiate church'. The French and Latin names alternate with *Oswaldestre* in records till 1300, after which *Oswaldestre* becomes the commonest one. Maesbury is well documented in the late thirteenth and early fourteenth centuries as one of the settlements in this large estate, and it seems clear that the centre of administration shifted from Maesbury, in the southern part, to Oswestry, on its northern edge, when the Norman castle was built there.

If there had been no question of an association with King Oswald of Northumbria, Oswestry would have seemed a normal specimen of a well-evidenced type of place-name in which the genitive of an Old English personal name (frequently dithematic) is combined with the word *tree*. Thirty-eight examples which are either settlement-names or names of meeting-places have been assembled (Gelling 1984: 212-13), and an uncounted number are to be found in the boundary clauses of Anglo-Saxon charters. Situation on a boundary is a marked characteristic of these names. I believe the original *Oswaldestrēow* to have been a boundary-marker on the northern edge of Maesbury. The Welsh and English traditions which made this the site of the battle of 642 may have been encouraged by a superficial resemblance between the name *Maserfelth*, by which Bede refers to it, and *Meresbyrig*. There was a similar tradition at a place called Oswald's Tump in Marshfield in Gloucestershire (Smith, A.H. 1964: 61), and attempts have also been made to associate *Maserfelth* with the Lancashire district-name Makerfield.

The church at Oswestry was dedicated to St Oswald probably because the place-name suggested him as the appropriate saint. There are parallels for this process, such as Atcham in Shropshire, Boston in Lincolnshire, and Warburton in Cheshire. The association was doubtless fostered by the priests who served there. The church is called *Ecclesia Sancti Oswaldi* in 1121 in the Shrewsbury Cartulary, and this is, by implication, the earliest record of the place-name. The misinterpretation of Oswestry as 'cross of St Oswald' becomes explicit, probably in the late twelfth century, when Gerald of Wales translates it as 'the tree of Oswald', and certainly in the thirteenth century, when the Welsh form *Croes Oswald* appears in records. But the battle of 642 is called *Maserfelth* by Bede and *Maes Cogwy* in the Welsh poetry, and nothing resembling those names is to be found in this neighbourhood. There is no way of demonstrating that the battle did not take place at Oswestry, but there is no firm evidence to show that it did. The occurrence of the personal name Penda in Penley, Flintshire, some ten miles from Oswestry, is of very doubtful relevance. Penley was translated into Welsh as *Llannerch Banna* (Charles 1938: 214). *Panna* is the correct Welsh equivalent of Penda; but this does not prove that the reference is to the king. Penda is the first element of other place-names, such as Pinbury, Gloucestershire, Pinley, Warwickshire, Pinvin, Worcestershire, and it is probable that other Mercians were called by it.[2]

The contexts in which place-names occur in *Canu Heledd* are mostly vague, but there is a precise reference to Baschurch, Shropshire, which is said to be the burial place of Cynddylan. The name is translated into Welsh as *Eglwysseu Bassa*, and Dr Rowland has pointed out to me that the use of the plural, 'churches', suggests that the poet imagined the place as a Celtic *clas* with many small shrines. The poet's choice of this settlement as Cynddylan's resting-place may have been partly due to the presence in the parish of the great earthwork called the Berth. Traditions of Dark Age activity there were perhaps current in the ninth–twelfth centuries as they were in later times. The poet may also have wanted a -church name for this context, and these are rare in England, Whitchurch being the only other one in Shropshire.

Baschurch is in the western half of Shropshire. The name *Tren*, which occurs frequently in the poems, is considered to be the River Tern in the eastern part of the county. Sometimes in the poems *Tren* seems to be a district-name: Cynddylan is said to have defended *Tren*, his patronymy, and the English are said to come through *Tren*. In other stanzas *Tren* is a settlement – an unfortunate, splendid, desolate town. It also occurs as a river-name, in some stanzas in which it is said, mistakenly, to flow into the Roden.

One stanza refers to Ercall. This is a place-name, probably of English origin, which belongs to two settlements, High and Child's Ercall, which are six miles apart and on either side of the River Tern. There is also a large hill called the Ercall, which is part of the same massif as the Wrekin, and lies six miles south-east of High Ercall. If, as seems probable, Ercall (Old English *Earcaluw*) was a district-name, the statement in the poem that 'the sod of Ercall is on brave men' could be a general reference to fighting over the eastern part of the north Shropshire plain.

In another stanza Heledd says that she has looked out from *Dinlle Ureconn*. This is naturally interpreted as a reference to the hill-fort on the Wrekin, but the form *Ureconn* can only be based on the English development of the ancient British name *Uricon*, since the British name would have become *Gwrygon* in Welsh.[3]

There are two other place-names in *Canu Heledd* which require consideration here: *Pengwern* and *Drefwen*. *Pengwern* is frequently named as the central place of Cynddylan's kingdom, his ruined hall being *Llys Bengwern* in the first stanza. Several identifications have been offered for *Pengwern*, starting in the late twelfth century with Gerald of Wales, who stated firmly that it was Shrewsbury. No conclusive case has been made for this or for any other identification, however. Dr Rowland concludes that 'the lack of precise topographical information in the poems makes any suggestion guesswork' (1990: 574). She considers that if Pengwern had been Shrewsbury the River Severn might have been expected to receive a mention.

One poem in the cycle concerns a place called *Drefwen*, literally 'white settlement'. This has naturally been associated with Whittington, near Oswestry, but statements in the poem about the position of *Drefwen* are self-contradictory, and in fact it may be a descriptive term meaning 'fair town' rather than a name for a specific settlement (*ibid.*: 593).

The use of place-names in this poetry is so imprecise that it is unwise to build on any of the possible identifications.

The English Record

If the story told in Welsh traditions of a bloody conquest of eastern Powys by Mercia in the seventh century be rejected, it is necessary to enquire when and how the transfer of this area to Mercia did take place. It cannot have been the result of a massive influx of English settlers, since the archaeological record shows that there was no reservoir of earlier-settled Angles in the counties immediately to the east. It must have been the result either of English conquest after Penda's time or of voluntary secession to Penda's kingdom by the Welsh inhabitants. The latter is the more probable.

The earliest documented event of the seventh century in the West Midlands is the Battle of Chester, which occurred between A.D.613 and A.D.616. From Bede's account of this battle (HE ii: 2), supplemented by Welsh and Irish sources, it emerges that King Æthelfrith of Northumbria defeated a British army led by a son of the king of Powys, and the victory was accompanied by the slaughter of a host of British monks from the monastery of Bangor Iscoed. This last episode is represented by Bede as a just punishment for the rejection by Welsh Christian leaders of St Augustine's bid for the overlordship of the church in Britain: in fact, it is in order to make this point that he introduces the account of the battle into his narrative. It is a reasonable supposition that Æthelfrith's incursion into north-west England was inspired by ambitions of adding Welsh territory to his expanding kingdom, and Powys was the obvious target for conquest. The conquest did not happen, however, probably because internal dissensions in Æthelfrith's kingdom became acute immediately after the victory.

Northumbria comprised the two ancient kingdoms of Deira and Bernicia, and Æthelfrith was a member of the ruling house of the northern one, Bernicia. He had control of both kingdoms while Edwin, the heir to Deira, was in exile, being sheltered by the formidable King Rædwald of East Anglia. In 616, at a battle on the River Idle in the north-east Midlands, Rædwald defeated and killed Æthelfrith, and Edwin was installed as king of Northumbria. This diversion may have enabled Powys to emerge intact from Æthelfrith's aggrandizing activities, but the memory of the pagan king's barbarous conduct at Chester and the perception of Northumbria as the enemy of the northern Welsh kingdoms would surely be motivating factors in the politics of the next generation of rulers.

It seems entirely natural that when an English warlord of outstanding abilities rose to power in the region immediately east of Powys and showed himself hostile to the major English kingdoms to the south, east and north, the rulers of Gwynedd and Powys should regard him as an ally. Their participation in the battle of *Maserfelth* poses no problems, nor does the presence of kings of Gwynedd in two of Penda's vital campaigns to the north, one of which culminated in the killing of Edwin of Northumbria in 633, the other in Penda's own defeat and death at the battle of the River Winwæd in 655. It is, however, very doubtful whether the princes of Gwynedd would have continued to join forces with him if he had recently overrun eastern Powys with fire and sword in the manner depicted in *Canu Heledd*.

Penda's main ally in 633 was Cadwallon of Gwynedd, whose hatred of Edwin and the Northumbrians was particularly fierce. Post-conquest Welsh writers, including Geoffrey of Monmouth, say that in his youth Edwin had been sheltered by Cadwallon's father, Cadfan, and had become Cadwallon's foster brother. The most recent assessment of these Welsh traditions, by Nora Chadwick (1963: 148ff.), is not as lucid as could be wished, and it is uncertain whether any credence should be given to them. If Edwin did have this relationship, it exerted no influence on his conduct after Rædwald of East Anglia installed him in his kingdom. He invaded north Wales, and is credited by Bede with taking possession of Anglesey. This provocation may have caused Cadwallon to form the alliance with Penda which led to Edwin's death. Penda has recently been described as a 'junior client' in this alliance (Brooks 1989: 167).

The permanent accession to Mercia of the areas which later became Shropshire and north Herefordshire can be seen as part of the process by which Penda enlarged the kingdom of Mercia between c.630 and the middle of the century. It does not seem possible that his achievement depended on conquest of all the various parts. Penda's Mercia is likely to have been a voluntary association of interested allies, cemented by the spoils from his frenetic warfare against Wessex, Northumbria and East Anglia. No record suggests that he ever fought against the Britons of Wales. The eastern part of Powys was probably absorbed into Mercia by agreement. Professor Davies (1982: 101-2) suggests that there had been two ruling houses in Powys, and a federal structure might have facilitated the accession of part of the kingdom to Mercia.

An outstanding problem of seventh-century history is the question of where Penda obtained an army for his first-recorded victory against the West Saxons at Cirencester in 628 (ASC, *s.a.*). Since the archaeological record precludes the existence of a reservoir of pagan Anglian manpower in western Mercia, the problem could be solved by assuming that he had already secured the support of the Welsh people of the West Midlands. Or, since he was not the first ruler of Mercia, he might have inherited this support from a predecessor.

Who was Penda, and what was the nature of the base from which he welded the Midland peoples into a kingdom which extended from the modern Welsh border to the Wash? In 1977 Professor Wendy Davies re-examined the English and Welsh sources - historical, annalistic and genealogical; and from these she concluded that Penda and his brother Eowa were joint rulers of Mercia in succession to a king named Ceorl. She identified two Mercian rulers before Ceorl, kings named Crida and Piypba. She suggested that Penda had ruled from as early as 610, sometimes jointly with Eowa, who was killed at *Maserfelth* in 642. This is very different from the interpretation of events by Sir Frank Stenton which was firmly based on *Bede's Ecclesiastical History*. Stenton considered that Penda became king in 632, and that 'in 628, for all that is known to the contrary, he may have been merely a landless noble of the Mercian royal house fighting for his own hand' (Stenton 1943: 45). If the beginning of Penda's reign could be put earlier than 632 this would make it easier to understand the power which he was wielding in the middle decades of the century. A period of diplomacy before he led his conglomerate kingdom into the aggressive wars of 628–55 would be a reasonable hypothesis, but a start to his reign in 610 would make him an old man when he led a great host to the battle of the Winwæd in 655.

The most recent study of the difficult problems posed by the chronology of Penda's reign offers a third scenario (Brooks 1989). Professor Brooks suggests emendation of the *Anglo-Saxon Chronicle*'s annal for 626 to read 'Penda succeeded to the kingdom and reigned thirty years and was fifty years old when he died.' The unemended statement that he was 50 when he became king is obviously corrupt. Brooks envisages Penda ruling intermittently from about the age of 20 until his death in battle aged 50. This is convincing, but it leaves little time for the cementing of alliances before his first success in battle in 628.

As regards the relationship between Penda and his brother Eowa, Professor Brooks suggests that they were rivals for the Mercian throne, not joint rulers, and that Eowa was a Northumbrian puppet. When he was killed at *Maserfelth* he may have been fighting alongside his Northumbrian overlord in order to maintain his possession of the throne of Mercia against Penda. On this view Penda would have lost the kingdom about 635 and recovered it after *Maserfelth* in 642. Professor Brooks points out that Bede says that after defeating Edwin of Northumbria at Hatfield in 633, Penda ruled the Mercians *varia sorte*, 'with varying fortunes'.

In considering the extraordinary nature of Penda's success in welding the various peoples of the Midlands into a single state, Stenton (1943: 39) laid much stress on the genealogy by which later Mercian kings claimed to be descended from Woden through Offa, king of Angeln, one of the chief heroes of Germanic legend. More recent studies discount this on the grounds that such genealogies were concocted after families had risen to positions of power and prestige. Dr David Dumville (1977b: 93) sums up his devastating attack on the traditional view of Penda's illustrious ancestry in the words 'The Mercian pedigree above Icil, which is a roll-call of legendary heroic names, is hardly to be taken seriously as a biological statement.' Historians agree that Icel was the founder of what became the Mercian royal house, and Professor Davies regards him as the leader of a migration from East Anglia.

A Mercian political unit must have been established in Staffordshire before Penda and Eowa emerged as rulers, but there is no evidence which would enable us to trace its growth. A calculation, based on the generations which separated Icel from his descendant Penda, concludes that 'we could therefore calculate a *floruit* for Icel at any time of our choice between c.450 and 525' (Brooks 1989: 163). We have seen that the absence of pagan Anglo-Saxon archaeology precludes the possibility that Icel was accompanied or followed into the West Midlands by a large body of Germanic immigrants. It is possible that the *modus vivendi* with the British people which must have been achieved if the story is to make any kind of sense was the work of the generations represented by the names Cnebba - Cynewald - Crida - Pypba which come between Icel and Penda in the section of the Mercian genealogy which modern historians accept as more likely to be genuine.

As regards the career of Penda, much remains obscure and all the suggested reconstructions give rise to difficulties. He must surely have been at least in his early twenties in 628, when he fought the West Saxons at Cirencester, and this would make him about 50 when he led a great army to his final battle in 655. There are other indications, such as the marriage of his sister between 642 and 645, and the term *adulescens* applied to his son Wulfhere in 658, that he is not likely to have been a very old man in 655. The necessity of regarding him as a young man in the late 620s, however, leaves little scope for him to have built up the support needed for his achievements. Professor Brooks's suggestion that he lost the throne between 635 and 642 raises doubts as to whether the conglomeration of peoples which made up the kingdom would have held together during that time, if it was indeed his personal prowess which had brought them into this state. The problem of how the huge Mercian kingdom was created is probably insoluble, but it certainly was created, and it is time to turn our attention to the nature of its component parts.

The Mercian Hegemony

It is agreed that the name *Mierce* means 'boundary people', but there have been differing views about whether the Welsh or Northumbrian boundary is referred to. I would take the name to mean that the founders of the kingdom were on the western fringe of the area of English penetration during the pagan period. Stenton considered that the name 'originally described the portion of the race in contact with its British enemies' (1943: 40); but, as stated above, there is no firm evidence for enmity between the sparse English settlers in the West Midlands and the Welsh farmers who must have outnumbered them. Their feeling of being 'boundary people' in relation to the mass of pagan Angles in the East Midlands must, however, have been strong.

The enlarged Mercia which Penda created is set out in the tax list, perhaps of the late seventh century, which is known as the *Tribal Hidage* (Dumville 1989). The opening statement of this text, *Myrcna landes is thrittig thusend hyda* - ('of the land of the Mercians [the tax] is of thirty thousand hides') - is glossed by the phrase *thær mon ærest myrcna [land] hæt'*. The verb is the third person singular present indicative of *hātan*, 'to name'. The text of the *Hidage* only uses the word *land* twice, but all the tribal names are in the genitive, which indicates that *land* should be supplied by the reader after each one. The gloss *thær mon ærest myrcna* [*land*] *hæt* means 'which is called the first land of the Mercians'. Behind this lies a district-name, *Ærest Myrcnaland*, 'Original Mercia'.

It is difficult to place the core of Original Mercia anywhere except in the later county of Staffordshire; but, as pointed out by Stenton (1943: 295), the figure of 30,000 hides is inordinately high. Bede (HE iii: 24) recognized northern and southern Mercians, settled on either side of the River Trent, and he ascribed 7,000 and 5,000 hides to these divisions. The area designated in the *Tribal Hidage* probably centred on Tamworth and Lichfield, but it may not (for reasons discussed below) have extended far to the south of Birmingham.

Before considering other entries in the *Tribal Hidage* which refer to our area, it is necessary to note the presence in the West Midlands of two units which functioned as sub-kingdoms within the Mercian hegemony. These are the Hwicce and the Magonsæte, and both probably came into existence as a result of Penda's assumption of authority in the region.

The territory of the Hwicce is believed to have been coterminous with the bishopric of Worcester, and that of the Magonsæte with the bishopric of Hereford. This correlation gives the Hwicce a large area comprising the later county of Worcestershire (except for the north-west tip), the south-west half of Warwickshire, and Gloucestershire except for the Forest of Dean and some land west of the River Leadon. The bishops of Worcester still called themselves *episcopi Hwicciorum* in the tenth century. The boundary through Warwickshire ran close to Stratford and Warwick. A field-name Martimow in the parish of Radway corresponds to *mercna mere* 'boundary of the Mercians' in a charter of A.D.969 (S 773), and this is on the boundary of the dioceses of Lichfield (later Coventry) and Worcester. This will be discussed in greater detail in the next chapter.

The territory of the Hwicce is outside the scope of the present volume, but the Magonsæte are wholly within it, and their kingdom must be considered in some detail. Their territory comprised what later became the northern half of Herefordshire and the southern half of Shropshire, roughly (but not exactly) the land between the River Severn and the River Wye. The area which later became the southern part of Herefordshire was the main part of a small Welsh kingdom of Ergyng, named from *Ariconium*, the Roman town near Ross. Professor Wendy Davies (1979: 74f.) has identified kings of Ergyng who ruled in the mid-sixth to early seventh centuries. She implies that when the last of these (Gwrfoddw, who founded churches at Bellimoor and Garway in 610 and 615) ceased to rule, the district passed into the control of the kings of Gwent. Ergyng (*Iercingafeld*, later Archenfield, in English speech) still had its own Welsh bishop, Cyfeiliog, in 914, when the Anglo-Saxon Chronicle notes that he was taken prisoner by marauding Vikings, and this ecclesiastical separateness emphasizes the absence of connection with the Magonsæte. The relationship between this district of Archenfield and English kings will concern us in later chapters, but Ergyng stands outside the story of the Magonsæte in the seventh century.

Traditions of the origin of the Magonsætan kingdom were preserved at the monastery of Much Wenlock in Shropshire, and a version of events can be reconstructed from a life of the foundress, St Mildburg, which was compiled there after the Norman Conquest (Finberg 1972: 197-224). The narrative (which is discussed in more detail in Chapter 6) tells of a king called Merewald who was the third son of King Penda. The *Vita Mildburgae* has been considered to be one of the works of the hagiographer Goscelin. This attribution has been challenged, but it is agreed that the text probably dates from the years after 1080, when the house was refounded as a Cluniac priory (Rollason 1982: 149-50).

The author of the *Vita Mildburgae* probably had some late seventh-century material, but none of this survives except in his narrative. The earliest surviving reference to the first Magonsætan king is found in the *Liber Vitae* of Hyde Abbey (Birch 1892: 83ff.). Though this text was written down c.1031, it must have originated before 974 (Rollason 1982: 28). The relevant statement says that St Eormenburg ('other naman Domne Eue') was given in marriage to 'Merwale Penda sunu cyninges' and became the mother of Saints Mildburg, Mildthryth, Mildgyth and Merefin. Rollason reads (1982: 42) 'Merwale Pendan sunu cynges', with *Pendan* instead of the *Penda* of Birch's text. The only other English-language source to mention the first king of the Magonsæte is the Peterborough insertion in the Anglo-Saxon Chronicle *s.a.* 656 (Clark 1970: 115). This reference, which is datable to c.1121, lists *Merwala* with the children of King Penda. Stenton (1970: 195 n.1) pointed out that *Merwale* in the Hyde text must be dative, since the princess was given to him, and that *-wale* is the correct dative for names ending in *-walh*, not *-wald*. Rollason's reading strengthens this argument, as it has another correct inflection, *Pendan*, genitive of *Penda*. On such grounds Stenton rejected the form *Mer(e)wald* which occurs in a number of Latin sources, including the part of the *Vita Mildburgae* which Finberg calls the Testament of St Mildburg. The king's name should have been put in the genitive in the Peterborough insertion, since it is the counsel of King Wulfhere's brothers and sisters which is referred to; but *Merwala* cannot represent an Old English or Middle English genitive. The grammar of the passage is inconsistent, however: it reads 'be his brothre ræd Æthelred and Merwala and be his swustre red Kyneburges and Kyneswithes and be se arcebiscopes ræd'. It looks as if the author intended *Merwala* to be nominative, like *Æthelred*.

It must be admitted, with regret, that the form of the name is not certain; but even if we could be sure that the second element was *walh* (which we have seen to be the normal term for a Welshman), it would be difficult to believe that this first ruler of the kingdom was actually Welsh. The hypothesis that Merewalh was a Welsh ruler installed by Penda has recently been proposed (Pretty 1989: 176); but surely a Welshman would not have become so completely Anglicized that no trace of a Welsh personal name would be found among his children.

Stenton (1943: 47) rejected the statements that Merewalh was a son of Penda on the grounds that there are no other names beginning with M- in the genealogy of the Mercian kings. But it has been pointed out by Finberg (1972: 219 n.2) and Sims-Williams (1990: 47-8) that this non-alliteration is not a strong objection to the relationship, as the nomenclature of the

Mercian royal house is not rigidly governed by the principle. There is another defence to hand if the true form of the name is taken to be *Merewalh*, as it is by Stenton. The literal meaning of *Merewalh* is 'famous Welshman', and a son of Penda could have adopted this name as being appropriate to his position as ruler of a people among whom the Angles must have been a tiny minority. It is to be regretted that this form of the name was not the one remembered at Much Wenlock.

In addition to rejecting the statement that the first ruler of the Magonsæte was a son of Penda, Stenton suggested that the alliteration of the names of members of the dynasty with the name of the kingdom indicated that this was an older dynasty, originally independent of Mercia; but there is no evidence for a connection of this kind between names of kingdoms and rulers. Merewalh of the Magonsæte may have felt that his adopted name went well with that of his small kingdom, but the coincidence can hardly be pressed further than that. The dynasty was short-lived. St Mildburg, the first abbess of Much Wenlock, was one of Merewalh's daughters, and the document known as *St Mildburg's Testament* refers to her father and to Merchelm and Mildfrith, her brothers. There is no evidence for any ruler of the Magonsæte later than these brothers, but the area probably survived as a distinct administrative unit until the time of the Danish wars, and the reorganization of the Midlands which happened afterwards. For some purposes the unit survived even later. An entry in the *Anglo-Saxon Chronicle* for 1016 records the flight from battle of Ealdorman Eadric with the *Magesæte*, indicating that an army had been raised from a group of people still using that name.

The name Magonsæte presents etymological problems to which an accepted solution has not yet been offered (Gelling 1978: 101-5). In the West Midlands, names for groups of people who constituted administrative units were characteristically formed by the addition of Old English -*sæte* 'dwellers' to the name of a prominent feature of the landscape. A high proportion of the features referred to in these formations had British names, but this may be a consequence of the fact that they are prominent landmarks rather than an indication of any deeper level of continuity. The Roman town of *Magnis*, near Kenchester, west of Hereford, has often been considered to be the *Magon-* of Magonsæte, but there is a serious phonological objection to this, as the -g- of *Magnis* could not have been a hard consonant at the date at which English settlers heard the name. A more likely connection is one with the place-names Maund Bryan and Rosemaund, east of the River Lugg, north-east of Hereford. Maund (earlier *Magene*) may be an Old English name for the flood-plain of the Lugg. The only available etymology, the dative singular or plural of *maga* 'stomach', modern *maw*, has understandably not found general acceptance, but it is not totally incredible as an Old English name for an area notorious for flooding. The name Maund occurs in a widely-spread group of place-names east of the Lugg, north of Hereford (Coplestone-Crow 1989: 12-13).

There is indeed no proof that the district-name Magonsæte ever referred to Merewalh's kingdom, though it was certainly in use by the year 800. The earliest surviving occurrence is in a charter of 811 (S 1264), where there is a reference to Yarkhill, Herefordshire, as being 'on Magonsetum'. The post-

Conquest biographer of St Mildburg does not use the name. He calls *Merewald* 'rex Westehanorum', and this is echoed in the appendix to Florence of Worcester, where *Merewald* is 'Westan-Hecanorum rex', and the list of bishops of Hereford is headed 'Hecana' with a subtitle 'Nomina praesulum Magesetensium sive Herefordensium'. No one has yet suggested a convincing explanation for this alternative name, and its true form is highly uncertain. Dr P. Sims-Williams (1990: 41-3) examines the varying versions of it and concludes that 'modern scholars who assert that the original name of the Magonsætan was *Hecani*, Western *Hecani*, or the like, are ... going further than the present evidence allows.'

It is time to return to the *Tribal Hidage*, and to endeavour to interpret the relevant entries in the light of what is known from other sources about the political geography of the West Midlands in the second half of the seventh century. The statement of the tax due from the Mercian heartlands is followed by the two statements 'Wocen sætna is syfan thusend hida. Westerna eacswa.' Emendation of *Wocen* to *Wrocen* is universally accepted, and the Wreocensæte of the north Shropshire plain are considered to be the unit of the second entry in the *Hidage*. These 'settlers' are named from the Wrekin which (as in other instances of such group-names) is on the border of their territory. Like that of the Magonsæte, their name survived the later organization into shires. A charter of 963 (S 723) grants land at Church Aston, south of Newport, which is said to be 'in provincia Wrocensetna'. An outlying pasture belonging to this estate was at Plaish, near Cardington, in the southern part of Shropshire, which invalidates the notion of a firm boundary along the Severn separating the Wreocensæte from the Magonsæte. An earlier charter (S 206), dated 855, refers to the fact that Viking raiders - 'pagani' - were 'in Wrecensetun'. Penda could presumably have made the Wreocensæte into a sub-kingdom if he had felt this to be expedient. A sub-kingdom could have existed briefly without any record surviving, but it seems possible that Penda retained direct control of the territory because he regarded it as being of particular strategic importance. It will be argued in a later chapter that the place-name evidence for Shropshire suggests a particularly tight administrative control by English-speaking rulers.

Who were the Westerne of the *Tribal Hidage*, the 'western people', whose assessment was the same as that of the Wreocensæte? Stenton (1943: 296) asserted that they 'should probably be sought in Chester and north Staffordshire'. More recent historians have considered Westerne to be another name for the 'Western Hecani' or Magonsæte, and this interpretation was for some time the orthodox one. Thacker (1987: 247), for example, says 'there is no express mention of Cheshire in the *Tribal Hidage*.' Opinion is now moving back towards Stenton's view, however (Sims-Williams 1990: 18). The people of Cheshire were as far west as those of Herefordshire and Shropshire, and the possibility of the name referring to them should certainly be remembered. Place-name evidence indicates that there were English settlers in Cheshire in the seventh century (Thacker 1987: 242ff.). It is clear at any rate that either the people of Cheshire or the Magonsæte are missing from the list. It may be worth considering the possibility that this reflects a situation before the Magonsæte were a separate unit. South

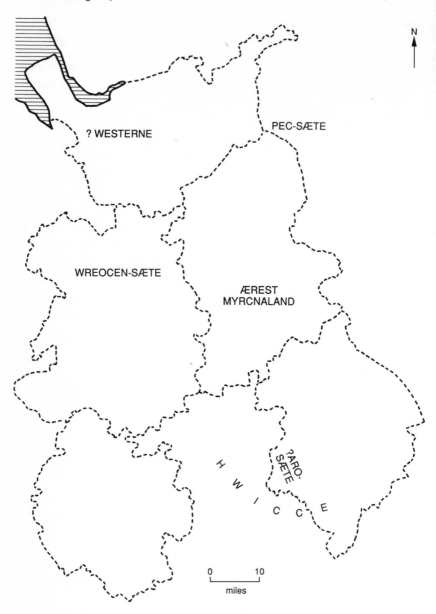

Figure 35 The units of the *Tribal Hidage*.

Shropshire and perhaps north Herefordshire might have been included in the territory of the Wreocensæte. This would make the name more appropriate, as the Wrekin is fairly central to the north-south dimension of such a territory. Also, the linking of Church Aston with Plaish in the tenth century indicates that some enduring territorial arrangements were established before there was a boundary near the Severn. The placing of the Westerne in Cheshire would give a smoother sequence to the clockwise progression which characterizes the opening section of the list, since the people who follow them are the Pecsæte, the dwellers in the Peak district (fig. 35).

An entry near the middle of the *Tribal Hidage* is considered to refer to the Hwicce under the garbled form *Hwinca*: they also have 7,000 hides. The only other people who may fall within our area of study are the Arosæte, a people allotted 600 hides. They can plausibly be placed by the River Arrow, a tributary of the River Alne which rises a few miles south of Birmingham and joins the Alne at Alcester, Warwickshire. The stream has given name to a settlement called Arrow, which is *Aru(u)e* in pre-Conquest sources. From this Celtic river-name the Anglo-Saxons might have formed a false nominative *Aro* on the analogy of such Old English nouns as *bearo* 'grove', oblique cases *bearwe*. At all events the Arosæte cannot be placed by the Herefordshire River Arrow because, although it developed to the same Middle English and modern form, that name appears as *Erge* in a charter of A.D.958, and *Aro* cannot be a form of *Erge*. A possible objection to placing the Arosæte south of Birmingham is that they would then be in the old diocese of Worcester, which is thought to be coterminous with the territory of the Hwicce; but they could have been absorbed into the Hwicce after the list was drawn up.

It is noteworthy that the *Tribal Hidage* does not list the Tomsæte, the dwellers by the River Tame, whose territory is known to have included the monastery of Breedon-on-the-Hill in Leicestershire and also some land (perhaps detached) south of Birmingham. They were perhaps the main component of 'Original Mercia'. Another group, probably much smaller, whose name has survived in a charter were the Stopppingas, whose territory lay round Wootton Wawen in Warwickshire. They are not likely to have been much less significant than the Arosæte. Their absence from the *Tribal Hidage* may indicate that they, too, were included in 'Original Mercia', but it is perhaps more likely that the inclusion of the Arosæte is atypical, and that many other units of comparable small size were omitted.

Modern historians date the *Tribal Hidage* to the late seventh century, giving it a context which will be discussed in the next chapter rather than that of the period of Penda's reign, which is the subject of this chapter. But it seems unlikely that any Mercian ruler between Penda and Offa exercised such a decisive influence on the political geography of the West Midlands, and the entries in the document which relate to this area may well reflect the situation in the middle decades of the seventh century.

6 Church and State in the Second Half of the Seventh Century

After Penda was defeated and killed at the Winwæd in 655 Mercia was for a short time at the disposal of King Oswiu of Northumbria. An area south of the Trent was given to Penda's son Peada, who had been appointed king of the Middle Angles in his father's time and had married Oswiu's daughter. When Peada was murdered in 656 his portion of the kingdom became, like the rest, a province of Northumbria; but this brief period of subjection ended in 657, when three Mercian ealdormen produced a son of Penda named Wulfhere who had been in hiding. Wulfhere regained his father's kingdom and enlarged it. He was succeeded by his brother Æthelred. Æthelred ruled from 674 to 704, when he retired into the monastery of Bardney in Lindsey (Stenton 1943: 84-5, 202).

Records of territorial losses and gains by Mercia under Wulfhere and Æthelred relate to Lindsey and to the lands along the middle Thames, where the area which was later Oxfordshire and Berkshire became debatable ground between Mercia and Wessex. No surviving record suggests that the western part of the Mercian kingdom was debated. If it be accepted that the annexation of eastern Powys and the creation of the kingdoms of the Hwicce and Magonsæte took place in Penda's time, it is reasonable to suppose that the administrative arrangements in those territories continued undisturbed until the end of the seventh century. Staffordshire must have seen more of the action, with the temporary division in 655 along the River Trent, and presumably a brief Northumbrian presence at the royal centre. The likely whereabouts of this centre will be considered in a later chapter.

Roman and Celtic Christianity

The most enduring of the developments in the West Midlands during the period 650-700 was the arrival of organized Anglo-Saxon Christianity. In the latter part of his reign Penda's Mercia was an island of paganism in a rising sea of Christianity, and the flood poured into it as soon as he was gone. Before considering the conversion of the pagan rulers of Mercia, however, we should enquire to what extent an earlier Christianity might have survived among their Welsh subjects.

The Christian traditions of Ergyng (south Herefordshire) predate Penda. The Book of Llandaff preserves charters by which arrangements were made for the local bishop to found monasteries at Bellimoor and Garway in 610 and 615, and Professor Davies (1982: 145) thinks it likely that two further Ergyng houses, Welsh Bicknor and Llandinabo, were founded in the late sixth century. Professor Thomas (1981: 267, and 273, fig. 51) thinks it possible to detect a sixth-century diocese of St Dubricius in this area. In later centuries there was a remarkable density of monasteries in Ergyng and its southern neighbour Gwent (Davies 1982: fig. 50). It is likely that Christianity here was continuous from late Roman times, but it need not be assumed that Ergyng and Gwent were typical of the Welsh Marches. Professor Davies suggests that the density of religious houses was much greater there than in any other part of Wales.

There is no way of knowing whether, but for the absorption into Mercia, similar developments to those in Ergyng might have taken place in Shropshire and Cheshire. If British people in the western part of Penda's Mercia had continued to practise Christianity they might have had difficulty in obtaining the ministrations of a bishop; but Sims-Williams (1990: 84) points out that there could have been British bishops whose credentials and activities were not recognized by Bede and his informants. As most early monasteries were either royal or episcopal foundations there would be little opportunity for them to be founded once the area was under pagan Mercian rule. It has been noted in Chapter 4 that there are some *ecles* place-names in Staffordshire and Cheshire which are likely to refer to Christian communities whose distinct entity was recognized by pagan Angles. In Herefordshire the hitherto solitary example of Eccleswall near Ross can be supplemented by Eccles Green in Norton Canon, nine miles north-west of Hereford, as a reference from 1392 is now available (Coplestone-Crow 1989: 152). There are no such names in Shropshire, where the absence of evidence for Christianity in late-Roman and sub-Roman Wroxeter has been noted in Chapter 2; but Shropshire has its full share of another type of evidence which may be relevant.

Traces of Celtic Christian traditions may be preserved by the round or oval-shaped raised churchyards which are found throughout the region, perhaps most frequently in Shropshire. This sort of churchyard is vaguely agreed to be a 'Celtic' feature, and is sometimes cited as evidence for a pre-English church site. It is very common in south-west and northern England (Pearce 1978; Thomas 1971). Dr Susan Pearce illustrates two churches in Cornwall with this type of raised oval graveyard: Lewannick and St Buryan (1978: plates 13a and 20). She gives a particularly clear description which deserves to be quoted:

> Characteristically, the present appearance of the graveyard is of roughly oval shape enclosed by a surrounding structure, usually with one entrance, which seems originally to have taken the form of an earth or earth and stone bank. Often the surrounding ditch has become a lane running around the perimeter of the site. Inside the enclosure, constant use has often raised the ground level above that of the surrounding countryside. The whole complex is known by the ... Old Cornish word *lann* which occurs as part of a number of relevant place-names in the form *lan*. Those sites which retain all or part of their original perimeters usually now have them marked by churchyard walls or hedges of varying antiquity. At those sites which take this form it is not known whether the enclosure was marked out first, or existing burials were enclosed.

Nor is the reason for the enclosure known with any certainty: the circular bank may represent the expression of a desire to separate the sacred from the profane, which had a long history stretching back beyond the Roman period (Thomas, 1971, 51-3). It may owe something to the example of the enclosed homesteads or 'rounds' which cluster thickly in the same broad area. The enclosed graveyard was enriched through the generations by the addition of various monuments and standing buildings. Sites like Sancreed in west Cornwall, Lewannick in east Cornwall, or Lustleigh in west Devon show all the characteristic *lan* features, and their pre-650 origins are demonstrated by the existence at the sites of early stone monuments. Nevertheless, there are a number of sites where a *lan* formation may be seen or suspected . . . but where any real dating evidence is lacking. The time at which it ceased to be customary to surround a cemetery with an embanked enclosure is a very difficult question, and there seems to be no reason why the process should not have continued into the ninth century or beyond. (Pearce 1978: 657-8)

It is presumably because of this last caveat (which is particularly relevant to our problem in Cheshire and Shropshire) that this type of graveyard is not used as evidence in the gazetteer of pre-Saxon graveyards which constitutes Appendix Two of Dr Pearce's book. One of the two churchyards photographed to illustrate the phenomenon is not listed there.

Professor Charles Thomas, in the passage which Dr Pearce cites, uses the term 'developed cemeteries' for the circular or oval enclosed burial-places to which buildings were added, 'leading', as he says, 'in many cases to medieval church sites and, in parts of Cornwall, Wales and southern Scotland, to parish churches surrounded by their graveyards'. His suggestion of continuity of sacred significance from pre-Christian, in fact from prehistoric, times does not much concern us here. Our problem is whether the occurrence in western Mercia of many sites which clearly resemble the final part of the sequence he envisages can be taken to indicate that there were Celtic Christian graveyards with, or without, churches before the coming of the English, and that these sites were patronized by the converted Mercians. Pending the discovery of archaeological evidence which demonstrates continuity from a sixth- or early seventh-century date at any one of these sites, the answer must be a reluctant negative. It does not seem likely that institutions or buildings survived from late Roman or immediate post-Roman periods in sufficient quantities to make a substantial contribution to the pattern of church-siting in later times.

The only thorough study of curvilinear churchyards in our area is Dr Alan Thacker's survey of those in Cheshire (Thacker 1987: 240 and fig. 36). In his survey of Anglo-Saxon Cheshire in the Victoria County History he plots churchyards of this type on a map which shows all Cheshire church-sites which, for various reasons, are believed to be of early origin. Eighteen curvilinear churchyards are included, and their distribution is biased towards the west of the county, particularly towards the Wirral (fig. 36). Dr Thacker considers curvilinear churchyards to be either sub-Roman or

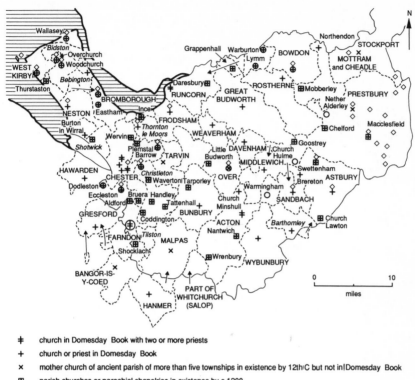

Figure 36 Early churches in Cheshire (from *VCH Cheshire I*, by permission of the General Editor).

‡	church in Domesday Book with two or more priests
+	church or priest in Domesday Book
×	mother church of ancient parish of more than five townships in existence by 12th/C but not in Domesday Book
⊞	parish churches or parochial chapelries in existence by c.1200
O	curvilinear churchyard
◇	cross(es) or other Anglo-Saxon sculptural fragment(s)
——	county boundary
- - - -	parish boundary
ACTON	medieval parish of over five townships
Tilston	medieval parish of five townships
Lymm	other ecclesiastical site

early Anglo-Saxon. He does not comment on whether the levels of the churchyards are raised above the surrounding ground. This is, however, a noteworthy feature of a number of examples in Shropshire.

The phenomenon has not been systematically studied or quantified in Shropshire, but some estimate of numbers can be made by consulting the marvellous series of re-drawn Tithe Award maps compiled by the late Mr H.D.G. Foxall. These show the churchyard shapes, though obviously fieldwork is required in order to ascertain whether the curvilinear ones are also raised. At least 60 likely examples appear on these maps. Random checking on the ground reveals some sites at which the churchyard is notably raised in addition to being curvilinear. These include Coreley, Easthope, Eyton on the Weald Moors and Diddlebury. A particularly fine

Figure 37 Stanton-upon-Hine Heath, Shropshire. Village and church as shown on Tithe Award map.

example can be seen at Stanton-upon-Hine Heath (figs 37 and 38); there has been an extension on one side, but without damage to the bank of the original enclosure. The little church at Abdon, by Brown Clee Hill, has a circular churchyard enclosed by an earth and stone bank, but the ground inside has not risen to the level of the bank-top. A fine Staffordshire example, very much raised, can be seen at Chapel Chorlton. Stoke Bliss provides a good specimen in Herefordshire, and not far west of the Herefordshire border there is a magnificent one at Old Radnor.

In spite of Susan Pearce's statement that 'constant use has often raised the ground level' I feel that it is sometimes necessary to postulate an initial mounding up with earth from the surrounding ditch. In some Shropshire instances – Coreley and Easthope for example – it is difficult to believe that enough burials have taken place to account for the level of the ground inside the churchyard.

Figure 38 Stanton-upon-Hine Heath churchyard (photograph M. Gelling).

It would be rash to postulate continuity from British Christianity at any specific West Midland church-site, but the frequent placing of churches within curvilinear, banked up enclosures may represent an Irish/Welsh tradition which lingered until it could influence the development of some of the places chosen for monasteries and churches in later centuries.

Curvilinear churchyards have also been surveyed in Cumbria (O'Sullivan 1980, 1985), and an early Anglo-Saxon date is considered likely for some of the churches characterized by them. No reference is made, however, to the presence or absence of raised ground surfaces inside the enclosures. The most recent study of church sites (Morris 1989) gives no credence to the suggested special significance of raised curvilinear churchyards. But the phenomenon is certainly one which deserves systematic study across the whole of northern and western Britain.

Mercia was not the last of the Anglo-Saxon kingdoms to adopt Christianity as its 'official' religion: that distinction belongs to the South Saxons, who were relatively isolated from outside influences. In Penda's reign Mercia was surrounded by Christian societies, in Wales, Northumbria, East Anglia and Wessex; and Penda's loyalty to the old gods did not prevent infiltration of the new faith. Bede tells us that Penda 'did not forbid the preaching of the Word, even in his own Mercian kingdom, if any wished to hear it' (Colgrave and Mynors 1969: 281). The rest of Bede's remarks on this matter suggest that Penda expected to see a real change of life in people who accepted the new faith, and that he disapproved strongly of the acceptance of baptism by people who did not take it seriously. Before the available information about the conversion in our area is considered, it will be useful to look at the evidence provided by place-names for the practice of the old religion.

Place-names Which Refer to Anglo-Saxon Paganism

English place-names which are considered to refer to pagan practices fall into two distinct groups: those which contain either the word *hearg* or the word *wēoh* (both meaning 'heathen shrine'), and those which contain the names of divinities (*Wōden, Thunor, Tīw* and the goddess *Frig*). These place-names have long been recognized as having very special significance, and they have been much studied. A useful summary of the literature can be found in the latest contribution (Wilson 1985).

The founders and early editors of the English Place-Name Society believed these names to be evidence of very early Anglo-Saxon settlement. In 1961, however, it was pointed out that the distribution pattern was not consistent with this interpretation, and the alternative suggestion was made that most of these names denoted sites where pagan practices continued exceptionally late (Gelling 1961). This need not be true of all the examples: Harrow north of London, for instance, has a particularly impressive site where a forerunner of the present church may well have succeeded the pagan structure. This place could have been known as 'the heathen shrine' even at a time when all communities had such centres. But several of the clusters on the distribution map (fig. 39) cannot possibly be seen as denoting early English settlement, and for some of them, such as that round Farnham in Surrey, the alternative explanation is particularly suitable. In our five counties, the most notable cluster occurs near Birmingham, where Wednesfield and Wednesbury refer to the god Woden, and Weeford (near Lichfield) has *wēoh* as first element. The god Tīw is difficult to identify in place-names with any certainty. A possible occurrence in a charter-boundary mark near Alvechurch, Worcestershire, is noted on the map, and if early references could be found to Tyseley in the south-east suburbs of Birmingham this might be admissible as a 'sacred grove of Tīw'. At present this interpretation of Tyseley is prohibited by the only available early spelling, which is *Tisseleye* from a surname in a subsidy roll of 1327; but the development to modern Tyseley is at variance with this form. The reference to Tīw in Tysoe, Warwickshire, seems wholly convincing. The *hōh*, or hill-spur, which stands opposite the church, is a striking topographical feature, and it has been conjectured that the district-name Vale of Red Horse refers to a now-vanished turf figure of a galloping horse, the emblem of the war-god. There was such a figure in the seventeenth century, when Dugdale mentioned it. It is believed to have been near the Sunrising Inn (VCH Warwicks V: 175). This is a mile north of Old Lodge Hill, the eponymous 'hill-spur', but it is reasonable to assume that a wide area was associated with the god.

Wednesbury also has an impressive site. The parish church stands on the summit of a rounded hill which is a conspicuous feature in the Black Country landscape, and it is possible that when the Anglo-Saxons first saw it there was a visible rampart which would have made it in their vocabulary

Figure 39 Place-names considered to refer to pagan Anglo-Saxon centres. Lost names in italics.

a *byrig*, or fort. If they established a shrine or temple to their chief god inside this fort, the site could have been Christianized later, and the parish church could be the successor of a much earlier one on the same spot. This hypothetical sequence, which obviously suits Harrow in Greater London very well, is supported by Pope Gregory's advice to St Augustine about the conversion of heathen shrines to Christian churches:

> For if the shrines are well built, it is essential that they should be changed from the worship of devils to the service of the true God. When this people see that their shrines are not destroyed they will

be able to banish error from their hearts and be more ready to come to the places they are familiar with, but now recognizing and worshipping the true God. (Colgrave and Mynors 1969: 107)

It will be seen from fig. 39 that Wednesfield ('open land of Wōden') marks the western limit of this type of name. They do not occur in Shropshire, Herefordshire and Cheshire, perhaps because there were never enough pagan Angles to establish centres of Germanic heathenism which were sufficiently notable. The cluster on the west side of Birmingham does not contradict the hypothesis of an area where paganism resisted the tide of Christianity long enough for its centres to become exceptional features of social life, and therefore to be mentioned in place-names. The examples which lie west of Birmingham are beyond the limit of pagan cemeteries, and this may be another indication that they represent the last remnants of the old religion.

Irish and Roman Christianity in Mercia

Bede's observations about Penda's tolerance of Christian missionary work in Mercia are made in connection with the account in the *Ecclesiastical History* of the conversion of Penda's son Peada, who was ruling a sub-kingdom composed of the people Bede calls Middle Angles. Peada entered into negotiations with King Oswiu of Northumbria for the hand of his daughter. This was the second such alliance between the two royal houses, as a daughter of Penda had already married Oswiu's son. In view of the personal enmity between Oswiu and Penda these arrangements seem surprising, but the complications of the relationships between the two families do not concern us here except as they affected the spread of Christianity into Penda's kingdom.

Oswiu made Peada's conversion a condition of his marriage, and Bede tells us that Oswiu's son, Alhfrith, who was already Peada's brother-in-law, added his persuasion. Peada was baptized in Northumbria, and when he returned home with his bride he brought four priests, Cedd, Adda, Betti, and an Irishman named Diuma. When King Oswiu took control of Mercia after Penda's defeat and death at the battle of the Winwæd, Diuma was consecrated bishop of the Middle Angles and the Mercians. Bede tells us that 'he won no small number for the Lord in a short space of time', but it is difficult to believe that his missionary activities or those of his immediate followers in this vast see can have penetrated deeply. Another Irishman, Ceollach, succeeded him, but resigned and 'returned' to Iona; and of Trumhere, who succeeded Ceollach, Bede says that although of English race he was consecrated bishop by the Irish. The distinctive Irish type of Christianity, for which St Columba's monastery at Iona, off the west coast of Scotland, was the centre of diffusion, must have been the dominant strain in Mercia in the reign of King Wulfhere. This Irish Christianity had been established in Northumbria by King Oswald, after the Roman church there had collapsed with the defeat and death of King Edwin. Bede does not say from whom Wulfhere accepted Christianity, but he notes that

Trumhere was the first bishop to serve under him, and this suggests that he did not entirely reject the ecclesiastical arrangements which had been made during Oswiu's supremacy. Trumhere may have been Wulfhere's appointment to replace Oswiu's Ceollach, but he sounds like a member of the same team.

Bede provides no information about the coming of Christianity to the Hwicce or the Magonsæte, and it is likely that the British people who formed the core of these kingdoms had a continuing Christian tradition from late Roman times. There were, however, traditions concerning the conversion of the Mercian rulers of the Magonsæte, and these were preserved at Much Wenlock and incorporated into the late-eleventh-century life of St Mildburg (Finberg 1972: 200). These traditions depict Merewalh as remaining pagan until about 660, when he was converted by a missionary priest from Northumbria named Eadfrith. He founded a church at Leominster and placed Eadfrith in charge of it. He made a second marriage to a Christian bride, a Kentish princess. She bore him three pious daughters, Mildburg, Mildthryth and Mildgyth, after which she returned to Kent to preside over a convent at Minster in Thanet. For the purpose of the hagiographical essay, the main consequence of these events was the foundation of the religious house at Much Wenlock about 680, and the establishment of Mildburg as its abbess. Much Wenlock is considered to have been a monastery with a house of monks and a house of nuns, ruled over by an abbess, like a number of others in England and on the Continent, because of a reference in a letter of St Boniface to a 'brother' who died and came to life again in the convent of the Abbess Milburga (Finberg 1972: 197).[1] In its English form the double monastery has been considered to represent a combination of Irish and continental usages (Stenton 1943: 161). In a thorough discussion of the evidence by Mary Bateson (1899) it is stressed that in England it was not considered peculiar to the Irish movement. Both Wilfrid and Boniface accepted it.

One of the salient differences between the Christianity diffused from Rome and that diffused from Iona was the much greater prominence given by Rome to practicalities. After the advocates of Rome won the debate at the Synod of Whitby in 664 the Northumbrian church adopted Roman usages, but the spirituality and asceticism of Iona remained characteristic of some of the priests who did not go back there after the synod. St Cuthbert is a very 'Irish' saint. In the Midlands, the meeting of Roman and Irish attitudes is seen in Bede's story about Archbishop Theodore providing St Chad with a horse.

Archbishop Theodore arrived at Canterbury in 669, having been appointed by the pope for the purpose of rescuing the English church from the demoralization caused by the devastating outbreak of plague which followed the Roman victory at Whitby. The first matter to engage his attention was the necessity of establishing manageable dioceses to which competent bishops could be appointed, and for this purpose he undertook a visitation of his province. There was no bishop in Wessex, Mercia or East Anglia. Trumhere's successor in the Mercian see had been a priest named Jaruman, who earned praise from Bede by stemming a relapse into heathenism among the East Saxons, having been sent to them for this purpose by King Wulfhere, who was overlord of their kingdom. The resources of the Mercian see must have been stretched to the utmost to encompass such a mission. Jaruman was dead by 669, and Theodore appointed Chad as bishop of Mercia and Lindsey (Stenton 1943: 131-3). Chad was a Northumbrian, and his formative years had been passed in the Irish Christianity which prevailed in Northumbria after King Oswald obtained a bishop from Iona. Austerity and humility were his salient characteristics, and he entered into his vast see with the intention of travelling round it on foot. Bede says:

> And because it was the custom of the reverend Bishop Chad to carry out his evangelistic work on foot rather than on horseback, Theodore ordered him to ride whenever he was faced with a long journey; but Chad showed much hesitation, for he was deeply devoted to this religious exercise, so the archbishop lifted him on to the horse with his own hands since he knew him to be a man of great sanctity and he determined to compel him to ride a horse when necessity arose. (Colgrave and Mynors 1969: 337)

Bede states that Chad had his episcopal seat at Lichfield, but says nothing of any reason for this choice of site. A reason is offered by 'Eddius' Stephanus, the contemporary biographer of St Wilfrid, who says that King Wulfhere invited the Northumbrian ecclesiastic Wilfrid into the Midlands on a number of occasions, that the king gave Wilfrid Lichfield as a seat for himself or someone else, and that Wilfrid gave the place to Chad (*Life of Bishop Wilfrid*, ed. B. Colgrave, ch. 15). It has been pointed out by J. Gould (1973) that Wilfrid is said by his biographer to have acquired church-sites in Northumbria which had been deserted by British clergy, and that it could be argued that he obtained Lichfield from King Wulfhere because it had been a British Christian establishment. It is suggested by James Campbell (1979b: 120) that Lichfield was appropriate because it was already in the seventh century the centre of a vast multiple estate, as it was at the time of the Domesday Survey.

It seems unlikely that a site which Wilfrid felt to be appropriate for an episcopal centre would have the same appeal for Chad, and if Stephanus' statement were discounted, and the choice ascribed to Chad, a different scenario could be envisaged. In this Lichfield could be seen as a place sufficiently encompassed by marsh and forest to offer the sort of isolation required by the Irish tradition. If the pagan place-names discussed above are accepted as indications of late-continuing heathenism, Lichfield could also have been a convenient base for primary missionary work. It would be reasonably close to the main royal residence if that was already fixed at Tamworth.

The cathedral established by St Chad is considered to have been the church dedicated to St Mary near which Bede says he was buried (HE iv.3; VCH Staffs XIV: 49). Bede further says that Chad's bones were afterwards transferred to a newly built church of St Peter. If the two churches stood close together they are both likely to have been within the site of the present cathedral. The Lichfield church which is dedicated to St Chad is at

Stowe, half a mile north-east of the cathedral. This is a twelfth-century structure. It is first recorded in c.1190, and at that time special honour was paid to a statue of the saint which it contained. Traditions that St Chad preached there go back to the thirteenth century, and a nearby well was traditionally associated with him in the sixteenth century (VCH Staffs XIV: 134-5, 146-7). One of the meanings of *stōw* is 'holy place', and it is likely that in place-names dating from before the Danish wars the word was used for sites with which saints were physically associated, either in their lifetime activities or in their burials (Gelling 1982c). Stowe may be the place to which Chad used to retire with a small company to pray or study, and which was the location of the death-bed scene which Bede recounts at considerable length (HE iv.3). The name Stowe is not recorded till 1221, however, and varying interpretations can be put upon the evidence relating to the origins and relationships of the churches in Lichfield.

Chad died in 672, and his two successors, Wynfrith and Seaxwulf, did not attract such devotion.

The Dioceses

It was during Seaxwulf's episcopate that the Mercian diocese was broken up into more manageable units. Bede tells us that Seaxwulf succeeded Wynfrith when the latter was deposed after displeasing Theodore by an act of disobedience, and it has been conjectured that the incident may have arisen from the bishop's opposition to the dismemberment of the see. There is no pre-Conquest source which describes the actual process of division, and the story has to be recovered from the appendix to the chronicle of Florence of Worcester, which is a twelfth-century work. This appendix contains confusions and errors, but Stenton's statement (1943: 134), 'Before 680 Theodore had created the diocese of Worcester for the Hwicce of the Severn valley, and that of Hereford for their western neighbours the Magonsætan' has commanded general acceptance.

The boundaries of the dioceses of Hereford and Worcester, as evidenced in later sources, have special interest because they are believed to be those of the kingdoms of the Hwicce and the Magonsæte. In Shropshire, the north-east boundary of Hereford diocese deviated from the Severn in order to exclude Astley Abbots and include Madeley and Little Wenlock and the detached area of Beckbury and Badger parishes (fig. 40). This inclusion reflects the endowment of Much Wenlock, and it is possible that the monastery's holdings north of the river were in the territory of the Magonsæte at the date of the foundation. West of Much Wenlock the boundary dipped south of the Severn for a considerable distance, bringing the line close to the village of Plaish, where an estate at Church Aston, near Newport, had outlying pasture in A.D.963. It is possible that in this area at the northern end of the Long Mynd the boundary between Wreocensæte and Magonsæte consisted of a belt of hill pasture rather than a fixed line. Similarly, the inclusion of estates north of the Severn in the endowment of Much Wenlock may indicate the sharing of a belt of woodland between the two peoples. After leaving a considerable block of territory south of the

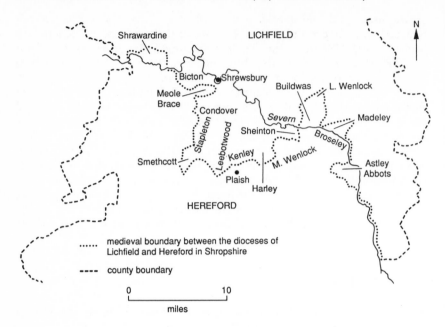

Figure 40 Part of the medieval boundary between Lichfield and Hereford dioceses.

Severn - extending from Sheinton in the east to Bicton in the west - in the diocese of Lichfield, the boundary returned briefly to the Severn. It then deviated to the north, giving Shrawardine to Hereford.

To the west and south the boundaries of the two dioceses were with Welsh kingdoms, and these would continue to fluctuate for centuries to come. Archenfield, as was noted above, still had its own bishop in A.D.914. After the diocese of Hereford had absorbed that of Ergyng its eastern boundary was with that of the diocese of Worcester. There is an eleventh-century description of the division between these two sees which indicates that it followed the Severn northwards as far as Minsterworth in Gloucestershire, where it turned west to run along the River Leadon. It then followed the crest of the Malvern Hills, after which it returned to the Severn and followed it to Quatford (Finberg 1972: 225-7). It is clear that the north-western projection of Worcestershire, bounded by Clifton-on-Teme and Rock on the east and by Tenbury and Bockleton on the west, belonged then, as later, to Hereford diocese, and so was presumably part of the kingdom of the Magonsæte.

The northern boundary of the Hwiccan diocese corresponded closely to that of Worcestershire, but its eastern boundary cut across the later shire of Warwick in a line running roughly from Tanworth to Tysoe (fig. 41). After the creation of new sees, this line, which is of vital interest to the historian, was preserved by the division between the archdeaconries of Worcester and Coventry. It has already been noted that the parish of Radway, on the Mercian side of the divide in Warwickshire, had a field-

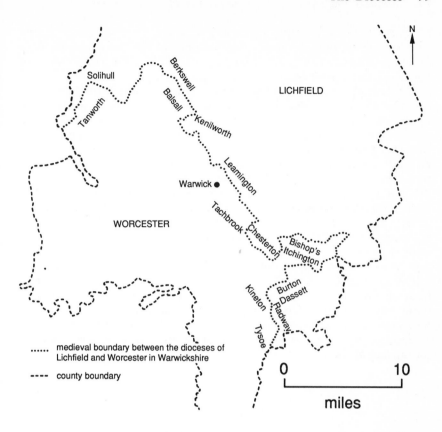

medieval boundary between the dioceses of
Lichfield and Worcester in Warwickshire

county boundary

0   10

miles

Figure 41 Part of the medieval boundary between Lichfield and
Worcester dioceses.

name, *Martimow*, meaning 'boundary of the Mercians'. Tachbrook is a
border parish on the Hwiccan side, and this name, which appears to mean
'brook which points something out', is believed to be another reference to
this ancient boundary.

Alterations to the Mercian see on its northern, eastern and southern sides
do not concern us so closely as the arrangements in the west. Adjustments
elsewhere continued into the first half of the eighth century, and these
reduced the diocese to limits similar to those which it had in the late
Middle Ages. It was still enormous, however, covering Staffordshire,
Derbyshire, Cheshire and large portions of Shropshire and Warwickshire.
One of the eastern divisions in the latter part of the seventh century was
the territory of the Middle Angles. These people sporadically had their own
see, fixed at Leicester, but this was not permanently established till 737.
Between about 692 and 702 the see of Leicester was under the charge of
Bishop Wilfrid, who was in exile from Northumbria and under the protection of King Æthelred of Mercia; but when he departed for Rome to assert
his claim to the see of York, Leicester was reunited with Lichfield under
the control of Headda, who had succeeded Seaxwulf as bishop of the

Mercians. The decade during which Wilfrid worked in the Midlands should be noted, as his influence must have diminished any remaining traces of the Irish influence which had been so pronounced in the earliest years of English Christianity here.

The Venerable Bede was not well placed as regards information about the see of Hereford. He several times mentions Putta, who was ejected from the Kentish see of Rochester as a consequence of an aggressive campaign of Æthelred of Mercia in 676, and he notes that Bishop Seaxwulf of the Mercians gave Putta land and a church; but he says nothing to suggest that he became a bishop in the Midlands. The appendix to Florence of Worcester names Putta as the first bishop of Hereford, but Stenton (1970: 193) regards this as a different person, and this view is endorsed by Sims-Williams (1990: 88 n.3). Bishop Putta of Hereford attests a charter of 681 (S 1167; Whitelock 1955: 444). The third of Putta's successors in Florence of Worcester's list is a priest named Walhstod, who is mentioned by Bede in his survey of the state of the English church at the end of the *Ecclesiastical History.* Bede says 'Walhstod is bishop of the people who dwell west of the river Severn.' *Walhstod* is an Old English noun which means 'interpreter', and in this instance (which is surely a nickname) the first element can be taken to mean 'Welsh' rather than 'foreign'. It is clear that the bishop of the Magonsætan see in Bede's day needed to be bilingual. This, however, is encroaching onto the history of the region in the eighth century, which is the subject of the next chapter.

7 The Eighth Century: The Building of the Dyke

Before Offa

Æthelred of Mercia retired in 704 to the monastery of Bardney in Lindsey. He was succeeded by Cenred, son of Wulfhere, who abdicated and went to Rome in 709, and the kingdom then passed to Ceolred, son of Æthelred, the last descendant of Penda to rule in Mercia. He died in 716. The throne was then obtained by Æthelbald, the grandson of Penda's brother Eowa, who had been killed at the battle of Maserfelth in 642. Æthelbald's reign was long and successful: he was the dominant figure in southern England for nearly 30 years (Stenton 1943: 201-2).

It may have been during the comparatively ineffectual rule of Cenred and Ceolred that Mercia's Welsh neighbours became aggressive. Sir Frank Stenton (in Fox 1955: xx–xxi) postulated devastating Welsh raids over Mercia at this time on the strength of his interpretation of a famous passage in Felix's life of St Guthlac. This text is translated in Whitelock 1955 (711). It has a rubric 'How he put to flight by his prayers visionary crowds of demons who were simulating a British army', and the story is nonsensical. Stenton, however, draws attention to the precision of the introductory sentence, 'Thus it happened in the days of Cenred, king of the Mercians, when the Britons, the dangerous enemies of the Saxon race were oppressing the nation of the English with war ...', and he concludes that this refers to actual Welsh raids rather than to demons in the Lincolnshire fens, where Guthlac's hermitage of Crowland was situated. Only a person skilled in the ways of hagiographers could evaluate the passage. The introductory sentence about Welsh aggression in the reign of Cenred slides into the account of Guthlac in his cell at Crowland being disturbed by a noisy crowd of people speaking the British language (which he recognized from experiences in exile), from whom he saved himself by chanting a psalm which caused them to disappear. Does the story indicate that Welsh raiders penetrated Mercia as far as the Lincolnshire fens, or did Guthlac have a hallucinatory experience caused by extra-sensory perception of Welsh attacks on the western parts of the kingdom? Guthlac was a member of the Mercian royal house, and his warlike youth might well have left him with a continuing interest in the military affairs of Mercia. Probably the story should not be taken literally as evidence for large-scale Welsh incursions. Stenton, however, links the raids mentioned by Felix to other evidence for a Welsh revival, noting that the *Annales Cambriae* record Welsh victories in 722, and that the inscription on the pillar of Eliseg (see above, p. 28) states that Elise king of Powys, who probably flourished in the same half century, recovered territory from the English. He considered that these

Figure 42 Offa's Dyke between Knighton and Presteign, looking south from SO 287683 (photograph J. Saunders, Offa's Dyke Association, Knighton).

Welsh victories led the Mercians to perceive the desirability of a fortified western frontier.

Æthelbald, whose personal life appears to have involved a good deal of violence, was murdered by his bodyguard at Seckington near Tamworth in 757, after a reign of 41 years. There was a disputed succession from which Offa, another descendant of Eowa, emerged as king. He ruled from 757 to 796. The confederacy of southern English kingdoms over which Æthelbald had presided had to be re-established by Offa, and Stenton (1943: 214) considered that it was towards the end of his reign, after his ascendancy was completely established in southern England, that he turned his attention to the delimitation of his frontier with Wales.

Offa's and Wat's Dykes (fig. 42)

Welsh annals record a battle at Hereford in 760 between Englishmen and Britons, a harrying of Dyfed by Offa in 778, an expedition into an unnamed part of Wales in 784, and another invasion of Dyfed in 796, the year of Offa's death. The attacks on Dyfed seem almost as surprising as the suggestion that Welsh raiders reached Crowland earlier in the century. The sequence of events cannot be fully understood from the fragmentary records, but it seems clear that there was no settled peace between Mercia and the Welsh kingdoms, and it is in this context that the construction of Offa's Dyke was undertaken.

This remarkable earthwork, 'the greatest public work of the whole Anglo-

Saxon period' (Stenton 1943: 212), was surveyed by Sir Cyril Fox between 1925 and 1932, and the results of this survey were published a generation later (Fox 1955). A note added to the posthumous third edition of Stenton's textbook (Stenton 1971: 212 n.2) refers to Fox's account as 'the definitive authority on the course and construction of Offa's Dyke'; but conclusions drawn from work undertaken in the last three decades show that Fox's work was not definitive, and that much more information could be recovered by a judicious combination of field work and selective excavation. Whatever the faults of his survey, Fox's account of his work is presented with admirable clarity, and this must make the process of revision easier for his critics.

Fox surveyed the Dyke from north to south, his work becoming progressively more hurried as he proceeded. He also surveyed the related earthwork known as Wat's Dyke, which he considered to run from the Dee estuary at Holywell, Flintshire, to Maesbury, near Oswestry, Shropshire, a distance of nearly 40 miles. More recent work on the northern portions of Offa's Dyke and on Wat's Dyke has been carried out by David Hill, with the assistance of extra-mural students of Manchester University, and accounts are contained in Hill 1974 and 1977. A detailed study of the southern two-thirds of Offa's Dyke was made by Frank Noble, the founder of the Offa's Dyke Association, and this was published posthumously (Noble 1983). It is hoped that a full report of David Hill's work will be published in the near future.

The Dyke is still regarded as a unitary work demarcating a line of which the southern end is at Tidenham on the Severn estuary, and the northern end is by the estuary of the River Dee in the old county of Flintshire, covering a frontier which is nearly 150 miles in length. At its most dramatic points the ditch (on the west) may have been 6 feet deep and the rampart 25 feet above it. A notable characteristic is the breadth, which Fox (p. 277) summarizes as 'nearly 60 ft'. The traditional ascription to Offa is not disputed.

Perhaps the most serious of the criticisms levelled against Fox is that he declared both Offa's and Wat's Dykes to be more intermittent than is the case, on account of failing to search in areas where they were not clearly visible. Wat's Dyke is in fact discernible in three areas where Fox declared it to be absent, as David Hill (1977) has demonstrated. Conversely, Hill 1974 demonstrates that Offa's Dyke is absent where Fox declared it to be present in some stretches in north Flintshire. The relationship of Offa's to Wat's Dyke, and to shorter stretches of roughly parallel linear earthwork further south, such as Rowe Ditch in Herefordshire, is not yet understood, and there is probably much to be discovered about the true line of all of them.

Fox was content to regard the Dykes as intermittent because this suited the hypothesis, widely accepted among scholars of his generation, that large areas of England were covered by dense oak forest ('untouched jungle' on p. 122) which discouraged settlement and made movement impossible. It is hoped that the survey of place-names which refer to ancient woodland in Chapter 1 of the present work affords a better-balanced interpretation of this aspect of the Dark Age landscape. There certainly was extensive woodland, but this probably influenced the nature of settlement rather than discouraged it; and the timber and other resources would be valued as an economic advantage both by Anglo-Saxon colonists and by communities established in these regions before the Mercians came.

The likely density of population at the time when the Dykes were built has an important bearing on the problems of the function of the earthworks and the logistics of the enterprise. The density of population would be related to the number of settlements, and there is circumstantial evidence bearing on this. It is impossible to demonstrate on any useful scale that villages, farms and hamlets were or were not in existence c.780, but some conclusions can be reached about the likely age of the land-units within which the settlements functioned, and this is an important piece of evidence for estimating the state of development of the landscape.

When enquiring whether an ancient earthwork antedates or postdates agricultural settlement, a convenient test to apply is whether the earthwork is used to delineate parish boundaries, or whether parishes are regularly bisected by it. Fox applied this test to Offa's and Wat's Dykes, and set out the results, with his usual admirable clarity, in Appendix III. But he was writing in advance of Desmond Bonney's seminal study of Wiltshire boundaries, which established the principle that when parishes ignore a linear feature, whether earthwork or Roman road, the land-units are likely to predate it, and where they make extensive use of such a feature the outlines of the units are likely to be more recent than the artificial line (Bonney 1972). Fox found that 18.6 per cent of the length he was able to trace of Offa's Dyke coincided with parish boundaries, and that 24.4 per cent was the corresponding figure for Wat's Dyke. The majority of parishes on the route of both earthworks are bisected by them, and it may be noted that when they are used for boundaries some of the units delineated are likely to result from fission of a larger area. The parishes of Esclusham-Above and -Below (Denbighshire) derive their affixes from the fact that one is west and the other east of Offa's Dyke. Newmarket (Flintshire) is obviously a late unit. Knighton, Whitton and Norton (Radnorshire) and Bishopstone (Herefordshire) have names which suggest late estate-division. Roman roads are much more conspicuous than the Dyke as parish-boundary determinants in Herefordshire. Some adjustments to Fox's boundary statistics may be required as corrections are made to his account of the lines of the two earthworks, but it is not possible that the dykes will emerge as major factors in parish layout. In the short stretches which are followed by administrative boundaries this may constitute evidence for late division of large estates.

Fox did not draw from his statistics the conclusion that the land-units along the Dykes were older than the earthworks, but that is the view which would probably be taken by most historians today. It seems incredible that if permanent settlements were established after A.D.800 the boundaries of their lands would not have been arranged so that one side ran along the Dyke. The same characteristic, of bisecting parishes, was pointed out by Desmond Bonney for the Wansdyke in Wiltshire, and he concluded that in that area the units which later became parishes were pre-Saxon, since Wansdyke is believed to be of fifth-century date. The units along Offa's and

Wat's dykes are not proved to be pre-English by their relationship to these barriers, but they may fairly be supposed to have been long-established in Offa's time. Fox regarded his statistics as having no importance, and remarked (303) that neither of the Dykes had any political significance 'when the parishes were fixed'. This is likely to be true, whether the boundaries predate or antedate the earthworks, but the practical convenience of operating within a land-unit which did not have a great earthwork running across it would surely have influenced the layout of newly created units at any time after the Dykes were made. The relationship of motorways to boundaries in our modern landscape is a legitimate parallel. Cows are seen being herded over motorway bridges because their pastures were established on either side long before the road was driven through the area.

Along the Offan frontier (as everywhere else in England) there was probably considerable scope for the expansion of settlement and the breaking in of new arable. But the whole strip of country is likely to have been settled, and the land to have been either under the plough, or systematically exploited for pasture or for timber production, within boundaries which neighbouring communities had agreed at a much earlier date. If no part of the boundary is assumed to have been crossing a landscape empty of people it becomes easier to conjecture how the work could have been accomplished.

There is general agreement that the Dyke was planned by a single authority, but two different views may be taken about who did the digging. One possibility is to assume that the work was undertaken by local communities, organized by overlords who had a statutory obligation to provide men for work on the king's fortifications. The other is to assume that it was carried out by a mobile workforce recruited by direct royal authority in more populous parts of Mercia. Fox took the first view in spite of his belief that considerable stretches of the border were uninhabited. On pp. 282–3 he says

> Each land-owning thegn on or near the border was made responsible for a certain length of the Dyke, proportionate to the extent of his estate or resources. I suggest that the other method, a labour force recruited by the State, paid by the State, and continuously employed over a period of years is ... not likely.

Related to the question of logistics is that of motive. How willingly would border thegns and the peasant farmers on their estates take part in such an enterprise? I suggest that they must have felt it to have had a practical purpose, and to have been a scheme which would bring them advantage. More recently Offa's Dyke has been compared, rather quaintly, with Stonehenge, and it is suggested that it can be seen as 'the last great prehistoric achievement of the inhabitants of Britain, in a tradition stretching back thousands of years' (Wormald 1982: 121). But Stonehenge is a structure of religious significance, and this would bring into play factors which are not relevant to an eighth-century linear earthwork. The Dyke would not command the moral fervour which enabled megaliths and cathedrals to be raised. Fox and Noble are agreed that the alignment is in

the main a military, therefore a practical, one. Fox says (198) 'the alignment
. . . was governed by one idea – that of visible control of enemy country',
and Noble concurs on the whole, though he suggests (6) that at its southern
end 'a show of strength against the kingdoms of Gwent and Glamorgan
perhaps overshadows the practical purposes which seem to dictate the rest
of the alignment and construction.' In order to estimate the degree of
usefulness which would be perceived by labourers from local settlements,
who were Mercians by allegiance whatever their ethnic origin, it is
desirable to consider the relationship of the Dyke to the actual division
between Welsh and English territory.

English Place-names West of Offa's Dyke

The presence of ancient English place-names west of the central and
northern portions of Offa's Dyke has naturally attracted the attention of
historians. The phenomenon is relevant to the origins of the earthwork in
the stretches which run from the north-west boundary of Herefordshire,
north of Kington, to a point west of Wrexham in Flintshire. Herefordshire
itself presents more complex problems, which are tackled below, and the
course of the Dyke at its northern end is too uncertain for this type of
discussion to be based on it. The stretch of Dyke which is relevant has
continued to bear a close relationship to the boundary between England and
Wales, and any English names to the west which would on general grounds
be considered to originate before the Norman conquest are likely to be pre-
Offan.

Fig. 43 shows English place-names which are west of Offa's Dyke in two
stretches. They are separated by a nine-mile zone in which the Dyke (at its
most impressive) is crossing the mountainous country of Clun Forest,
where settlement is very sparse. Stenton (1943: 214) considered these
English names to be proof that when the line was agreed between English
and Welsh rulers, some territory which had been English was ceded to the
Welsh. Noble (1983 *passim*) takes the contrary view that the actual frontier
was always to the west of the Dyke, and that the earthwork functioned as
a patrol line which would afford sufficient protection for English farmers
whose lands lay wholly or partly on the side towards Wales. Anticipation
of such protection could have been the motive for the vast effort required
to build the Dyke in the stretches adjacent to these names and in the
barren areas across the Clun uplands.

A notable feature of the names shown on fig. 43 is that in addition to
being of Old English origin they are remarkably free from Welsh influence.
The -tūn names do not exhibit the development to -tyn which occurs in
Prestatyn at the Dyke's north end and in Selattyn and Sychtyn in Shropshire, north of the stretch of Dyke shown on fig. 43b and respectively east
and west of it. Whether they were under Welsh or Mercian lordship, the
people of these townships must have continued to pronounce, and spell,
their names in the English manner for centuries after the Dyke was built.
An indication of the clarity with which the two languages were distinguished is afforded by the name Mainstone. This parish, in south-west

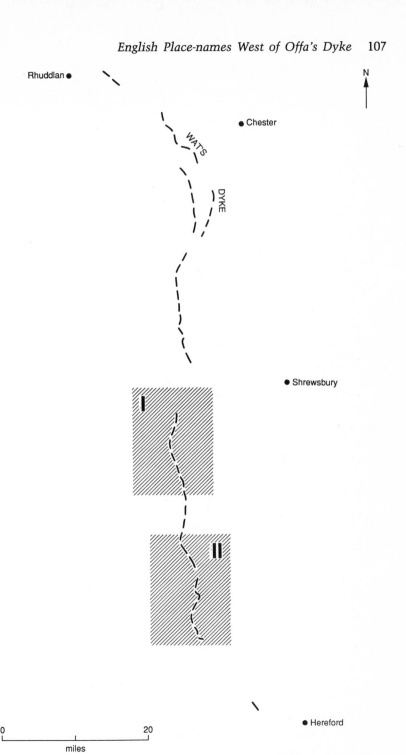

Figure 43a Map showing location of figures 43b (I) and 43c (II).

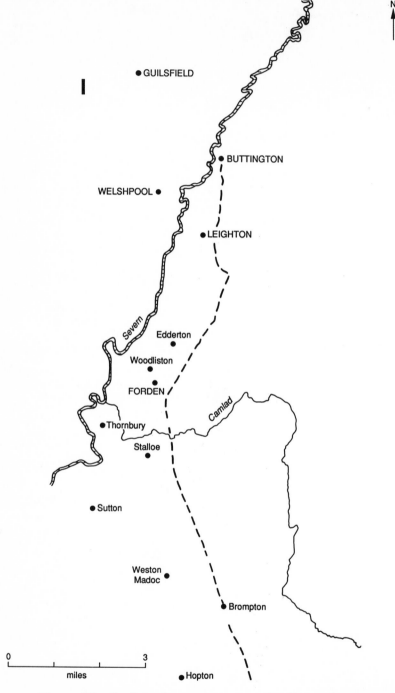

Figure 43b English place-names west of Offa's Dyke (I). Parish names are in capitals.

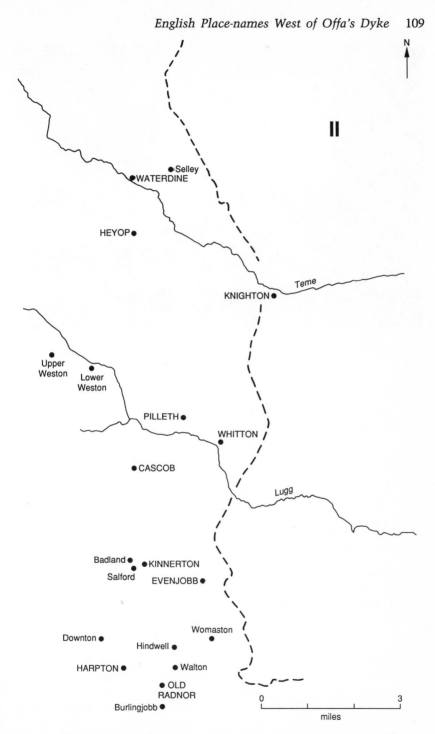

Figure 43c English place-names west of Offa's Dyke (II). Parish names are in capitals.

Figure 44   The stone of Mainstone (photograph M. Gelling).

Shropshire, is one of those bisected by the Dyke. The name refers to a 'strength stone', Old English *mægen-stān*, now housed in the church, which was used as a test of muscle-power by the young men of the neighbourhood (fig. 44). Confusion of the first element with Welsh *maen* 'stone' might have been expected, but early spellings regularly have *Meyn-*, *Mayn-* which, like the modern form, are more appropriate to the English word than to the Welsh one (Gelling 1990: 193-4). There is some distortion from normal English developments in these names along the border, as in Waterdine and Forden where *Waterden* and *Forton* would be expected, and the development of *hop* to -obb in several cases; but the majority of the names are as they would be in any English county.

The two names which seemed to Stenton to be specially significant as evidence of pre-Offan settlement west of the Dyke are Evenjobb and Burlingjobb. He took these to contain Old English *-inga-* and to refer to the type of settlement by pioneering groups which was supposed by his generation to be indicated by all *-ingas*, *-inga-* names. It is, however, far from certain that Evenjobb and Burlingjobb contain *-inga-*, the genitive plural of *-ingas-*, 'people of -'. It has been suggested that they should rather be classed with Buttington as names in which the connective particle *-ing-* is used to link a man's name to a word describing his estate (Gelling 1982). Butta, Berhtel and Emma, the men named in these compounds, were probably thegns of the Mercian or Magonsætan kingdoms who were given border estates in the seventh or eighth centuries. The generic of Evenjobb and Burlingjobb is *hop*, and the high incidence of this word in the names shown on fig. 43 is a consequence of the topography. This was the term used by the Anglo-Saxons for settlements in exceptionally secluded places. In some areas it denoted dry ground in marsh or cultivated ground in heath, but in north Herefordshire and south Shropshire it is regularly used for settlements in secluded valleys to which there is restricted access. At Evenjobb and Burlingjobb the sites are hollows rather than valleys, but both have the 'tucked away' quality which makes *hop* the appropriate generic.

The Functioning of the Dyke

As noted above there are differing views about the function of the Dyke, Stenton seeing it as the delimitation of a new, negotiated frontier with the Welsh, Noble as a patrol-line set back from an older frontier. Whichever view is taken it is necessary to envisage crossing-places as part of the original design. If the Dyke marked the frontier the builders could not have intended to preclude lawful traffic with the Welsh. If it was a patrol-line behind the frontier Mercian farmers would have been crossing it in their daily pursuits. There are numerous gaps through which the earthwork can be crossed today, but the problem is to decide which of these are original. Recent work has shown that Fox is not to be relied on in this matter. Dr David Hill excavated two of the gaps which Fox considered to be contemporary with the earthwork, and showed that the evidence indicates later origin (Hill 1977). Frank Noble considered each of Fox's proposed original gateways in the southern two-thirds of the Dyke, frequently disagreeing with his suggestions (Noble 1983). Only a massive campaign of excavation could enable progress to be made in this matter.

Excavation might also throw light on a possible association between the Dyke and some fortified sites in Montgomeryshire and Radnorshire to which attention was drawn in a recent paper (Musson and Spurgeon 1988) (fig. 45). Seven forts are discussed, six of them rectangular in shape. It is suggested that the three forts of this group which are very close to the Dyke – Old Mills Moat, Buttington and Nantcribba Gaer – might be Mercian works, as might a fort at New Radnor which is four miles west of the Dyke but in the midst of the English place-names mapped on fig. 43c. The other three forts – Cwrt Llechrhyd, Mathrafal and Plas-y-Dinas – are considered likely to be Welsh structures, perhaps built in imitation of Mercian ones. There is one outlying English name, Guilsfield, between Mathrafal and the Dyke (see fig. 43b), but both Mathrafal and Plas-y-Dinas to the north-east of it were probably outside Mercian territory. The fort which is the main subject of the paper, Cwrt Llechrhyd in Llanelwedd, is near Builth Wells, and this and New Radnor are a long way south of the others. Cwrt Llechrhyd is the most westerly of the seven and is most unlikely to be a Mercian work. It has, however, produced a radiocarbon reading which suggests a probable date of construction in the ninth or tenth centuries, and the structural similarity between it and the other six has led to this suggestion that they may all have a connection with the events of Offa's reign. For the moment it is only possible to note that the forts are available for study and excavation.

Traffic through the Dyke would need to be regulated, and one purpose of any linear earthwork at this date would be to hinder the theft of livestock.

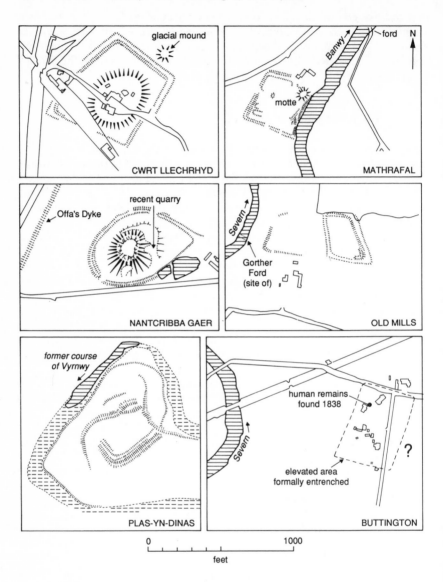

Figure 45 Possible Dark Age enclosures in the central Welsh Marches (from Musson and Spurgeon 1988, by permission of the Society for Medieval Archaeology).

Frank Noble thought that something of the manner in which the earthwork operated might be discerned from a law-code known as the Ordinance concerning the Dunsæte. This lays down rules for the procedures to be followed when stolen animals are suspected of being conveyed across a boundary between Welsh and English territory, and for the passage of people from one side to the other. The law-code comes from a later date, and the barrier in question is a river, not an earthwork, but it is very likely that it conveys an authentic hint of what the regulations along Offa's Dyke may have been. It is useful to discuss it at this point as it has a bearing on the next major problem: the political situation in Herefordshire in the reign of Offa.

The Ordinance Concerning the Dunsæte

There is a general agreement that the context of the Dunsæte Ordinance is a meeting which king Æthelstan held with the Welsh princes at Hereford c.930. The implications of this meeting for the history of Hereford will be considered in a later chapter. The law-code, which Stenton (in Fox 1955: xviii) called an 'enigmatical document', is published in facsimile with a translation in Noble 1983. In 1969 Frank Noble had initiated a sort of 'round robin' correspondence with a number of scholars in order to promote study of this text and in the hope of securing support for his hypothesis that the tenth-century code was an adaptation of an earlier one drawn up in Offa's reign to regulate traffic across the whole of Offa's border with the Welsh. This suggestion was received with great interest, but expert examination of the text, particularly by Professor Dorothy Whitelock, failed to uncover any evidence for a Mercian original behind the West Saxon. The correspondence was presented as an Appendix to Frank Noble's M.A. thesis, and may be consulted by application to the Open University. On pp. 33-4 of this Appendix Dorothy Whitelock's analysis of the dialectal characteristics is given, with the conclusion 'If there was a Mercian text the tenth century users of it have gone to very great and *unusual* care to eradicate any signs of such a text.' There can be no appeal against this verdict, but it is still legitimate to argue that the Ordinance deals with conditions on the English/Welsh border which are likely to have been much the same for several centuries. There may have been long-established ways of managing property disputes which were codified by Æthelstan's officials.

If the Dunsæte ordinance were not a codification of methods for settling disputes which had long been in practice among the people of the March, it is difficult for the modern reader to believe that they would have understood it. All the written law-codes of the Anglo-Saxon period were 'composed for persons familiar with the general circumstances' (Whitelock 1955: 333) and their wording is elliptical, but this one is more than usually cryptic. The setting is a situation in which Welshmen are living on one bank of a river and Englishmen on the other. There are elaborate procedures to be invoked 'if anyone follows the track of stolen cattle from one river bank to the other'. One provision limits wergilds (compensation payments for homicide) to half the normal sum for Welshmen killed by Englishmen and Englishmen killed by Welshmen in the vicinity of the boundary river. Another states that 'Neither is a Welshman to cross over into English land, nor an Englishman to Welsh, without the appointed man from that land, who shall meet him at the bank and bring him back there again without any offence.' This last provision seemed to Frank Noble to echo a situation in which crossing-places on Offa's Dyke were manned by officials who controlled the passage of travellers to and from Wales.

Archenfield

Who were the Dunsæte (who never appear in any record but this), and how could an English king issue laws which were binding both on English and Welsh people? The only possible region for them seems to be south Herefordshire, the territory which is called *Ircingafeld* in the Anglo-Saxon Chronicle for 915, and which had earlier constituted the Welsh kingdom of Ergyng. The river, which is not named in the Ordinance, is generally considered to be the Wye. If Ergyng had become part of Mercia before the time of the Ordinance, it might have been divided into two portions, an eastern one in which English law and customs prevailed, and a western one in which the laws and customs were mostly Welsh. This situation could have led to the necessity for a special law code dealing with disputes between people of the two parts.

Archenfield is the modern name for an area bounded by the Rivers Wye, Monnow and Worm (which are shown in fig. 34); but in order for the Dunsæte to be regarded as the people of Ergyng it would be necessary to assume that the district originally included land to the east of the Wye, and there is evidence that this was so. The Roman town of Ariconium, from which the name Ergyng is derived, is itself east of the Wye, and for it to have been more or less central the kingdom would have had to extend as far east as the Rivers Leadon and Severn. This would mean that the diocesan boundary between Hereford and Worcester (described on p. 98) was in its southern part the boundary of Ergyng. Other evidence for the original extent of Ergyng is shown on fig. 46 (Coplestone-Crow 1989: 2–5).

The Ordinance speaks of the river as dividing English from Welsh, and the place-name evidence presented on fig. 34 is consistent with this. Between the Rivers Wye and Leadon the only surviving ancient British names noted are Ross and Penyard. The other two names mapped in the area east of the Wye are Eccleswall and Walford. Eccleswall ('Christian-community spring') can be interpreted as a pagan English reference to the Christianity of Ergyng which is likely to have been continuous since Roman times. Walford is one of a small group of names in which *walh* is uninflected: it means not 'ford of the Welshmen', but 'Welsh ford', and the settlement is less than half a mile from the River Wye. The phenomenon, discussed on p. 70, of Welsh names of post-Roman type which are likely to be part of an uninterrupted sequence of Welsh nomenclature, is confined to the west side of the river.

Thus it makes sense to locate the Dunsæte on either side of the Wye, and to regard them as the people of an earlier kingdom of Ergyng which extended to the Leadon and Severn, and which had received dense English settlement in its eastern part (fig. 47). It is still necessary to consider how and when this kingdom passed from Welsh to English rule, and why the name Dunsæte was applied to its inhabitants.

The date at which Archenfield came under English control is a matter for

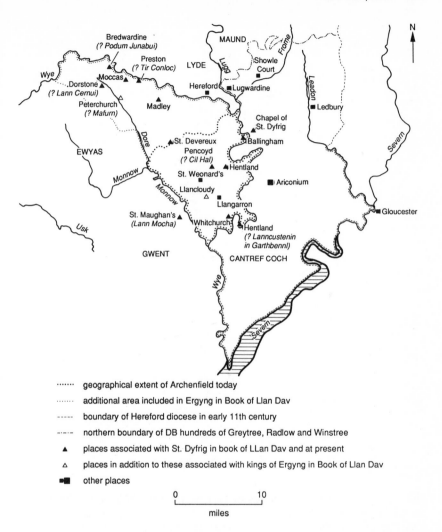

Figure 46 The kingdom of Ergyng (from Copplestone-Crow 1989).

conjecture. A sparse framework for guesses is provided by the few events which are mentioned in surviving records. It has been noted above that independent Welsh rulers of Ergyng ceased to be mentioned c.620, and that the district probably passed into the control of the kings of Gwent after that. Professor Wendy Davies (1982: 102) says that the loss to the English of political control in Ergyng happened in the later ninth century, but she gives no reason for considering this to be the date. It may have happened a century earlier. It must, however, be later than c.750. An entry in the Book of Llandaff (Davies 1979: 113–14) records that King Ithel of Glywising (which had incorporated Gwent) returned 11 churches to Bishop Berthwyn after Saxon devastation in the Hereford area. The account mentions King

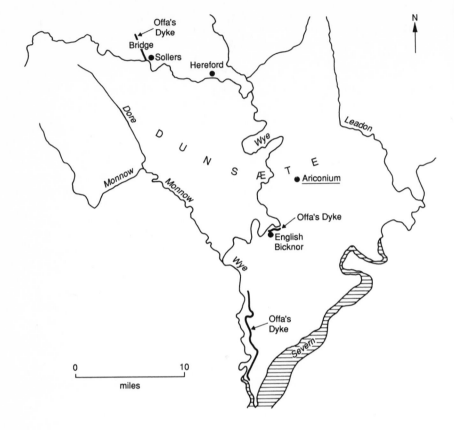

Figure 47   The territory of the Dunsæte.

Æthelbald of Mercia, and Professor Davies dates it c.745, and links it to the annal in the Anglo-Saxon Chronicle for 743, which records that Æthelbald and Cuthred (of Wessex) fought against the Britons. The restored churches are named, and this record seems to establish that Archenfield was conquered by Æthelbald but regained after a brief period by Ithel of Glywising. Noble (1983: 11) notes that grants in Archenfield by Welsh kings terminate in the reign of Ithel's son. There appears to be no reason why political control in Ergyng should not be assumed to have passed to the Mercians in the later eighth century, in the reign of Offa. Several Welsh sources record a battle at Hereford in 760. If Offa obtained Archenfield then, or later in his reign, he would have been able to include the district in his frontier arrangements. This was Frank Noble's conclusion; and it is difficult to see how the frontier line to north and south could have been effective if there was a large gap between, over which the Mercians had no control.

Frank Noble (1983: 11) thought that the Welsh of Archenfield 'were brought into the position which they still occupied in 1066 in the reign of

Offa'. The customs of the Welsh of Archenfield are set out in Domesday
Book, and are said to date from before 1066. They indicate a continuance
of Welsh law together with a surprising enthusiasm for escort duties and
military service. If Archenfield had this special position in Offa's Mercia,
it is not clear why the Offan boundary should have run through the eastern
or central part of its territory, though Fox and Noble both assume that it
did so. The Dyke probably does not appear in Archenfield, though Noble
(13-16) looks for corridors of land 'which must be taken into consideration
when searching for any traces of the line which may have been marked out
by Offa'. Fox considered the Dyke to be totally absent from Bridge Sollers
(on the Wye, 6 miles west of Hereford) to English Bicknor on the Severn,
27 miles to the south; and he concluded from this that 'the Wye is, broadly
speaking, the frontier throughout' and that 'the whole of Ergyng, then, the
Hereford bridgehead apart (?), remained in Welsh hands' (211-12). This idea
of Hereford occupying a bridgehead, with the territory around it either in
Welsh hands or, on the English side of the Wye, covered by dense, unoccupied forest, will be considered when the evidence for the early history of
the city is discussed in Chapter 9. Our present concern is with the Dyke
and the political and administrative arrangements within which it functioned.

Fox thought there must have been a boundary along the Wye because
Archenfield, which he regarded as the district west of the Wye, was under
Welsh government. Noble thought that the inhabitants of Archenfield had
become a buffer state, but that

> Offa's line from sea to sea would either have had to mark them off
> from the Welsh of Upper Gwent, or form a boundary between
> them and Offa's other Magonsætan subjects who would have to
> observe Mercian taxes and services.

I should like tentatively to advance another possibility. If the people of
Archenfield had accepted Offa's rule on terms which allowed them to keep
their own customs, Offa could have told them to make their own
arrangements for securing their western and south-western boundaries
against Welsh neighbours who were still under Welsh rule. If labour on
fortifications was not part of their customs it would have been imprac-
ticable to raise a dyke. But it would have been in their own interests to
keep hostile Welsh forces from crossing their border, and they would share
the concern of all Offa's western subjects about cattle raiding. If they could
be relied upon, by whatever means, to prevent Welsh armies and raiders
from penetrating their territory, then the gap in the patrolled border would
not be an embarrassment to the English people north and south of Ergyng.
Prowess at keeping out invaders could have led to the custom described in
Domesday Book; 'When the army advances on the enemy, these men by
custom form the vanguard and on their return the rearguard' (DB i, f. 179b).

If it were to be assumed that the boundary, instead of following the Wye
or a more direct marked-out line northwards from Bicknor to Bridge Sollers,
went west along the Wye and then up the Monnow and perhaps along the
Dore, a problem might seem to be posed by the positioning of the Dyke so

far to the east when it reappears on the north bank of the Wye at Bridge Sollers. The Dyke is here assumed, however, in accordance with Frank Noble's interpretation, to be set back anything up to three miles from the actual frontier; and this assumption would place the greater part of north-west Herefordshire comfortably in Offa's Mercia. Some of Fox's forest may really have existed along this frontier west of the Dyke: see the cluster of *lēah* names shown on fig. 7. But there is a cluster of English place-names west of the *lēah* names which must be admitted to be outside the reach of any conceivable protection provided by the Dyke or by the people of Archenfield. The ones which appear in Domesday Book are Huntington, Whitney, Middlewood, Clifford, Winforton, Moor, Cusop (a Welsh/English hybrid) and Harewood. Two of these, Whitney and Clifford, are likely to be relatively early names, and all of them are free from Welsh influence. It is necessary to assume that there was an enclave of English-speaking people south-west of Kington which was beyond the Offan frontier. Their presence may at a later date have influenced the boundary of the county. It might be in this area that Elise of Powys recovered land from the English, probably before Offa's time. It would be at the southern extremity of his kingdom.

The intermittent nature of the Dyke in north Herefordshire, from Bridge Sollers to Titley, was explained by Fox (176) mainly in terms of 'uncleared jungle'. The place-name evidence mapped on fig. 7, however, does not suggest that the area was so densely wooded in the middle Saxon period as to be uninhabited. Some provision must have been made for the areas where the Dyke did not reveal itself to Fox's survey.

The two final provisions of the Dunsæte Ordinance state:

> Formerly the *Wentsæte* belonged to the *Dunsæte*, but more correctly they belong to the West Saxons: and they have to send tribute and hostages there. But the *Dunsæte* also need, if the king will grant it to them, that at least they should be allowed hostages for peace.

The significance of this clause has not yet been elucidated, but it is convenient to consider the identity of the Wentsæte together with that of the Dunsæte in the context of this type of province-name as manifested on the west boundary of Mercia.

Wentsæte has been interpreted, reasonably, as meaning 'people of Gwent'. It could, however, be 'people whose territory adjoins Gwent', and it might refer to a relatively small administrative unit lying between Gwent and Ergyng in the vicinity of Monmouth. If the Dunsæte are the people of Archenfield, their province was a large one, and this contrasts with the characteristic size for '-sæte' groups along the border, which is something corresponding to the hundredal divisions discussed in Chapter 8, rather than to half a county. The district, place, or natural feature called *Dun*, from which the Dunsæte took their name, has defeated all attempts at identification. It is not likely to be the Welsh word meaning 'fort', as that would have given **Din*. It is most probably the Old English word *dūn*, modern *down*, perhaps used in the sense 'mountain'; but it would be very difficult to identify a suitable mountain.

-sǣte Names Along the Dyke

Dunsǣte and *Wensǣte* can be seen as the southernmost items in a line of *-sǣte* names extending up the Dyke to the north-west corner of Shropshire. The others are shown on fig. 48. *Meresǣte* ('dwellers by the boundary'), *Rhiwsǣte* ('dwellers by the mountain called Rhiw') and *Stepelsǣte* ('dwellers by a steep place') were names of hundreds. *Halhsǣte* (probably 'river-meadow dwellers') persisted in the later form *Alcester* into the sixteenth century as the name of a district in the parish of Church Stoke, Montgomeryshire. *Temesǣte* ('dwellers by the River Teme'), later *Tempsiter*, was the name of the southern portion of the Honour of Clun.

This series of names has a regular, organized look, and it is possible that they originated in administrative arrangements made by Offa as part of his organization of the border. If there was some reorganization of local government units in connection with the building and functioning of the Dyke, the coining of the name *Dunsǣte* for the people south of Hereford might have been part of the same process, and its use in Æthelstan's law code might be an archaism.

Burton and Associated Names

Evidence for the defence of Mercia against attacks from Wales is not confined to linear earthworks. There is also a significant series of place-names derived from the Old English compounds *burhtūn*, *byrhtūn*, *byrigtūn*. These may be respectively translated, according to the grammatical case of the first element, as 'fort-settlement', 'settlement of a fort' and 'settlement at a fort'. The commonest modern form is Burton (which can be from any of the three forms), but Bourton, Boreton and Broughton also occur. The genitive form, *byrhtūn*, gives two Buertons in Cheshire and a Bierton in Buckinghamshire. The form in which the first element is in the dative gives seven Berringtons and one Burrington, and this form is the most westerly, occurring in Gloucestershire, Worcestershire, Shropshire and Somerset.

A case has been put forward recently (Gelling 1989) for considering all the names of this type which have been traced, numbering about a hundred, to be remnants of a system of defensive posts and army mustering-places which survived in Mercia until the catastrophe of the Danish wars in the latter part of the ninth century. It is too soon to say whether this suggestion carries any conviction among historians. An alternative interpretation would be that defended settlements grew up by private initiative in areas which were especially vulnerable. The distribution map for the whole country is shown in fig. 49. For present purposes it is desirable to look at the positioning of such names in our five counties.

'Burton' names are especially numerous in north Herefordshire, all of Shropshire, and west Cheshire. They are not distributed primarily along Offa's Dyke, though some of them are close to it. The two series which stand out most clearly on the map are running along the valleys of the Rivers Severn and Teme, as if intended to overlook major east/west travel

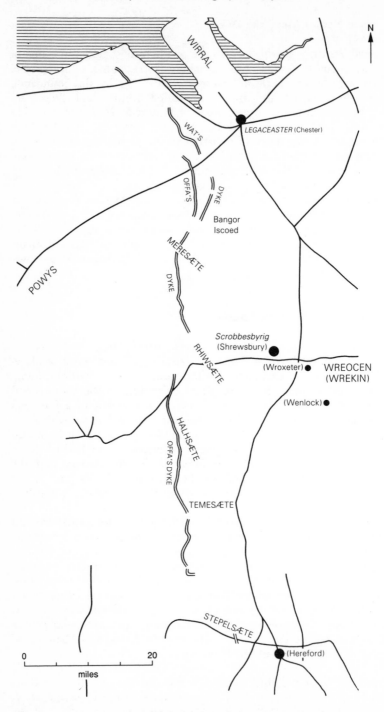

Figure 48   *sǣte* names along Offa's Dyke.

Figure 49 Burton and associated names.

routes. A similar arrangement can be seen in Yorkshire, along the Rivers Ouse and Ure, where the names are clearly related to a major route through the Pennines.

The distribution of *burhtūn*, *byrhtūn* names in Staffordshire and Warwickshire is markedly different. There are three in each county, and they are evenly spaced, as are the three examples in Leicestershire and Kesteven.

Other names shown in fig. 49 include 10 which contain Old English *burhweard*, 'fort guardian'. Seven of these are in Cheshire, Shropshire and Herefordshire. In Gelling 1989 it is suggested that there were officials with the title *burhweard* who had charge of a group of defence posts and were given estates from which to operate. The seven names in the Marches are Burwardsley and Brewer's Hall in Cheshire; Brosely and Burwarton in Shropshire; a Domesday manor called *Burwardestone* which lay partly in Cheshire and partly in Flintshire; another Domesday *Burardestune* which can be firmly identified with Bollingham House in Eardisley, Herefordshire; and Treverward in the parish of Clun, Shropshire, which is *Treboreward* in 1284, an obvious Welsh version of Burwarton, as Trebirt in Llanfair Waterdine is an obvious Welsh rendering of Burton. Upper and Lower Trebirt are about half a mile west of Offa's Dyke, and Treverward is less than two miles north-east, on the English side. This treatment of the names by Welsh speakers may have been a way of coping with technical terms for which they had no exact equivalent.

If these names referred to elements in an organized system of defence against invaders, this is likely to have been independent of, and probably earlier than, the building of the Dyke.

Recurrent -tūn Names

Shropshire has more 'Burton' names than any other county in the western half of England, and this is typical. Repetition of settlement-names which may be suspected of referring to a specialized function is the dominant characteristic of the toponymy of this shire. Shropshire has 10 Astons, 9 Westons, 6 Nortons and 7 Suttons. The comparative figures for Cheshire are 5, 2, 1 and 7. Warwickshire has 2 Astons, 3 Westons, a single Norton and 2 Suttons. Definitive figures are not available for Herefordshire and Staffordshire, but it is clear that directional *tūn* names do not occur in either county with the same sort of frequency as they do in Shropshire. Similar comparisons can be made for Upton (5 in Shropshire, 4 in Cheshire, 2 in Warwickshire), Middleton (4 in Shropshire, 2 in Cheshire, 1 in Warwickshire) and Newton (10 Shropshire and Cheshire, 2 Warwickshire). In some instances, perhaps in most, these names refer to the position, locational or chronological, of a settlement in a larger economic unit, and in the western part of Mercia they may sometimes be descriptions employed by Mercian administrators in preference to earlier British names. The argument is perhaps stronger with reference to recurring compounds of *tūn* with words for a topographical feature. Eaton ('river settlement') occurs 6 times in Shropshire, 3 in Cheshire, once in Warwickshire. The figures for Hatton ('heath settlement') are 4, 2 and 2, for Moreton ('marsh settlement') 4, 3 and 2, for Wootton ('wood settlement') 4, 0 and 3. It is very likely that the Shropshire Eatons (for instance) are settlements which were perceived by Mercian administrators as having a special function in relation to the major rivers by which they were situated (Gelling 1990: 114-15), and that the English appellative which expressed this concept gradually displaced an earlier British name.

The point about recurrent *tūn* names is introduced here because it forms part of the material which might be considered to be evidence for a particularly tight Mercian administrative organization in Shropshire. The second half of the eighth century - the reign of Offa - would be a likely date

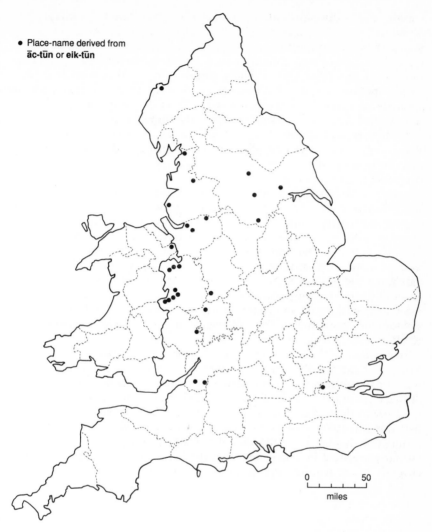

● Place-name derived from
āc-tūn or **eik-tūn**

0 ⊢─┴─┴─┴─┴─┤ 50
miles

Figure 50 Place-names derived from *āc-tūn* and *eik-tūn*.

for the establishment of these names, as there is good evidence that *tūn* did not become a fashionable place-name element until about A.D.750.

Finally, readers may like to exercise their imaginations on the unsolved problem of the distribution of names derived from Old English *āc-tūn*, 'oak settlement'. As can be seen from fig. 50, the distribution is a curiously limited one, and Shropshire has more instances than any other county. The standard explanations of Acton/Aughton are that the name means 'farm built of oak', 'farm by an oak-tree', or 'farm among oak-trees'. It is, however, difficult to explain the limited distribution if any of these is accepted, since they must have been equally appropriate in many areas where the name does not occur. Compounds of *tūn* with some other tree-names, e.g. Ashton/Eshton and Alderton/Allerton/Ollerton/Orleton, are fairly frequent but more widely distributed. The only such compound which shows similar preferential distribution to Acton/Aughton is Thornton, which has a predominantly East Midland and north-country distribution, 16 of its occurrences in major names being in Yorkshire. It is clear that something in the significance of the compound *āc-tūn* made it specially applicable to settlements in the West Midlands, and that *thorn-tūn* denoted a type of settlement especially common in Yorkshire.

A tentative explanation of Acton based on the characteristics of the eight Shropshire examples is that places so called had special functions in the processing or distribution of oak timber. The places can easily be seen as component parts of large multiple estates. The four 'minor' names are situated in large parishes which contain a number of settlements, and Acton Reynald (which can be classified as a 'major' name because it appears in the Domesday Survey) is similarly placed in the large parish of Shawbury. As regards the three Actons which became parishes – Acton Burnell, Acton Round and Acton Scott – the areas of the parishes are modest, quite different from those of Rushbury, Shawbury, Lydbury North, Baschurch and Ruyton-XI-Towns, where the 'minor' Actons lie. The hidage given in Domesday for the five Actons mentioned there is three for Acton Pigott, Acton Reynald and Acton Scott, three-and-a-half for Acton Burnell, and four for Acton Round. The splitting up of large composite estates might result in the creation of just such units as these.

To account for the geographical distribution, it would have to be assumed either that the handling of oak timber became a specialized function for subordinate settlements at the period when English names were replacing British ones in the West Midlands and in Yorkshire, or that the pre-English economy of those areas had been characterized by such specialization, and that this was recognized in the new English names. In support of the first assumption it may be noted that the work on bridges and fortifications regularly specified in land-grants from the latter part of the eighth century onwards would require large supplies of timber.

8 The Danish Wars and the Formation of the Shires

Secular and Ecclesiastical Politics Before the Danish Wars

Whatever local administrative arrangements prevailed in the western part of Mercia at the end of Offa's reign (and the account offered in Chapter 7 is, of course, highly conjectural), these may be supposed to have continued in operation without serious disturbance for the first half of the ninth century. The years from Offa's death in 796 to the appearance of the sustained Viking menace in the 860s saw important developments in secular and ecclesiastical politics, but nothing which happened is likely to have been accompanied or followed by much interference in the processes of local government. More-or-less settled peace is required for minor administrative rearrangement, and total disaster, such as befell Mercia in the latter part of the century, is the likely condition for major change.

In secular politics, the period after Offa's death saw the steady erosion of Mercia's supremacy over other English kingdoms. Wessex became independent of Mercian overlordship in 802, when Egbert became king; and a war between Mercia and Northumbria in 801 ended in a peace on equal terms (Stenton 1943: 223, 294). Cenwulf, a distant kinsman of Offa who succeeded to the kingship on the death of Offa's son after a reign of a few months, had authority outside the ancient kingdom in Sussex, East Anglia and Kent, as did his brother, Ceolwulf, who reigned from 821-3. But their successor, Beornwulf, was defeated by Egbert of Wessex at Wroughton (anciently *Ellandun*) in Wiltshire in 825, and the men of Kent, Essex, Surrey and Sussex submitted to Egbert after that battle. The East Angles revolted against Beornwulf before the end of the year, and an attempt to subdue them led to his death. His successor, an ealdorman named Ludeca, inherited a kingdom reduced to Mercia, Lindsey, Middle Anglia and the provinces of the Hwicce and Magonsæte, apart from the anomalous retention south of the Thames of the area which later became Berkshire. In 829 Egbert of Wessex became briefly the immediate ruler of Mercia, but Wiglaf, Ludeca's successor, regained his kingdom in 830.

By contrast with these unsuccessful campaigns to east, south and north, the Mercians under Cenwulf and Ceolwulf waged successful war in the west against their British neighbours. Welsh sources record Mercian raids in north Wales, between the rivers Clwyd and Elwy, and the penetration of Snowdonia in 816; and in 818 Cenwulf harried the Britons of Dyfed. Cenwulf died at Basingwerk in Flintshire in 821, and Stenton (1943: 230) conjectures that he was preparing for another Welsh expedition. His successor, Ceolwulf, is credited by the *Annales Cambriae* with the destruction in 822 of the fortress of Deganwy at the mouth of the Conway, and the conquest of the kingdom of Powys (AC 89). It is not likely that any attempt was made to retain Powys. That kingdom became a victim of inter-Welsh rivalry and was absorbed into Gwynedd in 855 (Davies 1982: 110). These Mercian campaigns are only known from Welsh sources, and the Mercian successes and the tribute derived from them may have been greater than these sources suggest, and sufficient perhaps to offset Mercian defeats (or, at any rate, lack of gains) in other quarters.

The ecclesiastical politics of the reign of Cenwulf are comparatively well documented, as a number of contemporary accounts have survived. Offa had secured the elevation of Lichfield into an archbishopric, but in 798 King Cenwulf wrote to Pope Leo III urging a return to Pope Gregory's suggested arrangement whereby there were to be only two English arch-bishops, seated in London and York. Stenton ascribes this move to a desire on Cenwulf's part to have the southern archbishop at London, where he would be under Mercian protection, rather than in Kent, where Mercian authority did not prevail owing to a revolt which had broken out shortly before Offa's death. The plan came to nothing. The pope refused to sanction the removal of the archbishop's seat from Canterbury, and the restoration of Mercian authority in Kent rendered it unnecessary from Cenwulf's view-point. The archbishopric of Lichfield was, however, abolished by a provin-cial council in 803, and this seems to have been accepted without opposition in Mercia. Cenwulf had indicated his consent in the letter of 798, and Archbishop Hygeberht of Lichfield had resigned before the council was held (Brooks 1984: 118-27; Stenton 1943: 225-30).

King Wiglaf of Mercia regained his kingdom from Egbert of Wessex in 830, beginning what he himself called in a charter of 831 his 'second reign' (S 188). This lasted 10 years. London remained in his control, as did the region south of the Thames from Ashbury in the west to Cookham in the east (Gelling 1976: 840), but the Mercians did not initiate any movement of aggression against Wessex. Wiglaf was followed in 840 by a king named Beorhtwulf who appears to have ceded the Berkshire lands to King Æthelwulf of Wessex. Sir Frank Stenton suggested that a unique coin with the name of Beorhtwulf on one side and that of Æthelwulf on the other may commemorate the transfer (Stenton 1971: 245n.). The position of Wessex as the dominant partner in this friendly relationship was dramatically confirmed in 851, when a Danish army stormed Canterbury and London and drove King Beorhtwulf into flight before being defeated by the West Saxon army led by King Æthelwulf. The *Anglo-Saxon Chronicle* also records that in 853 Burgred, who had succeeded Beorhtwulf as king of Mercia in 852, asked Æthelwulf for help against the Welsh and was given the assistance of the West Saxon army led by the king. It is possible that the Welsh had been taking revenge for the maraudings of Cenwulf and Ceolwulf, a generation earlier. This campaign was followed by the marriage of Æthelwulf's daughter to Burgred.

This was not a period of military glory for Mercia, and Burgred did not prove an effective leader when the Danish raiding became the full-time activity of a 'great army' which remained in England year in and year out. It is suggested in Chapter 7 that 'Burton' place-names may preserve a record of an ancient Mercian system of defence posts. If so, it was a system which proved totally ineffective against the Danish army. After a successful campaign in Northumbria (based on York), in 866-7 the Danes took winter quarters at Nottingham, and Burgred asked Wessex for help in spring-summer 868. He was joined by King Æthelred and his brother, the future King Alfred, but there was no battle, and the campaign ended with the Mercians buying peace, and the return of the Danish army to York in the autumn of 868.

Partition of Mercia

We are concerned here not so much with the well-documented and well-known stages of the Danish wars as with the consequences for western Mercia of the partition of the kingdom which the Danes imposed in A.D.876. Burgred resigned (or was deposed) in 873, and the Danes, who were then at Repton, placed one of his thegns named Ceolwulf on the throne, on the condition that Mercia should be at their disposal if they wished to occupy it. Four years later they appropriated the eastern half of the kingdom and granted the western half to Ceolwulf. Ceolwulf was described in the *Anglo-Saxon Chronicle* as 'a foolish king's thegn', but his reputation has risen among historians in recent decades. His coins issued from London show that the same moneyers worked for him and for King Alfred, and he must have been recognized and respected by the West Saxon ruler (Stenton 1971: 252n.). Perhaps the arrangements of 873 and the terms made in 876 represented the best that any leader could have secured. It is clear that any defensive organization which existed in the Midlands before the Danish wars was totally unable to offer protection against Viking armies, and the conglomerate nature of the kingdom may have made it difficult to set another system in operation quickly. The Mercian state had for centuries been geared to the defence of its western, northern and southern borders; the eastward direction from which the Viking threat came may have made matters more difficult.

Ceolwulf ruled western Mercia until 879. The circumstances in which his reign ended are not recorded. He had no successor as king, and by 883 the English part of Mercia had been placed by King Alfred under the control of Ealdorman Æthelred, who married Alfred's sister, the Lady Æthelflæd, a few years later.

We have no exact knowledge of the boundary which the Danes agreed with Ceolwulf in 877. There is, however, a treaty, probably drawn up in 886, which divided the south Midlands into a southern and western portion, to be ruled by King Alfred, and a northern and eastern section, controlled by the Danish King Guthrum. The first clause of this treaty declares: 'First concerning our boundaries: up the Thames, and then up the Lea, and along the Lea to its source, then in a straight line to Bedford, then up the Ouse to Watling Street' (Whitelock 1955: 380). Because the final point in this boundary is Watling Street, it has been widely assumed that the English-Danish boundary through the central Midlands ran along the Roman road. The conventional interpretation of the 886 treaty was challenged by Professor R.H.C. Davis (1982), and one of the criticisms which he made was that on maps showing areas of Scandinavian settlement the thick black line which purports to represent the 886 agreement is continued along Watling Street to the east boundary of Shropshire, though the text of the treaty gives no warrant for this. In fact the line between English and Danish Mercia may well have turned north at the northern tip of Warwickshire and have followed the line which later became the boundary separating Staffordshire, Cheshire and Lancashire from Derbyshire and Yorkshire.

Professor Davis considered that nothing was said in the document about the line of the boundary after it reached Watling Street because King Alfred was negotiating an agreement with the Danish king of East Anglia about territory in the south Midlands which Wessex had taken over from Mercia. He was not negotiating about the division between Mercian and Danish land.

Boroughs and Shires

The modern county boundaries of the Midlands came into being as a consequence of the Danish wars. They were the result of a new system of establishing military centres. By no means all the places chosen for such centres became county towns, but some did, and the special administrative role of Chester, Hereford, Stafford, Shrewsbury and Warwick is likely to have crystallized as a result of this policy. In western Mercia the fortresses were mainly the work of Æthelflæd, the Lady of the Mercians, who ruled the kingdom after the death of her husband, Æthelred, in 911, and probably for some years before that while he was incapacitated by illness. The version of the *Anglo-Saxon Chronicle* which is known as the Mercian Register records the building or restoration of 'boroughs' (i.e. fortified places, Old English *burh*, dative *byrig*) at Chester in 907, *Bremesbyrig* in 910, *Scergeat* and Bridgnorth in 912, Tamworth and Stafford in 913, Eddisbury and Warwick in 914, Chirbury, *Weardbyrig* and Runcorn in 915, and *Cledemutha* (now Rhuddlan) in 921. This last fort was built by King Edward after Æthelflæd's death in 918 and his assumption of direct rule in Mercia in 919. The main text of the *Chronicle* records that in 919 King Edward built a *burh* at Thelwall (on the Mersey near Warrington) and occupied Manchester 'in Northumbria'. These forts are shown on fig. 51. The north-west frontier of Mercia was being strengthened, not against the Welsh, who accepted Edward's overlordship in 918, but against the threat presented both by the Norwegian Viking bases established round the Irish Sea, and by the Norse kingdom of York, whose king, Sihtric, raided into Cheshire as far as Davenport in 920. Chester became the focus for the defence of a wide region.

The Role of Chester During the Danish Wars

The cluster of Burton place-names round Chester could be seen as an indication that earlier Mercian administrators had regarded the area as a particularly vulnerable one. The town itself appears to have been

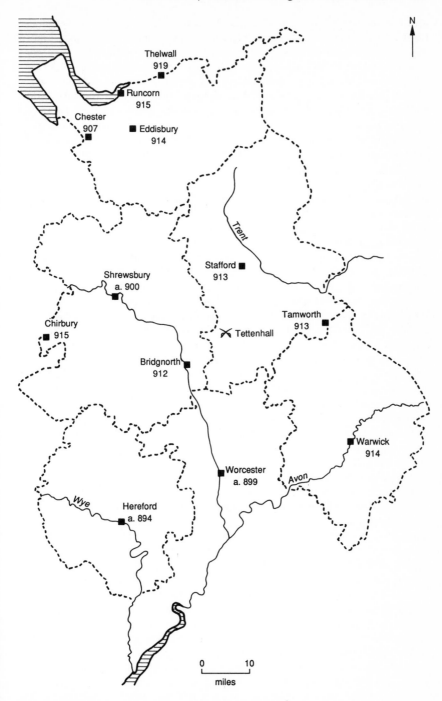

Figure 51 The forts of the Danish wars.

uninhabited in 893, when it was seized and used as a base by Danish raiders from Essex. The *Anglo-Saxon Chronicle* notes that in that year a highly-mobile band of Danes 'went continuously by day and night till they reached a deserted city in Wirral, which is called Chester' (Whitelock 1955: 187). They were besieged but not dislodged by an English army, which ravaged the surrounding countryside causing them to move out of the city in 894 because there was no food. They raided in Wales and then made their way back to Essex.

There is archaeological evidence for the building of a timber hut to the west of Lower Bridge Street in the late ninth century, and finds from this area include a silver brooch of that date and sherds of a Carolingian vessel of the eighth-ninth century. This may suggest that the desertion recorded in the *Chronicle* was a temporary phenomenon, following a period when Chester had been a functioning centre (Mason 1985; Thacker 1987: 250).

The strategic importance of Chester was again demonstrated after a group of Norwegian Vikings, expelled from Dublin in 902, established a colony in the vicinity (Wainwright 1948). This immigration, under the command of a Norse leader named Ingimund, was not noted by contemporary English chroniclers; but the story is preserved in some detail in a later Irish text, which has been accepted as a reliable source in spite of having been infiltrated by a great deal of folklore. Ingimund and his Norse followers left Dublin and tried to establish themselves in north-west Wales, but were expelled by the Welsh king, Clydog. After this they arrived in north-west Mercia and entered into negotiations with Æthelflæd. She gave them lands near Chester, but her tolerance of their presence broke down when they decided to occupy the city. Æthelflæd assembled an army and defended Chester successfully, and the restoration of the defences in 907 can obviously be connected with these events. Associated developments within the city will be considered in the next chapter. Here it is appropriate to note the developments in the organization of the area whose defences centred on Chester.

After the Danish wars Chester was the administrative centre for an area considerably larger than the modern county. It was larger to the north because an area round Manchester had been annexed from Northumbria in 919. That, at any rate, is the date suggested by Thacker (1987: 252), and the conjecture is eminently reasonable. As noted above, the *ASC* annal for 919 records the occupation of 'Manchester in Northumbria' by a Mercian army sent by Edward the Elder. The extent of the area made dependent on Chester at that time may be revealed by Domesday Book, where all Lancashire south of the River Ribble is included in the Cheshire folios. The lands 'between Ribble and Mersey' are, however, treated in an appendix, not as an integral part of Cheshire, and the Mersey must always have been recognized as the ancient boundary between Mercia and Northumbria. The name Mersey is Old English *gemǣresèa*, 'river of the boundary'. Tame, now restricted to one of the head-streams, was perhaps the name of the whole river in pre-English times.

The Cheshire of the late Anglo-Saxon period was much larger, also, in the west. The Domesday folios include all Flintshire and a great deal of Denbighshire. Most of the Welsh estates, like the south Lancashire ones, are surveyed in a discrete section at the end of the Cheshire folios. The exceptions are Bettisfield, Worthenbury and Iscoyd, which later formed a detached part of Flintshire called Maelor Saesneg ('English Maelor'), as opposed to Maelor Gymraeg ('Welsh Maelor') which was part of Denbighshire. These three estates, which had passed from Earl Edwin to Earl Hugh, were probably felt to be more closely associated than the other Welsh districts with the English lands dependent on Chester.

The west boundary of Cheshire could only reflect territorial agreements (voluntary or otherwise) between English and Welsh rulers. The east boundary, with Derbyshire, may also be arbitrary, reflecting the division into English and Danish Mercia imposed upon King Ceolwulf. It does, however, follow river-courses, of the Etherow, Goyt and Dane. To the north and south Cheshire has natural boundaries. The northern one roughly follows the Mersey, the southern one is closely related to a major watershed (see Chapter 1). When it was stripped, in the post-Conquest centuries, of areas of north Wales and southern Northumbria, Cheshire may have been the least artificial of the West Midland shires.

Before considering the formation of Herefordshire, Shropshire, Staffordshire and Warwickshire, it will be useful to consider the place-name evidence for Norse and Danish settlement in the West Midlands.

Norse Place-names and Norse Settlement

Since 1965, when Professor Kenneth Cameron delivered his inaugural lecture entitled *Scandinavian Settlement in the Territory of the Five Boroughs: The Place-name Evidence*, there has been an ongoing debate about the likely relationship of place-names in the Old Norse language to density of settlement by people of Danish or Norwegian stock. A number of studies by Professor Cameron have demonstrated that a convincing case can be made for considering that many of the very numerous Old Norse names in the East Midland counties were coined for new settlements made by Danish farmers on land which was under-exploited by the English in the late ninth century. This demonstration, which is based largely on a study of drift geology, led to the hypothesis which has become known as Kenneth Cameron's secondary migration theory (Cameron 1976: 18). This postulates the peaceful infiltration of Danish peasant farmers into areas which were under the control of Viking armies, and the acceptance of these newcomers by English farmers in situations where expansion of settlement was possible and may even have seemed advantageous. This hypothesis has been rejected by some historians (e.g. Professor Peter Sawyer, 1974: 108) and subjected to considerable qualification by other (e.g. Dr Gillian Fellows-Jensen, 1978: 368–72). Fellows-Jensen 1978 explores all possibilities, but the Summary concedes that 'The establishment of most of the *bý*s must reflect an intensification of settlement in the Viking period that was presumably caused in part at least by an influx of settlers from Scandinavia.' Less cautious scholars, such as myself, continue to believe that there is an equation between Norse place-names and Norse settlers.

True Old Norse place-names, as opposed to names which contain late

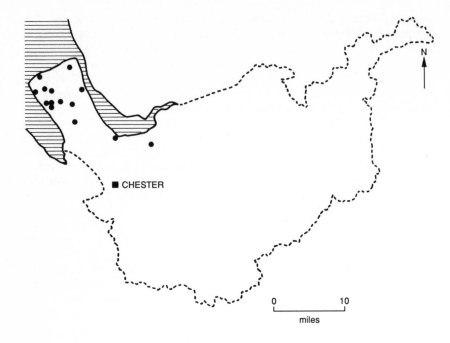

Figure 52   Norse place-names in Cheshire.

Old English or Middle English words adopted from Scandinavian speech,
are rare in the West Midlands as a whole, but there is a group in the Wirral
which deserves careful study.

Norse Place-names in Cheshire (fig. 52)

Wainwright (1948: 161-5) assumed that the Norse names which occur in
the northern half of the Wirral peninsula were the direct result of Ingimund's invasion, a view which continues to be held (Thacker 1987: 249).
These names are at some distance from Chester, however, and it is not
certain that they represent the 'lands near Chester' which Æthelflæd gave
to the refugees from Dublin. They may rather represent an infiltration of
Norwegian farmers which would be a mini-version of the secondary migration postulated by Cameron in eastern England. It is interesting that as
early as 1948, before the mass of work on Scandinavian place-names in
England which began with Cameron's inaugural lecture in 1965, Wainwright's close study of the names in the Wirral led him to say (165) that
'it leaves one with the impression that the Norsemen were generally
content to occupy the poorer lands left uncultivated by the English.' The
'Norsemen and Danes' who were incited by Ingimund to attack Chester
could have been the lords of ancient English villages nearer the city, which
they had taken over without causing changes of name. The northern end
of the Wirral may have been a relatively under-developed area in which
Norsemen of less exalted status could find land for the establishment of

new settlements, which would naturally be named in their own tongue.

The core of the Norse place-names in north Wirral consists of a group ending in -by: Frankby, Irby, West Kirby, a lost *Kirby* in Wallasey, Pensby and Raby. Whitby and Helsby stand apart from these, overlooking the marshes by the Mersey estuary, north of Chester. For the fullest discussion of the qualifying elements in these names Fellows-Jensen 1985 should be consulted. Her account subsumes and in some instances expands the suggestions of earlier scholars.

Whitby, though treated here as a Norse name, may be a Scandinavianized version of an English *Hwītanbyrig* 'white manor'. (Greasby, not listed above, is certainly a Scandinavianized -*byrig*). Kirby means 'church settlement', and this is likely to be a Norse name for an English village which had the attribute, rare at that date, of a village church. The other names are very likely to refer to new settlements. Irby is 'of the Irishmen'. Pensby has a British hill-name as first element (*v.* Chapter 4). Raby, with the first element *rá* 'boundary mark', is on the southern edge of this Norse enclave. Helsby probably means 'shelf settlement' which suits its position on the edge of marshland. Arrowe has been considered to derive from Norse *ærgi* 'shieling', and this may be correct, but Fellows-Jensen (1985: 61) makes the interesting suggestion that it is a doublet of the Herefordshire river-name Arrow, in which case it would be a British survival to add to Pensby.

Other Norse names shown on fig. 52 are topographical. Meols is from Scandinavian *melr* 'sandbank', and early spellings suggest that Tranmere is a compound of Scandinavian *trana* 'crane' with the same element or a related word meaning 'pebbly shore'. Scandinavian speech has affected the form of the English name Birkenhead. Larton is a Norse/English hybrid with *leirr* 'clayey ground' as first element, and Storeton is another such with *storth* 'brushwood, plantation' as qualifier. Thurstaston is the *tūn* of a Scandinavian named Thorsteinn: this is a type of name which elsewhere is considered likely to refer to an ancient English settlement taken over by an upper-class Scandinavian (Cameron 1976: 19-20), and it is noteworthy that only one instance occurs in this group of names.

A particularly significant item in this cluster is Thingwall, derived from a term which Norsemen used for their assembly-places. It means 'open place of the assembly'. In the Isle of Man and in Iceland this was the name of a national assembly, but in Thingwall in Cheshire and Lancashire the name must refer to humbler gatherings, perhaps functioning in the same sort of way as the English hundred or the Danish wapentake. The Wirral was later a single hundred, named in Domesday from Willaston, two-and-a-half miles south of Thingwall; but there could have been two administrative units at an earlier date, the northern one catering for a largely Norse community. Dr Barbara Crawford (1987: 206-10) cites place-names in Scotland and the northern isles which refer to Norse assembly-places for territories of varying size.

Thingwall may suggest that there was a Manx–Norse element in the Wirral settlers (Fellows-Jensen 1985: 373). That there was an Irish element is indicated by the curious name Noctorum (Irish *cnocc-tírim* meaning 'dry hill') and by Irby. There is indeed archaeological evidence, discussed in Chapter 9, for an Irish Sea trading centre at Meols.

Thus the evidence is consistent with a hypothesis that Norse exiles from Dublin who bargained with the Lady of the Mercians may have obtained overlordships of estates near Chester, and that their presence in this capacity facilitated the immigration of Norse farmers from various Irish Sea colonies into a relatively undersettled part of the Wirral. Helsby and Whitby, which are closer to Chester, could be new settlements made viable by draining of marsh.

The Cheshire names which can be considered to indicate Norse settlement are mapped on fig. 52. The maps showing Scandinavian, hybrid and Scandinavianized names in Fellows-Jensen 1985 indicate the presence of some elements of Norse speech at widely scattered points in the county, mostly in the eastern half. Many of the items mapped, however, such as Holme near Tarvin and Mickledale near Frodsham, would not be considered to indicate Norse settlement, but rather a Norse element in the Middle English vocabulary. The same caveat possibly applies to the names Booth and Toft. It is doubtful whether a case could be made from place-names for the taking of English land anywhere in Cheshire by Norwegian and Danish settlers except in the Wirral and on the south bank of the Mersey estuary. There are a number of Norse personal names, like Cnut in Knutsford and Aggi in Agden, but these could belong to landowners of the eleventh century.

The Scandinavian colony in the Wirral was a small one, and geographically separated from similar colonies in Lancashire. After the abortive attempt to occupy Chester these settlers caused less trouble to the English rulers of Mercia than the native English did. It may be that King Edward's visits to Cheshire in 919 and 921 were partly connected with unrest among the English people of the area, who resented his assumption of power in Mercia after Æthelflæd's death (Thacker 1987: 254). Certainly in 924 there was a revolt by the men of Chester in alliance with the Welsh, and the campaign by which Edward suppressed this was the last of his career. He died immediately afterwards at the royal vill of Farndon, on the Cheshire/Flintshire border (Stenton 1943: 335).

Shropshire and Herefordshire During the Danish Wars

Cheshire saw a great deal of action in this period, not because it was subject to Norse settlement, but because of the greatly increased activity in all the lands in and around the Irish Sea. This caused the western defences of Mercia to be concentrated round Chester and along the Mersey, whereas in Offa's reign the central area of the defence system was probably Shropshire.

Shropshire, like every other part of the kingdom, was subject to Viking raids. In fact the area saw some of the earliest attacks, as is known from a charter of A.D.855 which states that the 'heathen' were then in the territory of the *Wreocensæte* (S 206). At a later date action is recorded at the important crossing-place on the River Severn at Bridgnorth, though the place is not referred to by that name. The *Anglo-Saxon Chronicle* records that the Danes wintered in *Cwatbrycge* in 895–6 and built a fort there;

under the year 910 it is noted in Æthelweard's *Chronicle* that a band of Northumbrian Danes crossed the Severn at *Cwatbrycg* before being defeated at Tettenhall in south Staffordshire; and the Mercian Register records that in 912 Æthelflæd built one of her fortresses at *Bricge*.[1] There is no reason to think that these campaigns were accompanied by any settlement. The place-names of Shropshire reveal minimum influence from Norse vocabulary, and there is not a single instance of the name-type exemplified by the Cheshire Thurstaston.

Herefordshire place-names reveal even less Norse influence in their vocabulary than those of Shropshire. There are some compounds of *tūn* with personal names which are ultimately of Old Norse origin (as *Hrolf, Swein, Arnketill, Thored* and *Thorkell,* in Rowlestone, Swanstone, Arkstone, Durstone and Thruxton), but it is not likely that any of these go back to Scandinavian settlements of the ninth and tenth centuries. Some of them may even be post-Conquest. Compounds of *tūn* with names of post-Conquest landowners are mainly a feature of south-west England, and Herefordshire is the only one of our counties in which they occur. There are several proven instances in Herefordshire, such as Turnastone from Ralph de *Tornai* and Walterstone from *Walter* de Lacy. The Arkstone type of name, however, is perhaps more likely to date from before the Norman Conquest and to have arisen in the early eleventh century, when Norse personal names were commonly used by landowning families all over England. A Danish follower of Cnut, named Ranig, was appointed to the earldom of Herefordshire, and two others, Hakon and Eilaf, became earls of Worcestershire and Gloucestershire (Williams, A., 1986: 2, 6). Many Danish noblemen obtained English estates in the reign of Cnut, and this context would suit Thruxton, which is recorded in Domesday Book. Dr John Insley (1985: 46–52), quoting work by E.J. Dobson, notes that some of the Scandinavian personal names recorded in the West Midlands persisted in use till the thirteenth century, when they occur in documents in the archives of Hereford Cathedral. A different view can be taken of Thurstaston in Cheshire because that is in an area where both Norse peasant settlement and the taking-over of estates by tenth-century Vikings are likely to have occurred, and where there is no reason to think that aristocratic Danes became landowners in the early eleventh century.

Norse Place-names in Staffordshire and Warwickshire

The place-names of Staffordshire show some influence from Old Norse vocabulary, as in the use of *gata* for street-names in Tamworth, and the occurrence of *holm* in names like Cat Holme where there is less reason than in Shropshire and Herefordshire to suspect substitution for an original Old English *hamm*. The only place-name evidence for actual Scandinavian settlement, however, is found in the northern tip of the shire. Swinscoe and Thorpe are the two names in this area which have always been recognized as Old Norse. Swinscoe is 'swine wood', with *skógr* as generic, and Thorpe is the regular Danish term for a secondary settlement. More recently, (Wrander 1983: 34), it has been suggested that Ilam is a Norse name

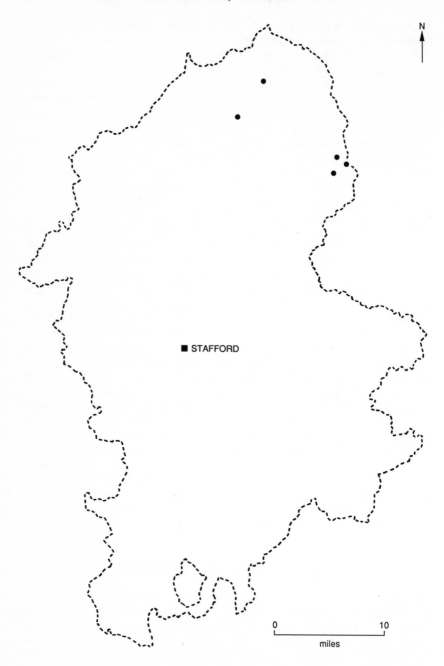

Figure 53   Norse place-names in Staffordshire.

meaning 'at the pools' from the dative plural of *hylr*, and this is more convincing than the earlier explanation of it as a pre-English river-name. Another addition to this group is Leek, which, like Leake in Nottingham-shire, Lincolnshire and the North Riding, should be ascribed to an Old Norse word meaning 'brook' (Gelling 1984: 25). There is a settlement called Hulme to the north east of Leek. If these names are accepted as indications of the presence of Norse-speaking farmers, they represent a small colony moving into an upland area which, like the northern part of the Wirral, may have been underpopulated at the time. Leek would probably not have been anybody's first choice for a settlement-site. These names are plotted on fig. 53.

There are a few Danish and partly Danish names in north-east Warwickshire. This is one of the two areas where such names spill over onto the English side of Watling Street. The other, in Northamptonshire, contains a larger group. Names plotted on fig. 54 are Griff which means 'pit' (perhaps 'coal-pit'), Wibtoft 'Vibbi's homestead', Copston 'Copsi's estate', Monks Kirby 'church village', Thurlaston 'Thorleifr's estate', Toft 'homestead' and *Holm*. The last place, now Biggin Mills in Newton parish, is likely to be of genuine Old Norse origin since it is recorded in Domesday Book. It has seemed safer to omit three -thorp names (Eathorpe, Princethorpe, Stoneythorpe), as they may derive from Old English *throp*. Other possible specimens which have been rejected are Willoughby, which is suspected of being a ring of willows with Old English *bēag* as generic, and Rugby, which is probably a refashioned English name in *-byrig*. The Danish presence in Warwickshire was slight. One of the aristocratic Scandinavian landowners referred to above gave his name as an affix to Wootton Wawen. Wootton is one of several estates which the Domesday Survey records as having been held before the Norman Conquest by Waga. The personal name is more fully recorded in other documents as *Wagene, Wagan, Wagen*, and it is an Anglicized form of Old Danish *Vagn*.

The West Midlands under Edward the Elder

The Norwegian and Danish presence in north-west Cheshire, north Staf-fordshire and east Warwickshire was slight, and not likely to have had any discernible effect either on political history or on the ethnic composition of the people of our five counties. The use of the area as a base for the conquest of the Danelaw by Æthelflæd and then by her brother, King Edward, however, had a drastic effect on its administrative organization.

When Edward seized power in western Mercia in 919 he had, with the help of his sister, obtained the submission of the Danes of East Anglia and most of the eastern Midlands. Stenton (1943: 319-20) ascribes the success of Edward's campaigns partly to the resounding defeat of the Northumbrian Danes at the battle of Tettenhall in 909 (Whitelock 1955: 192), since this left the more southerly Danish armies without support from Northumbria. Edward's seizure of Tamworth in 918 was followed by the submission of the princes of Wales; and having acquired this authority over English Mercia and the British peoples beyond Offa's Dyke he was able to turn his

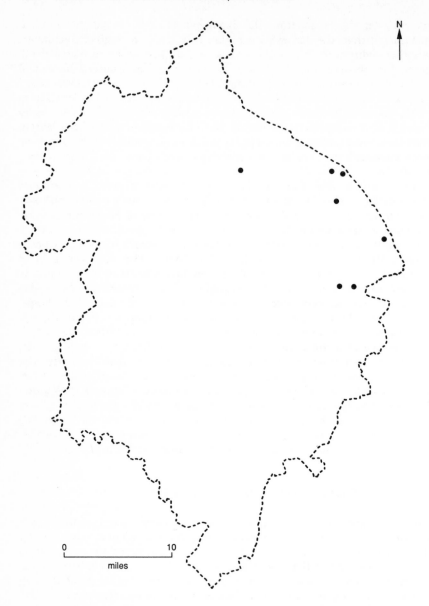

Figure 54   Norse place-names in Warwickshire.

attention to the reduction of the last independent Danish colonies south of the Humber, in the regions which centred on Lincoln and Nottingham. When they surrendered without fighting, the English frontier had been carried to the Humber.

In the wars of 911–20 a crucial role was played on both sides by fortified sites where detachments of the English or Danish armies were stationed. The choice of sites made by the Danish leaders can be inferred from the recorded events of the war and from later administrative history. Most of the sites fortified in western Mercia by the rulers of Mercia and Wessex are listed in the Mercian Register and the *Anglo-Saxon Chronicle*. Two of the most important, Hereford and Shrewsbury, do not occur in these lists, probably because they had been fortified earlier than the others.

Hereford is spoken of as a *burh* from which fighting men were obtained in the campaign of 914, when King Edward defeated a Danish force which came from Brittany and which captured Bishop Cyfeiliog of Archenfield when ravaging the lands within reach of the Severn estuary. There is a reference in an earlier annal, for 894, to 'every borough east of the Parret and both west and east of Selwood, and also north of the Thames and *west of Severn*' from which an army was assembled to defeat the Danes at Buttington in Montgomeryshire, and this may fairly be taken as indicating that Hereford was fortified then (Whitelock 1955: 187, 194–5). There is no information about the fortification of Shrewsbury, though Stenton (1943: 322) considers that the application of the word *civitas* to the place in a charter of 901 (S 221) may be an indication that it already had this status by then. It would be a comparatively small operation to erect defences which would block access to Shrewsbury by land.

Hereford and Shrewsbury, like Worcester, became garrison towns while the war against the Danes was still in its defensive stage. A document (Whitelock 1955: 498) has survived which describes the agreement made by Æthelred and Æthelflæd with Bishop Werferth of Worcester about the maintenance of the fortifications which they erected in response to the bishop's request. This was towards the end of Alfred's reign. The extent to which the boroughs of the Danish wars were also centres of population and trade will be discussed in the next chapter. The main purpose of the Worcester document may fairly be conjectured to be the securing of funds for the upkeep of the walls, but its text relates specifically to the division between lay and ecclesiastical authorities of dues obtained mainly from the market. These include 'land-rent, the fine for fighting, or theft, or dishonest trading, and contribution to the borough wall – as regards the market-place and the streets'. A similar situation, with a major trading-centre within defensive walls, seems very likely at Hereford and Shrewsbury, but less so at some of the later boroughs, such as Eddisbury (which is an ancient hill-fort) and the lost sites of *Bremesbyrig, Scergeat* and *Weardbyrig*. Stenton (1943: 528) notes, however, that there is a surviving coin of Æthelstan which was struck at *Weardbyrig;* and Æthelflæd issued a charter from *Weardburh* in 915 (S 225).

The date at which some of the Midland boroughs became administrative centres is not precisely known, and opinions vary between the early tenth and the early eleventh century. Before discussing this problem it will be useful to note what it was that the shire system replaced. Unlike Wessex, where the shire system was in operation before the end of the eighth century (Stenton 1943: 290), Mercia appears to have functioned until the catastrophe of the Danish wars with an older system based on areas described in Latin documents as *regiones* or *provinciae*. These were probably in origin associations of people rather than arbitrarily demarcated areas.

The Early Administrative Units of the West Midlands[2]

Modern cognizance of *regiones* or *provinciae* depends on chance references like that in an eighth-century charter which describes Wootton Wawen (Warwickshire) as being 'in regione quae antiquitus nominatur Stoppingas' (S 94). This region-name (which did not give rise to a settlement-name) means either 'people of the hollow' or 'followers of a man named Stoppa'; and its occurrence proves that the *-ingas* formula, which is the commonest way of forming region-names over much of the eastern half of England, extends at least as far west as the Birmingham area. This being so, such formations may have occurred sporadically to the west of the Birmingham plateau, and Birmingham itself, and such a name as Oddingley in eastern Worcestershire, may be evidence for provinces called *Beormingas* and *Oddingas*. It is more doubtful, however, whether -ingham names in Shropshire and Cheshire should be viewed in this light.

There were various methods of forming province-names, the typical one to the north and west of Birmingham being the addition of the word *sǣte*, 'settlers, inhabitants', to the name of a prominent topographical feature, often a name of pre-English origin. Such formations include *Tomsǣte*, 'dwellers by the River Tame', a province which stretched from the Birmingham area at least to Breedon in Leicestershire, and which had its own ealdorman, and *Pecsǣte*, the people of the Peak District. The use of the formula in the western part of Mercia, in names like *Wreocensǣte*, *Magonsǣte* and in a series of items along Offa's Dyke has been discussed in Chapters 5 and 6. There appears to be no surviving evidence for any ancient region or province in the area which became Cheshire.

The units which we know about are of varying sizes. The provinces of the *Tomsǣte* and *Wreocensǣte* were probably too big to be governed from a single centre, as that of the *Stoppingas* might have been. Our knowledge of the system is sketchy, but it is clear that the emphasis is primarily on groups of people (*-ingas*, *-sǣte*) who recognized a certain cohesion among themselves, and only secondarily on the area which these peoples inhabited. This contrasts with the West-Saxon shire system, by which designated areas were administered from royal estates, such as Southampton, Dorchester, Wilton and Somerton. Stenton (1943: 291) thinks that the names Dorset, Somerset and the obsolete *Wilsǣte* preserve traces of earlier associations of people akin to those of the Midlands. The analogy is not perfect in the case of Dorset, where the reference is to the town of Dorchester, not to a natural feature like the Wrekin or the River Tame; and it is possible that *Wilsǣte* and *Sumorsǣte* are abbreviated forms of *Wiltunsǣte* and *Sumortunsǣte*. There is probably no firm evidence that a system resembling the Midland one ever existed in Wessex (Gelling 1976: 842-3), but if it did it was presumably superseded by the shire system on account of the greater efficiency which could be obtained by having local government units of more regular size.

The Shires

It is probable that a version of the West-Saxon shire system was imposed on the parts of Mercia which were under his direct control by King Edward in the last years of his reign, though we have no explicit indication that the new system was functioning earlier than a reference to Cheshire in the annal for 980 in the *Anglo-Saxon Chronicle* (and even this could be an anachronism by a chronicler writing c.1046). The main reason for ascribing the creation of the West Midland shires to Edward is that they show no respect for the traditional divisions between the peoples who made up the composite kingdom of Mercia. After 920 Edward was in a position to over-ride local loyalties, and it must have been apparent that there was need for a more effective and more regular system. There is, however, a rival school of thought which asserts that the West Midland shires are more likely to have acquired their modern outlines in the early eleventh than in the early tenth century. More will be said of this when the early history of Warwick is discussed in Chapter 9. The most recent discussion concludes that 'the Mercian shires were in existence in the tenth century, even though they were not called shires until the early eleventh century' (Whybra 1990: 106).

In the eastern half of the old Mercian kingdom shires emerged which corresponded to the districts occupied by the various Danish armies between which the country had been divided. A key factor in the arrangements is likely to have been the selection of a defensible settlement as the central place in each unit. This was obviously a major determining factor in western Mercia, also. Chester and Hereford had particular strategic importance in relation to the directions from which sea-borne military threats came. Shrewsbury and Warwick were at points where roads converged on river-crossings (though in the latter case Stratford-on-Avon would have served at least as well). Stafford, however, can never have been a natural crossroads, as marshy ground would have made access difficult except from the north. One of its assets may have been the comprehensive view over the country to the west which is obtained from the site later occupied by the castle; but perhaps it was mainly a *faute-de-mieux* choice, necessitated by the awkward position of Tamworth, the traditional centre of Mercian government, on the boundary between English and Danish land. Something will be said in the next chapter about what is known from archaeology of the early history of these shire towns. Here is it appropriate to consider the districts which were assigned for their upkeep and which were governed from them.

Warwickshire was an aggressively arbitrary creation, joining a large area which had been part of the Hwiccan sub-kingdom to a north-eastern half which was part of the old Mercian heartland. The line between the two areas is known from its survival as an ecclesiastical boundary (v. Chapter 6 and fig. 41). Warwick lay precisely on the boundary between these two ancient kingdoms, and the choice of this place as the centre of the new unit may have been intended to emphasize the demise of the older arrangements. This consideration may also have applied to Shrewsbury, which was on the boundary between Magonsætan territory and that of the Wreocensæte (also discussed in Chapter 6, v. fig. 40). The annexation to

Shropshire of the northern part of the ancient Magonsætan kingdom left Hereford with a relatively small shire in which the area which had been the ancient Welsh kingdom of Archenfield was a major component.

The need to have the chosen centres well within the areas of their allotted shires possibly explains some discrepancies of size in the West Midland units. Worcestershire, another small shire, was perhaps squeezed by the necessity to give Gloucestershire an adequate amount of land to the north of its shire town. But the precise reasons for the new boundaries are probably not recoverable. Shropshire was given a more generous allotment of land south of Shrewsbury than seems obviously necessary. Cheshire, as noted above, was given territory which at a later date lay in Lancashire, and some land in north-east Wales.

The Hundreds

It was probably also in connection with the military dispositions of the early tenth century that the new shires were divided into the smaller administrative divisions called hundreds. This local government device, like that of the shire, appears to have been transplanted from Wessex. The historical problems connected with its origin are complicated and as yet unsolved, but there is no doubt about the importance of the hundred organization in the late Anglo-Saxon state and in the centuries after the Norman Conquest. The hundred court, which met every four weeks, was the main means by which both law and the burdens of taxation were disseminated in the countryside. The hundredal units, because of this close relationship to everyday administration, were much subject to alteration, and the arrangements which can be deduced from Domesday Book had, in most shires, been greatly modified by the thirteenth century. A shining exception to this is presented by the five hundreds of Staffordshire, which kept their outline, practically unchanged, down to modern times. These are shown on fig. 55, together with the places at which the courts assembled. The other Midland counties had a greater number of hundreds in 1086, and these were subject to violent alterations in succeeding centuries.

Special interest attaches to the names of the hundredal divisions because in many cases it is obvious that they are the names of the meeting-places, and the nature of the sites thus made known to us suggests that they may have served much older units in more primitive times. Sometimes the primitive name is lost, and has been replaced by that of a royal estate, but we have a great deal of material from which to deduce information about the early sites. The typical hundred meeting-place was in a sort of 'no man's land', situated as far away as possible from the settlements of the community it served and on a boundary between two or more estates; often they were also near a main road or a river-crossing. A tumulus, a stone or a tree were the sort of objects likely to be chosen as markers for the spot. Indeed, artificial tumuli were sometimes erected for the purpose (see Chapter 3). The names of the five Staffordshire hundreds are Seisdon, Cuttlestone, Offlow, Pirehill and Totmonslow. Seisdon may mean 'Saxon hill', with reference not to the presence of English among Welsh but to the

Figure 55 **The Staffordshire hundreds.**

presence of some Saxons in a predominantly Anglian community. The village of Seisdon, which lies six miles south-west of Wolverhampton, is overlooked by a small hill, which was presumably the meeting-place. There is a junction of several parishes on the other side of the hill from the village. Cuttlestone means 'Cuthwulf's stone', and the name survives in Cuttlestone Bridge, one mile south-west of Penkridge. This is not on a parish boundary, but it is typical in other ways, as there is no settlement, only a very fine bridge at a junction of roads and waterways. It can be recommended as a place which conveys the atmosphere of an ancient assembly-site. Offlow ('Offa's tumulus') has been discussed in Chapter 3. The hill lies on the north boundary of Shenstone, with Watling Street a short distance to the south. Regrettably the name has been left off recent Ordnance Survey maps. Pirehill, possibly 'look-out hill' is a small hill two miles south-south-west of Stone, of similar size to the one at Seisdon, but a fairly commanding eminence in thinly settled, marshy land. Totmonslow ('Tatmonn's tumulus') is a hamlet in Draycott in the Moors, in high moorland two miles south-west of Cheadle.

There were 12 Domesday hundreds in an area comprising the later Cheshire and some adjacent Welsh territories. Four of the names – Chester, Willaston, Rushton, Middlewich – reveal nothing about early meeting-places, but the remaining eight are more informative. There are two 'mounds', *Roelau* (modern Ruloe) and *Bochelau* (modern Bucklow Hill), both of which are lost. *Warmundestrou*, also a lost site, is 'Wærmund's tree'.[3] *Tunendune* (lost) is 'Tuna's hill'. The Welsh district, *Atiscros*, is now called Croes Ati in Flintshire, and the pedestal of a stone cross was still to be seen there in 1772 (Charles 1938: 233).

Domesday Warwickshire had ten hundreds, four of these – Barcheston, Coleshill, Marton and Stoneleigh – bearing only the names of the settlements to which the meetings had been transferred. The remaining six include three 'mound' names. Brinklow and Pathlow survive, and are both typical meeting-places. The lost *Tremlau* means 'three mounds', probably a group of tumuli. *Honesberie* was probably named from a small round hill of the type for which *beorg* is used in place-names. *Fexhole* and *Ferncumbe* are unusual hundred-names, referring respectively to a hollow and a short, broad valley (*cumb*) of a type which is rare in Warwickshire.

Enough has probably been said to indicate the nature of the hundredal divisions in western Mercia. The Herefordshire units numbered 20, so were smaller than those discussed above. Particularly interesting as meeting-place names are a number which refer to trees – Hazeltree, Cutsthorn, Winstree, Greytree and Bromsash – and to mounds – *Thornlaw*, Radlow and Wormelow. *Wulfheie*, later *Wolphy*, is 'wolf enclosure' (Gelling 1978: 211). Shropshire, in spite of the frequency of *hlāw* in its place-names, had in 1086 only a single meeting-place marked by a mound, *Rinlau* in the south-west. Three others, *Alnodestreu*, *Witentreu* and *Condetre*, are 'tree' names, and a stone was the marker for *Colmestan*. The interesting use of two *-sæte* names, *Mersete* and *Ruesset*, is noted in Chapter 7 (see also Gelling 1978: 211-14). The fact that new hundreds which appear in the twelfth–thirteenth centuries frequently have names of the types which are instanced here from Domesday Book, and that some of the sites to which they refer are similarly on boundaries and away from habitations, suggests either that there were a great many recognized ancient meeting-places available for use as required, or that the traditional notion of what a meeting-place should be like was carried over into the Norman period. The second hypothesis, which seems the likelier one, is akin to the suggestion made in Chapter 6 about raised curvilinear churchyards.

The Administration of Mercia after the Danish Wars

The secular administration of western Mercia was very different in the last two centuries of the Old English period from what it had been earlier. It is fortunate that no authority was concerned, in the troubled years of the Danish wars, to alter the ecclesiastical geography, since it is through the survival of ecclesiastical boundaries that we can define some of the units which were swept away by the reorganization.

The overall administration of the hundreds and shires of Mercia was in the hands of one or more ealdormen (Williams, A., 1982). The precise arrangements for the western shires between 919 and 940 cannot be ascertained, but there is evidence which suggests that in 940 three ealdormen were appointed to the region which Æthelred had governed in the time of King Alfred. Æthelmund appears in connection with the north-western provinces, Ealhhelm in central Mercia and Æthelstan in the south-east. In 957, when Edgar, the younger brother of King Eadwig was ruling Mercia while his brother still held Wessex, the Mercian council (*Myrcna witan*) was in operation, as is shown by a document concerning a dispute over land in Middlesex (Robertson 1939: 90-3). Dr Williams regards this and the use of two of the old tribal names of Mercia in charters of 958 and 963 as evidence for the assertion of some degree of identity within the West Saxon kingdom. The Magonsæte are named in a Herefordshire charter of 958 (S 677) and the Wreocensæte in a Shropshire grant of 963 (S 723). A reference to the Pecsæte in the recently discovered charter of 963 for Ballidon, Derbyshire (Brooks *et al.* 1984) can be added to these. The recurrence of these tribal names in the middle years of the tenth century may indicate that local administration was not always at that time organized in terms of the new boroughs and the territories assigned to them.

9 Towns and Trade

There are not many settlements in our five counties which had in the pre-Conquest period characteristics indicative of a status for which the word 'town' is appropriate. The ones which can be so termed are here considered to be Tamworth, Stafford, Warwick, Coventry, Hereford, Shrewsbury and Chester; and this chapter will set out such information as is available about the origins and early history of these places.

Tamworth's special status derives from its having been the administrative centre of the Mercian kingdom, and that of Hereford derives partly from its being the likely seat of administration in the early kingdom of the Magonsæte. Hereford later became a shire town, so it requires discussion here on that score also, together with the shire towns of Stafford, Warwick, Shrewsbury and Chester. Coventry is a later comer, but a brief account is included here as there are some grounds for considering that its urban status predates 1066.

There would be little point in attempting a close definition of the word 'urban' as applied to these places. It is here taken to mean that a proportion of the inhabitants spent most of their time in the practice of various crafts, in consequence of which there had to be a market at which they could sell their manufactures and purchase food and clothing. Chester, however, is in a different category from the other towns listed, as it must also have had an additional category of inhabitants who earned their living by the management of long-distance trade in luxury goods.

Tamworth

No available evidence throws light on the choice of Tamworth as the seat of the kings of Mercia, and there is as yet no evidence bearing on whether this arrangement goes back to the days of King Penda, when the greater Mercian confederation was engineered. The evidence of the name suggests, however, that there was a settlement here in Celtic-speaking times. The River Tame has a considerable number of settlements on its banks, but only Tamworth and the nearby Tamhorn are named from it. The river-name is pre-English, and use of a river-name was one of the commonest ways of denoting settlements in the Romano-British period. It is reasonable to assume that the name of the river was already pre-empted for a settlement here when the English arrived, and that English speakers accepted this, adding a term in their own language which suited the role of the place in their administrative arrangements.

The earliest surviving reference to Tamworth is probably contained in a memorandum written at Peterborough which records a transaction of A.D. 675-92. This says that when King Æthelred sold an estate to the newly founded monastery at Breedon (in Leicestershire) the transaction was confirmed at a place called *Tomtun*. Stenton (1970: 182) translates the passage:

> When this was done, King Ædilred in his chamber in his own *vicus* called *Tomtun*, joining hands with the queen and bishop Saxwulf, placed a turf from the land on a gospel-book before many witnesses in confirmation.

The gospel-book which was treated in this cavalier fashion must have been one of the earliest of its kind, but that is not what concerns us here. The immediately relevant point is the location of the ceremony. The identification is not capable of proof, but there is general agreement that *Tomtun* can be regarded as an earlier name for Tamworth.

Tomtun is one of the small group of names recorded before A.D.730 which have *tūn* as generic. There are only six of these (Cox 1976: 51). At a later date, when *tūn* became the commonest of all place-name generics, a variety of meanings must be allowed for, but in the first century of the Anglo-Saxon settlement the word may have had a more limited sense. James Campbell's investigation (Campbell 1979) into the Latin and Old English words for settlements which were used by Bede and by the composers of early charters led him to postulate that English *tūn* and Latin *vicus* both meant 'royal vill' at an early date. The 'functional' type of *tūn*-name, discussed in Chapter 7, was being formed before 730. Two such, Acton Beauchamp in Worcestershire and Wootton Wawen in Warwickshire, are included in Cox's list. But *Tomtun*, and comparable names like Taunton, Somerset, were probably coined a good deal earlier than Acton and Wootton, and could be using *tūn* in an earlier sense.

The later name of Tamworth appears in records in the reign of Offa, two of whose charters, both dated 781, cite the place where the grants are made as *in Tamoworthie, in regali palatio in Tamoworthige* (S 120, 121). A charter of Cenwulf, dated 799, amplifies this by saying *in vicu regio æt Tome worthige*, and one of Burgred, dated 855, calls the royal seat *in vico qui Tomweorthin nuncupatur* (S 155, 207). At some time in the course of the eighth century the generic *tūn* was replaced by the generic *worthig(n)*, probably for a specific reason which had to do with a change in the nature of the settlement.

In order to arrive at satisfactory conclusions about the precise significance of English place-name generics it is necessary to supplement the traditional forms of place-name study - regional surveys and alphabetical dictionaries - by monographs which make a country-wide investigation of individual terms. This sort of study has not yet been undertaken for the group of words *worth, worthig, worthign*. The discussion of Tamworth in Gelling 1970 glanced at the problem:

> The second element of Tamworth is Old English *worthig* which is a derivative of the word *worth* ... It is generally considered to have much the same meaning as *worth*, and is especially characteristic of the south-west of England, where it often has the

modern form -worthy . . . Away from the south-west, it is very rare, and the spellings for Tamworth show that in this name it had been assimilated to *worth* by the time of the Norman Conquest. Another Midland instance is *Northworthig*, the earlier name of Derby. It has been suggested that -*worthig* in the spellings for these two names is due to West Saxon scribal practice, and does not represent the local form. But the earliest spellings for Tamworth are from Mercian charters, and there is every reason to think that they are the true local forms. The meaning 'enclosure' does not seem altogether adequate for Tamworth, which was the seat of the Mercian kings. Possibly at a very early stage of the settlement in the Midlands *worthig* developed a meaning akin to that of *burh*, and was used for sites of considerable importance.

It was also noted under Derby that in the English name *Northworthige* 'north' might be understood in relation to the *worthig* at Tamworth. A much wider study of the place-name element is needed before the meaning can be recovered, and for the moment it can only be said that the use of this group of words in literary Old English suggests that they had a strong connotation of 'enclosure'. There are no occurrences of *worth, worthig* or *worthign* in names recorded before A.D.730.

If the change from *tūn* to *worthig* in the name of Tamworth signifies an enlargement of the enclosed settlement-area, this could indicate that during the eighth century the population grew to include people not directly concerned with the maintenance of the royal household; but there is no reason to think that Tamworth was a trading centre as well as the site of the palace. In the south and east of England in this period a number of royal centres in some ways comparable to Tamworth had associated trading settlements (Old English *wīc*), adjacent but outside the walls, as at Canterbury, London and York, or some distance away which is the suggested relationship between Winchester and Southampton (Old English *Hamwīc*).[1] The Mercian royal centre differs from these southern and eastern towns, however, in being neither on a Roman site nor on a navigable river. It is at a meeting-place of numerous roads, but there is no reason to think that its position was exploited for commercial purposes on a significant scale until after the Danish wars. The *wīc*s of the West Midlands were the salt-producing centres in Worcestershire and Cheshire, whose activities are discussed later in this chapter.

Tamworth is fortunate to have been both well excavated and well published. A series of excavations[2] was begun in 1960 with the aim of investigating the circuit of the medieval town walls wherever redevelopment projects made this possible. These culminated in 1971 with the discovery of a pre-Conquest water-mill in Bolebridge Street (fig. 56).

The Tamworth mill is a discovery of great interest, but it is difficult to evaluate in terms either of regional or national history. This was only the second mill-site of the Anglo-Saxon period to be found in England, so there is no corpus of comparative archaeological material, though there are frequent references to mills in Anglo-Saxon charters (Bullough 1977). At the Tamworth site conditions were suitable for the preservation of wood, and

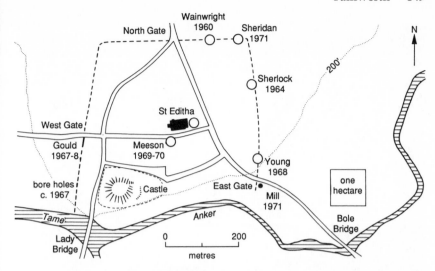

Figure 56 The Saxon defences of Tamworth (from *TSSAHS* XIII).

the excavators found massive timber remains of the undercroft, the walls of the mill-pool, and the emplacements for the wheel-race and the outfall. They also recovered a practically complete paddle. The wood has been assigned by radio-carbon dating to the eighth century.

The wheel is believed to have been horizontal, which occasions surprise, as horizontal mills are characteristic of the peripheral regions of the British Isles. They are technologically less advanced than mills with vertical wheels, and this latter type might have seemed more appropriate in the capital of Mercia. The other excavated mill-site of the Anglo-Saxon period is at Old Windsor, on the River Thames. Here there was an ambitious structure employing three vertical water-wheels, but when this was destroyed in the ninth or tenth century it was replaced by a horizontal mill like the one at Tamworth. The eventual replacement of the horizontal by the vertical mill in medieval England presents unsolved problems of dating and causation (Holt 1988: 5, 117ff.). A model of a conjectural reconstruction of the Tamworth mill was made by Mr F.W.B. Charles, and this is shown in fig. 57. The detailed excavation report has not yet appeared.

A less unexpected result of the Tamworth excavations was the discovery of the defences constructed by the Lady Æthelflæd in A.D.913. Consistently underlying these defences was a small ditch with the imprint of a palisade, and the excavators suggest that this represents an eighth-century enclosure associated with the palace complex, perhaps the feature which caused the town to be renamed with -*worthig* as generic.

No trace has been found of a slighting of the 913 defences, such as could have been ascribed to the events of A.D.940, when Olaf Guthfrithson, king of Dublin, having occupied York, led a great raid over the Midlands in the course of which he 'took Tamworth by storm' (Whitelock 1955: 202). In the same raid the Vikings captured Wulfrun, the mother of Wulfric Spott, whose estates in the Midlands, as listed in his will, give a valuable

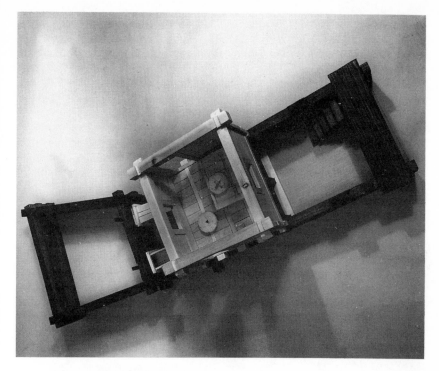

Figure 57 The Tamworth mill, reconstruction by F.W.B. Charles (photographs Martin Charles).

indication of the realities of landed power in late Anglo-Saxon England. The provision made in this will for his 'poor daughter' (who was presumably either disabled or mentally deficient) suggests that her household was located at Tamworth.

A mint was established at Tamworth by King Æthelstan, but the number of surviving pre-Conquest coins with this mint signature is not large. Dr D.M. Metcalf has provided statistics for boroughs whose mints are represented among surviving coins of the reign of Æthelred the Unready, and his tables show consistently low figures for Tamworth (Metcalf 1978). The Tamworth excavations of 1960-71 produced only one pre-Conquest coin, found by Dr Wainright in 1960. This was a silver cut halfpenny of Edward the Martyr, minted at Torksey, in Lincolnshire, and dating from 975-9. The find was of great interest to numismatists since Torksey coins are extremely rare. It cannot, however, do much to relieve the general impression of failure to thrive as a commercial centre which emerges from archaeology and records. When Mercia was no longer a kingdom the town lacked the royal patronage which had been so important in its earlier history. From the tenth through to the fourteenth century the picture is one of consistent poverty (Gould 1969: 38-41).

Tamworth receives scant attention in Domesday Book, where there is no entry relating specifically to the borough. There are, however, three

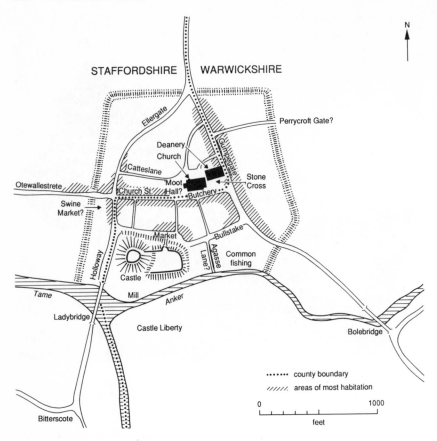

Figure 58   Tamworth and the county boundary (from *TSSAHS* XIII).

references to burgesses. These occur in the entries for Wigginton and Drayton Bassett in Staffordshire, and for Coleshill in Warwickshire. A total of 22 burgesses is credited to Tamworth, but the eight who are entered under Drayton Bassett, which is two-and-a-half miles south-west of the borough, are said to belong to that manor and to work there like the other villeins (DBi, f.246d).

The connection between Coleshill and Tamworth would be possible at the time of the Domesday Survey because the county boundary between Staffordshire and Warwickshire actually bisected the town (fig. 58). This arrangement continued till 1890, part of Tamworth which contained the castle being in Warwickshire and the remainder, including the church, in Staffordshire. Tamworth became a border town when Mercia was divided between English and Danish rulers, and the choice of Warwick and Stafford as shire centres led to its being bisected by the county boundary.

Tamworth's chances of thriving as a commercial centre might have been greater if the cathedral had been within its walls. The separation, by six miles, of the diocesan centre at Lichfield from the royal palace denied Tamworth the stimulus which might have come from ecclesiastical gatherings and from the visits of pilgrims to the tomb of St Chad. Possession of the cathedral did not, however, lead to the growth of an urban centre at Lichfield. C.C. Taylor established in a classic paper (1969) that Lichfield was a newly created town of the mid-twelfth century. The bishopric had been transferred to Chester in 1075 and to Coventry in 1102, but later bishops perceived the value of the continuing pilgrim traffic at Lichfield, and this caused them to plant the town. The success of the town subsequently enabled the place to recover its cathedral status. The settlement at Lichfield before the Norman Conquest was probably not entirely insignificant (Slater 1985), but it was not yet a town.

Stafford (fig. 59)

It is improbable that Stafford was a trading centre before the *burh* was created in 913, and far from certain to what extent it became one after that event. The use of *ford* as generic suggests that Stafford is one of the earliest settlements in the region to acquire its English name, but this particular ford cannot have been a major road-junction (above p. 141). The first element of the name is *stæth* 'landing-place'. This probably does not indicate a great volume of traffic on the river,[3] but the difficulties of road transport on three sides of the town may have led to regular use of the River Sow by local traffic, and this may have necessitated a carefully maintained landing-stage.

A good deal of excavation has taken place in Stafford in the last decade. It is established that the place was a centre for manufacture of pottery in the tenth century, and that this pottery was distributed to Worcester, Hereford, Shrewsbury and Chester. The other main pre-Conquest activity revealed by excavation is the storage and processing of grain. This evidence has led Professor Martin Carver to suggest that the *burh* functioned as a collecting-point for tax in the form of grain, and had been assigned responsibility for producing a supply of pottery.[4] Its trading activities may have been very limited until after the Norman Conquest.

The minster church at Stafford has a rare dedication to St Bertelin, an obscure saint who may have been a Mercian prince. It is possible that the Lady Æthelflæd was responsible for this and for another Bertelin dedication at Runcorn in Cheshire. She showed special sympathy to Mercian cults, such as those of St Mildburg and St Werburg (Thacker 1985: 18-19).

The Domesday account of Stafford which is placed at the beginning of the Staffordshire folios enumerates the houses available for burgesses. Nearly a third of these houses (52 out of 162) were unoccupied. The population of the town in 1086 has been calculated as at least 750 (Darby and Terrett 1954: 206). Supplementary entries tell of six plough-teams, a mill, two parcels of meadow and a wood, so there was a strong agricultural element in the borough.

The evidence relating to Tamworth and Stafford suggests that urban life and commercial activities were poorly represented in pre-Conquest

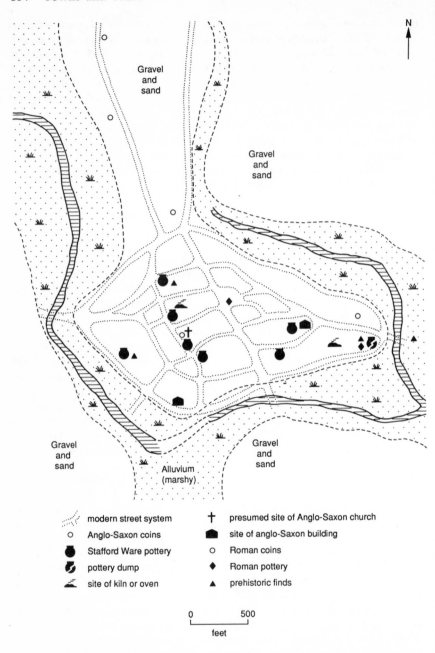

N

Gravel
and
sand

Gravel
and
sand

Gravel
and
sand

Gravel
and
sand

Alluvium
(marshy)

	modern street system	†	presumed site of Anglo-Saxon church
o	Anglo-Saxon coins		site of anglo-Saxon building
	Stafford Ware pottery	o	Roman coins
	pottery dump	♦	Roman pottery
	site of kiln or oven	▲	prehistoric finds

0   500
feet

Figure 59 Anglo-Saxon Stafford (from M. Carver, *Underneath Stafford Town*, by permission of Birmingham University Field Archaeology Unit).

Staffordshire. Tutbury had become a town by 1086: the Domesday account says 'In the borough around the castle are 42 men who live only by their trading: with the market they pay £4.10s.' This was a post-Conquest development consequent on the building of Henry of Ferrers's castle. It may have been helped by the absence of serious competition elsewhere in the shire.

Warwick

The origins of pre-Conquest towns are notoriously difficult to ascertain, and those of Warwick are among the most obscure. Archaeology has so far contributed nothing, and the only established fact is that the place was furnished with a *burh* in 914. It has been considered that the *burh* was new-founded on what geographers call a greenfield site. A valiant attempt to refute this view was recently made by Terry Slater (1983). This presents what is probably a definitive collection of evidence which might support the view that a trading centre existed at Warwick before 914; but the case is tenuous, as the author freely admits.

The name Warwick is anomalous. Other early towns considered here have names which refer to their Roman origins (Chester), to their enclosed or fortified status (Tamworth, Shrewsbury), or to an important river-crossing (Hereford, Stafford). Warwick, like the last two, is at a river-crossing, and one would have expected an ancient settlement-name here to have *ford* as its generic, such names being frequent to east and west along the River Avon. It is very difficult to envisage any other meaning for Warwick than 'dwellings by a weir'. the name is plural: pre-Conquest spellings which reveal this are *Wærinc wicum* 1001, *Wærincwican* 1016, *Wæring wicum* c.1050, *Wærincg wican* eleventh century. These plural forms are only counterbalanced by *Wærinc wic* in the D version of the *Anglo-Saxon Chronicle* (this and the form dated c.1050 above are the *Chronicle* entries which record the building of the *burh*, but they are given the date of the surviving manuscript rather than the date of the event). The dative plural ending *-um* has caused the development to -wick. In names which contain *wic* in its now-established early sense of 'trading centre', there is a strong tendency for the word to be used in the singular, and to develop to modern -wich, -wych. It must be admitted that the earliest reference to one of these trading centres, Fordwich in Kent, is *Fordewicum* in a charter of A.D.675. But since the next surviving reference, a charter of A.D.747, already has *Fordwic* and since the modern form indicates that the singular was normal in Old English, it may well be that *Fordewicum* has been given a Latin inflection (Dornier 1987: 93). However that may be, it seems clear that 'trading centre' is not a strong probability for *wic* in Warwick.

Mr Slater's paper explores the possibility of equating Warwick with the lost *villa regalis* of *Werburging wic* or *Werburgewic* where two Mercian charters of the early ninth century were issued, and I admit to having made moderately encouraging noises when I was consulted about this suggestion. The difficulties, however, are formidable. It would have to be assumed that *Werburging wic* (not *Werburgewic*) was the common form. This would mean 'settlement associated with a woman named Werburh'. It would then have to be assumed that this name was shortened by dropping *-burg*, leaving *Weringwic. Dropping something from the middle was the usual way of shortening long names in the late Old English period – this has happened, e.g. in the development of *Liccidfeld* to Lichfield. But I can find no parallel for shortening a place-name by dropping the second element of a dithematic personal name, and it is more likely that the connective *-ing* would be dropped causing *Werburgingwic* to become *Warburwick. Warwick probably contains *wæring, a side-form of the recorded *wering*, 'dam'. Another name likely to contain *wæring is Warrington, Lancashire. 'Dwellings by a weir' is a satisfactory etymology, and a simple explanation of a place-name is generally to be preferred to a more ingenious one. The name tells against, rather than for, a pre-burghal origin for the town of Warwick.

Mr Slater adduces other reasons for regarding Warwick as an early 'central place'. It was at the centre of a large estate held before the Norman Conquest by Earl Edwin of Mercia, and many of Earl Edwin's manors were earlier Mercian royal manors. He also considers that the church of All Saints, which stood in the precincts of the Norman castle, is likely to have been an unrecorded early Saxon minster church. Such attributes 'are not proof that a town was emerging', but they show 'that given the right conditions a town was rather more likely to succeed here rather than elsewhere in the vicinity'.

The site of Warwick, a prominent sandstone knoll beside the River Avon, is eminently defensible, but it is not altogether clear why the rulers of western Mercia felt the need for a military centre on the north-east boundary of Hwiccan territory. Mr Slater suggests (1983: 3) that 'its prime purpose was to protect and secure the north-east flank of the old Hwiccan sub-kingdom by controlling the mid-Avon valley', and he points to the Domesday record of contributory burgesses provided exclusively by vills in south-west Warwickshire as evidence that the function of Warwick was to protect the area (fig. 60). He is not convinced that the marking out of the area which became Warwickshire occurred at the date of the founding of the *burh*, but regards it as equally possible that the north-eastern part of the later county was administered from Tamworth in the tenth century. He is inclined to favour the view that the shiring of Mercia should be ascribed to the early eleventh, rather than the early tenth, century (Taylor, C.S. 1957). But it seems easier to understand the choice of Warwick as a shire town if it is seen as part of a policy, carried out by a strong ruler, of imposing new administrative patterns deliberately intended to slight ancient Mercian loyalties; and Edward the Elder slots into this scenario better than Eadric Streona, the treacherous associate of King Æthelred Unræd and King Cnut. Eadric is said by a Worcester chronicler writing in the late eleventh century to have 'joined townships to townships and shires to shires at his will; he even amalgamated the hitherto independent county of Winchcombe with the county of Gloucester' (Whybra 1990: 6). But it is more likely that he was tinkering with a system already established by a stronger authority than that he was creating a new administrative geography.

Whether or not it was an ancient settlement, Warwick throve between

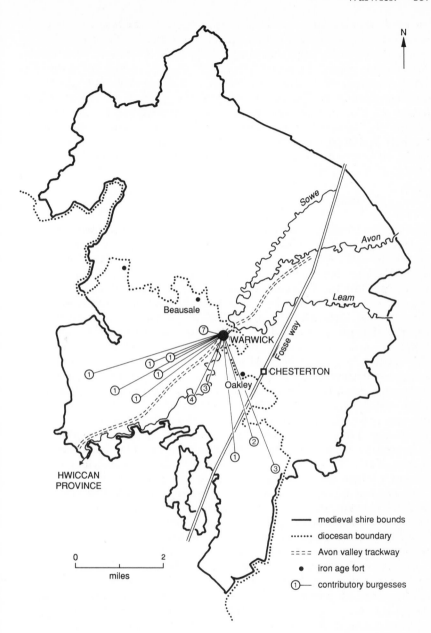

Figure 60 Warwick's contributory burgesses (from Slater 1983).

the creation of the *burh* and the Norman Conquest. The Domesday account credits the town with 248 houses, 22 burgesses and 100 'bordars'. This has been taken to imply a population of at least 1,000 (Darby and Terrett 1954: 303). A more recent discussion (Dyer 1985: 96, 102) estimates the figure at 1,500. The hundred bordars are mentioned in the description of the manor of *Cotes*, later Coten End, on the northern edge of Warwick. Professor Dyer points out that they are said to be, ('with their gardens'), *extra burgum*, 'outside the borough'. This implies that they are dependent on the borough for their livelihood. The town may have been a more notable trading centre in the late eleventh century than it was in the later Middle Ages.

? Parker 1016

Coventry

The best evidence for considering Coventry to have been a town before the Norman Conquest is probably the transfer of the seat of the bishopric from Chester by 1102. After the conquest, in 1075, Archbishop Lanfranc decreed that cathedrals should be moved from villages to towns, and in accordance with this ruling the Mercian see was transferred from Lichfield to Chester. A desire for centrality may have prompted the move back to the Midlands, albeit not to Lichfield. The attractions of Coventry would include the wealthy monastery, founded by Leofric and Godiva in 1043; but unless Lanfranc's ruling was flouted there must have been a trading community also. Such a community is likely to have grown up in association with the monastery in the decades following its foundation. The late Professor Ralph Davis considered that the existence of burgage tenure in Coventry in the 1120s and the granting of the laws and customs of Lincoln to the town in the time of Earl Ranulf II (1129-53) indicated a degree of urban development which was likely to have taken some time to accomplish (Davis 1976). Coventry is only recorded as a rural estate in Domesday Book, but Davis suggested (17-19) that there might also have been an incipient town of Coventry which was omitted from the final compilation.

Excavations in Coventry have as yet produced no stratified evidence of settlement before the thirteenth century, but there are scattered finds of pre-Conquest date. These comprise a tenth-century cross, a seventh/eighth-century sceat, a ninth-century brooch, a Viking-type axe head, and a wooden vat dated c.1000 (Rylatt and Gooder 1977: 10).

The name Coventry, even more than is the case with Warwick, tells against the settlement being a natural 'central place' with an immemorial pre-eminence in its region. Coventry belongs to an interesting class of names which consist of the word 'tree' with the genitive of an Old English personal name, in this case a masculine name *Cofa*. The whole corpus of settlement-names with *trēow* has recently been examined (Gelling 1984: 211-18) and this study led to the conclusion that a great many of these names belonged originally to trees which were boundary markers between Anglo-Saxon estates, one of whose owners was named in the compound. In these cases the settlements, often still on parish boundaries, are likely to be of later origin than most of the surrounding villages. If they have become parishes, the shape and size sometimes suggests late origin, as with

Bartestree in Herefordshire, a small parish lying between the larger units of Lugwardine and Weston Baggard. Such an origin is supported by the earliest documentation of Elstree, Hertfordshire. Oswestry, as explained above (pp. 74–5), is a boundary name which came to denote a large parish because the place supplanted the earlier centre of Maesbury. In other instances the eponymous tree may have marked a central meeting-place for a large land-unit with scattered settlements. This seems the likeliest explanation of Coventry, and of Aymestrey, a large Herefordshire parish. The growth of the town of Coventry at such a meeting-place may plausibly be associated with the foundation of the monastery in 1043.

NB . S. orbung's
Cuthbert 1016

Hereford

The see of Hereford is believed to have been created before 680, in the time of Archbishop Theodore. It is not necessary to assume that the bishop's seat was at Hereford from the beginning, though Stenton (1970: 193) considered that it was there at least as early as the mid-eighth century. This was a deduction from the fact that in 803 a council of the province of Canterbury was attended by Wulfheard 'Herefordensis ecclesiæ episcopus', accompanied by an abbot, three priests and one or two deacons, and an act of this council speaks of certain monasteries which were given to the church of Hereford 'in ancient days'. If the testimony of William of Malmesbury could be accepted there would be further evidence for the bishop being at Hereford in the first half of the eighth century. Writing c.1125 in his *Gesta Pontificum* William gave the text of an inscription which he claimed to have seen on a cross in Hereford. This is a composition by Bishop Cuthbert (736–40), stating that he constructed a burial-place for six people: three of his predecessors, Walstodus, Torhtere and Tirhtil, the *regulus* Milfrith (one of the sons of King Merewalh) 'cum conjuge pulchra Quenburga', and 'Oselmi filius Osfrith' (a totally obscure character). This was accepted as genuine by Stenton (1970: 195), and such a mausoleum could easily be envisaged as the porticus of an eighth-century church, or perhaps a crypt, as at Repton, Derbyshire.

These two supposed pieces of evidence for the original location of the see at Hereford have, however, been questioned recently (Sims-Williams 1990: 90–1, 339). The possibility of another location is suggested by a twelfth-century letter in which Gilbert Foliot, former bishop of Hereford, asks the bishop-elect to confirm the rights of a church at *Lideburi* 'for the sake of the episcopal see which it held long since and out of reverence for the holy bishops whose bodies lie there'. The bishops of Hereford owned two places to which this could refer, Ledbury in north Herefordshire and Lydbury North in south-west Shropshire. The Shropshire place acquired the affix *North* in the thirteenth century to distinguish it from Ledbury. Foliot's statement could be construed as evidence that one of these places was the original site of the Magonsætan see, though, as Sims-Williams observes, the reference might be to a former Welsh see. As regards William of Malmesbury's claim to have seen Bishop Cuthbert's composition on a cross in Hereford, Sims-Williams points out (91 n.19) that he is not likely to have seen it *in situ*. A variant version of the 'inscription' was copied by John Leland from a manuscript at Malmesbury, and that is probably where William saw it. The connection with Hereford may be no more than an inference because the verses referred to bishops of the see which became Hereford.

Perhaps the only firm reason for believing the see to have been at Hereford from the beginning is the difficulty of finding a reason why it should have been transferred there if it was originally at a place more comfortably within the Magonsætan kingdom. Sims-Williams suggests that the monasteries given to the church of Hereford 'in ancient days' might have been acquired before the church was a cathedral; but since there was a church which owned monasteries here in the mid-eighth century, it seems simplest to assume that this church was the cathedral.

Hereford Cathedral has a joint dedication to St Mary and to St Ethelbert, king of East Anglia, who is stated in the *Anglo-Saxon Chronicle* to have been beheaded in 794 by order of King Offa. In an early eleventh-century list of saints his body is said to be 'at the bishop's seat at Hereford near the River Wye'.[5] There are later legendary lives of St Ethelbert which represent the murder as having taken place at the royal vill of *Suttun*, and Stenton (1970: 195) accepts the identification with Sutton Walls four miles north of Hereford, and regards this central fact in the story as authentic. It is assumed that Ethelbert was visiting Offa. To atone for the murder Offa was believed to have been a lavish benefactor to the cathedral.

There were two minster churches in Hereford. The cathedral is referred to as St Ethelbert's in the will of the Shropshire thegn, Wulfgeat of Donington, which may date from c.975 (S 1534). Wulfgeat's legacy to St Ethelbert's is followed by an identical one to St Guthlac's; and a later document, from the mid-eleventh century (Robertson 1939: 186), cites the two households of these minsters as witnesses to a purchase of land.

There is no documentation for the foundation of St Guthlac's. D.A. Whitehead has argued that it might have been an earlier foundation than the cathedral, and that the dedication to Guthlac, some of whose relics it possessed, might have replaced an original one to St Peter (Whitehead 1980: 3). His belief that Guthlac did not become a cult figure until the tenth century has, however, been contested on the grounds that Guthlac occurs in a Mercian martyrology dependent on a Latin exemplar written before 850 (Thacker 1985: 6). It may be that king Æthelbald introduced the cult of Guthlac to Hereford in the early eighth century, since the saint was his kinsman. But the archaeological evidence suggests that the church may have had an earlier origin, whatever its original dedication. The church stood on Castle Green until the twelfth century, when it was moved to another site because of horrific events in the war between Stephen and Matilda. Excavations on Castle Green have demonstrated the presence there of a church and a cemetery which may have been in use as early as the late seventh century. Whitehead suggests that this cemetery was the first resting-place of the six corpses for which Bishop Cuthbert built a new repository. When St Guthlac's was moved from the castle after 1140, the new establishment in the Eye Street suburb was dedicated to St Peter, St Paul and St Guthlac. Whitehead argues that this may be

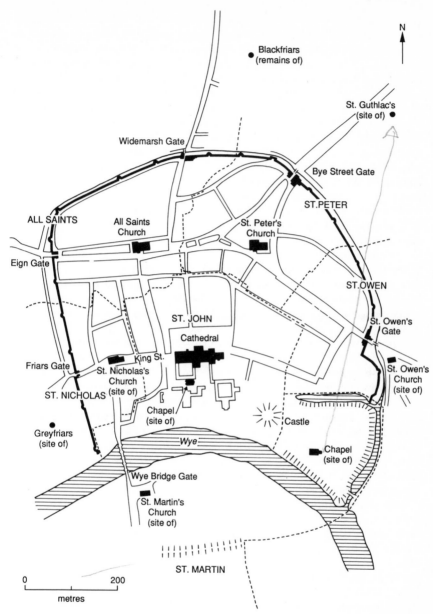

Figure 61 The centre of Hereford, showing parish boundaries and streets as in 1757 (from Whitehead 1982, by permission of CBA).

evidence for an original dedication to St Peter, which would be appropriate for a seventh-century minster. If the earliest suggested date for St Guthlac's be accepted, continuity with pre-Anglo-Saxon Christianity seems possible, and this could have been a reason for the choice of Hereford as the bishop's seat.

A series of excavations undertaken at Hereford in the 1960s and 1970s has enabled the development of the town around the two minsters to be traced (fig. 61). Hereford can be considered to have been an 'embryo town' in the mid-eighth century, with the two religious establishments standing on a gravel terrace near the ford across the Wye, a north–south road crossing the Wye, an east–west road passing immediately north of the cathedral and Castle Green, and 'probably a few houses close to the crossroads' (Shoesmith 1982: 91). There were traces of a defensive work on the marshy western side. This early phase is believed to have been followed at some date between c.750 and c.850 by a deliberately planned expansion of the city to the west of the cathedral; and the grid pattern which remains a feature of the streets is considered to have originated at this date. In the middle of the ninth century the city was enclosed by a ditch and gravel bank which formed the first stage of the defensive sequence. This enclosed the primary grid pattern of streets and the cathedral, but apparently excluded St Guthlac's and the cemetery.

The building of the second stage of the defences in the late ninth or early tenth century brought St Guthlac's and the cemetery within the enclosed area to the east. An increase in population is suggested by the evidence from the cemetery. In stage three of the defences, a few years later, the timber work of stage two was replaced by stone. The secondary grid pattern of streets in the east of the city was probably in use by this time. This was the city which became part of the *burh* system, and was selected as the centre of a shire. In A.D.930 it hosted a meeting of King Æthelstan with the Welsh princes, and they promised him tribute. Also at this meeting Æthelstan appointed the River Wye as the boundary between Welsh and English, an act presumably intended to legitimize the operation of Welsh and English customs in distinct parts of an area which was an integral part of the English kingdom. The Ordinance concerning the Dunsæte (above pp. 113-14) is considered to have been composed as a result of this meeting. The situation of Hereford on the boundary with land which was independent of English rule at least as late as the reign of Offa is the next point which requires consideration.

Early interpretations of Hereford's origins supposed that there was a Roman fort on the gravel terrace by the River Wye. This theory has not been conclusively disproved, but the evidence for Roman occupation is now considered to point rather to 'a third or fourth century temple, shrine or small wayside settlement – perhaps associated with one of the fords across the Wye' (Shoesmith 1982: 82). The crossroads north-west of the cathedral, which is likely to have been the nucleus of the earliest non-ecclesiastical post-Roman settlement, is part of the Romano-British road system, but the exact route of the north–south road is not recoverable within the city, so the precise position of the river-crossing is not certain. The Roman town of *Magnis* was at Kenchester, four miles north-west of Hereford, and the crossing of the Wye adjacent to that place must have been more frequented than the Hereford one until the end of the Roman period. It is possible that the collapse of a bridge at the higher crossing diverted traffic to the ford at Hereford. From these considerations it emerges that the function of Hereford as a central place cannot be projected back into the Roman period.

A recent reference has been made to 'the sees of Worcester and Hereford, both of them on Roman urban sites' (Sims-Williams 1990: 143), but the available archaeological evidence from Hereford does not support this claim.

It is not certain that Hereford was the original centre of authority for the sub-kingdom of the Magonsæte. King Merewalh is credited with the foundation of the minster church at Leominster, and this great estate has seemed to some commentators (e.g. Shoesmith 1982: 90) to be a likelier location for his chief residence. But the fact that eventually (if not originally) the bishopric was centred at Hereford strongly supports the claim of the place to be the principal royal centre. On the whole it seems best to accept Hereford as Merewalh's 'capital'. It was a border town, since all the land south of the Wye was in Archenfield, and that district was not under English rule till at least the reign of Offa (see above, pp. 114-16). A partial comparison might be made with Bamburgh, the earliest seat of the kings of Bernicia, which is a 'bridge-head' site on the east coast of Northumberland; but there does not appear to be a true parallel for the siting of an early 'capital' on a boundary with a potentially hostile state. The people of Merewalh's kingdom must have been mostly Welsh, however, so perhaps the political division between English and Welsh territory did not constitute a major factor in everyday life.

Offa may have obtained control over Archenfield after the battle of Hereford in A.D.760 (AC 88), and the archaeological evidence for the early planning of the street system may point to his direct concern with the city at that date.

The name Hereford, which means 'army ford', is consistent with the supposition that this was perceived as a vital site from the beginning of Mercian involvement. The name is repeated in Little Hereford, also in Herefordshire but 18 miles north, and there are other examples in Devon, Huntingdonshire and Worcestershire. The reference may be to a ford which was wide enough for an army to cross in broad ranks. Leominster, the rival candidate for Merewalh's 'capital', has as first component the pre-English district-name *Lene*. This also would be appropriate to a place with early administrative importance, but the failure of Merewalh's minster to become the cathedral of the Magonsætan see appears to rule out Leominster as the main centre of his kingdom.

Hereford was one of several places in Herefordshire where castles were built in the mid-eleventh century by Norman officials of Edward the Confessor. Stenton (1970: 199) suggests that a Norman military colony was established in the shire to counter the threat posed by the king of Gwynedd, Gruffydd ap Llewelyn, who made himself ruler of all Wales at this time and embarked on a war of conquest in Herefordshire. A Norman named Ralf became earl of Hereford, and built a castle there. 'Frenchmen from the castle' are said to have fought with Gruffydd 'quite close to Leominster' in 1052 (ASC *s.a.*). Gruffydd allied himself with Ælfgar, the exiled English earl of Mercia, and in 1055 they defeated Ralf's combined English and Norman forces outside Hereford (*ibid.*). A Welsh source, the *Brut y Tywysogyon*, says that the Saxons fled to their castle (*gaer*), which Gruffydd entered and pillaged, and Welsh and English sources record the burning of the town. The *Anglo-Saxon Chronicle* also says that the cathedral was sacked and burnt, but part of the building, at least, must have been reasonably intact in 1056 when, according to Florence of Worcester, Bishop Æthelstan was buried in it (Whitehead 1982: 15).

The Welsh victory was immediately countered by Earl Harold, who collected a force at Gloucester and pursued the enemy west beyond the River Dore. The *Anglo-Saxon Chronicle* states that Earl Harold had a ditch made about the town (i.e. Hereford), and Florence of Worcester amplifies this, saying that the town was 'fortified with gates and bars and with a broad deep ditch'. Whitehead (*op. cit.*) points out that this was a reversion to the traditional *burh* defences, ignoring Ralf's innovatory castle. From this base Harold concluded a peace with Ælfgar at Billingsley, four miles south-south-west of Hereford. The Welsh danger disappeared for a time in 1063, when Gruffydd was killed by his own people after being defeated by Harold. In the absence of statements to the contrary it seems likely that the people of Archenfield maintained their English allegiance during Gruffydd's attempted conquest.

The account of Hereford at the beginning of the Herefordshire folios of Domesday Book credits the town with more than 200 burgesses before the Conquest, and the survey also refers to an unquantified community of French burgesses, and says that there were seven moneyers in King Edward's time. The number of moneyers and the presence of the French burgesses (who could have been there before the Conquest) suggest a thriving trading centre.

Shrewsbury (fig. 62)

Unlike the Magonsæte, the Wreocensæte had neither a recorded ruling dynasty nor a bishopric; and since Shrewsbury was not an ecclesiastical centre its documentary history begins later than that of Hereford. We have no references until the early tenth century, when the settlement may be assumed to have come into prominence as a military centre. Æthelflæd and Æthelred were there in 901, when they issued a charter granting land to Wenlock Abbey (S 221). The charter was given *in civitate Scrobbensis*, and it is probable that the town had been provided with defences by then, and that it was functioning as a trading centre. Surviving coins from the Shrewsbury mint date from the reign of Æthelstan (924–39) onwards. The first reference to the shire (*Scrobbesbyrigscire*) occurs in the *Anglo-Saxon Chronicle* under the year 1006.

Shrewsbury lacks early archaeological evidence, as well as documentation. The archaeological problem was set out admirably by Professor Martin Carver (1978), though his discussion is slightly marred by inexpert treatment of place-name evidence. Carver dismisses claims that there was a Roman occupation and a British palace with the succinct statement 'The debate about the town's origins . . . has been informed by little more than a species of antiquarian mysticism' (226). Concerning the spurious impression which has been conveyed by chance finds of Roman coins and other objects, he observes that 'the ability of the later town to attract ancient

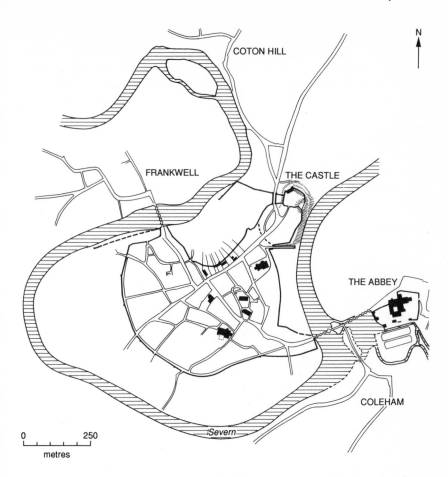

Figure 62 The topography of Shrewsbury (N. Baker).

artefacts means that care must be taken to establish the provenance of finds and eliminate any chance of displacement' (248). Some of the finds recorded from Shrewsbury have obviously been brought there from Wroxeter in comparatively recent times.

Carver admits that 'archaeology has so far nothing to offer to the Shrewsbury of the 5th-8th centuries' (249), but he does not regard this as positive evidence that there was no occupation during those centuries. It is to be seen, rather, as a consequence of the nature of Shrewsbury's geology and topography, both of which were unfavourable for the building up of stratified occupation levels. 'High, soft sites such as Shrewsbury may experience a gradual lowering of the ground level as it is exploited' (225).

As regards the military use of Shrewsbury at the time of the Danish wars, Carver endorses the view put forward in Chapter 8, that a *burh* could have been formed easily by throwing a barrier across the landward side. 'All the earliest levels of the town, however, are suspected of damage or removal by later earthmoving operations, and nowhere more than . . . across the neck of the peninsula' (253).

There is no way of knowing how far back beyond 901 (when it was *civitas Scrobbensis*) the origins of Shrewsbury may lie, or what the relationship of this defensible site is to the undefended Roman capital at Wroxeter. There are other sites in the vicinity which have been suspected of having a chronologically intermediate position as centres of authority. There is the Iron Age fort called The Berth, near Baschurch, which could well have been re-occupied by a Dark Age ruler in search of a citadel. Only very limited excavation has been carried out at The Berth, and Dark Age finds may await discovery there. And there is the crop-mark site in a field called Frog Hall, four miles east of Shrewsbury, which archaeologists interpret as a series of timber halls resembling those which have been excavated at the Northumbrian royal centre of Yeavering. The Yeavering halls were occupied in the time of King Edwin and destroyed in one of Penda's invasions. The Frog Hall site, like Wroxeter, is totally without natural defences.

The name Shrewsbury (Old English *Scrobbesbyrig*) is most plausibly interpreted as 'fortified place of the scrubland'. About this, also, there has been much speculation. E. Ekwall, in a rare lapse of judgment, introduced a curious red herring in the form of a Norman settler called Richard Fitz Scrob who was established in north Herefordshire in the reign of Edward the Confessor, and who is commemorated in the place-name Richard's Castle (Ekwall 1960: 420). The Norman surname Fitz Scrob is not, however, evidence that there was an Old English personal name *Scrobb* which could, at a much earlier date, have entered into the place-name Shrewsbury. Carver (1978: 228 n.1) mentions the Norman family-name Scroop, which is also irrelevant. There is good evidence in English place-names for an Old English word *scrobb, a by-form of the recorded *scrybb* which meant 'belt of scrubland' (Gelling 1990: 267-71).

The Domesday Survey gives an account of Shrewsbury at the beginning of the Shropshire folios. The customs of the town, like those of Hereford, include the provision of men for the king's hunting and for expeditions by the sheriff into Wales; and the burgesses of both towns had escort duties in relation to the king and the sheriff. In the present context, however, it is information about the numbers of burgesses and moneyers which is particularly relevant. The Shrewsbury account opens with the information that there were 252 houses in the time of King Edward, and as many burgesses in these houses. It also states that the king had three moneyers there. This is fewer than the eight who have been identified as working there in the reign of Æthelstan,[6] and fewer than Domesday ascribes to Hereford. Perhaps the best evidence that Shrewsbury was a potentially important trading centre is the presence of 43 French burgesses, though these are less likely than the French burgesses of Hereford to have been there before the Norman Conquest. It is probably the presence of these Frenchmen which accounts for the place-name Frankwell (*Frankevilla* c.1222). This suburb of Shrewsbury across the Welsh Bridge is a 'free town', like the documented borough planted by the bishopric of Winchester in the Isle of Wight, where this name alternates with that of Newtown.[7] There appears to be no record of the Shropshire plantation other than the name.

It obviously dates from after the Conquest and the building of the castle, but it perhaps constitutes evidence that Shrewsbury in the reign of King Edward had the potential for commercial development.

Chester

There is no doubt about the Roman origins of Chester, the last of the shire towns to be considered here. The place was *Deva* in Roman times, this being the British river-name which has developed into modern Dee. The Romans established a legionary fortress here, and civilian settlements grew up to the west and south of it. The Anglo-Saxons called the site *Legaceaster*, which Bede rendered into Latin as *civitas Legionum*: and the prefix referring to the Roman legions remained part of the name until the eleventh century. A long series of coins from the Chester mints has LEG, LEGCEST, LEIGCE, LECEST, LEIC and the like for mint signatures (Dodgson 1981: 3–4). The Welsh name contemporary with English *Legaceaster* was *Cair Legion*. Professor Dodgson (*ibid*. 7) suggests that 'The reduction of the place-name to simplex Chester must be taken as a result of the political and commercial importance of the place, whence it could be known as *the* Chester, needing no identifying qualification.' From the fourteenth century to the eighteenth the city was also called *Westchester*, which Dodgson interprets as a reflection of its role as the principal port in north-west England, especially important for traffic with Ireland.

It is always difficult to decide whether the English place-name generic *ceaster* refers to impressive but deserted Roman ruins, or whether it implies a sub-Roman occupation. At Chester it has been demonstrated that the major public buildings of the Roman town survived, some of them at least until the tenth century (Thacker 1987: 238); but up to 1985 archaeology had uncovered no certain evidence of sub-Roman habitation. There is now a possibility of this inside the north wall of the legionary fort at Abbey Green, where there are traces of alteration to a building in the late Roman period, and of occupation after the alteration. There are also sherds of imported pottery from the eastern Mediterranean, which cannot be dated closely within a range of second to sixth century. This is possible, but far from conclusive, evidence for sub-Roman activity.

There is not yet sufficient evidence to prove continuity of occupation, and it is not certain that Chester had urban status before the time of the Danish wars. But at least the regional centre of this area did not shift away from Chester after the Roman period, as that of the region to the south did from Wroxeter. Thacker (*ibid*.: 239) suggests that the British dynasty defeated by the Northumbrian king Æthelfrith at the battle of Chester in A.D.616 may have been ruling from the city.

Chester and its region were not annexed to Northumbria in spite of Æthelfrith's victory, and by the late seventh century the area was firmly within the Mercian sphere of influence. The strategic importance of Chester in the Danish wars of the ninth and tenth centuries has already been discussed (above, pp. 128–31). Such evidence as has been found for the Æthelflædan defences and for any associated planning of the town's internal layout is summarized in Thacker 1987: 250-1.[8] He concludes that it is likely that the Roman walls were used, and that the survival of major public buildings such as the principia and legionary bath-house caused the later street pattern to be closely related to the Roman one.

Like Hereford, Chester contained two minsters, St Werburgh's and St John's. The latter was believed in the twelfth century to have been founded by King Æthelred of Mercia in 689 (*ibid.*: 168). The Lady Æthelflæd is credited in later tradition with the translation of St Werburg's relics from Hanbury in Staffordshire, and with the refoundation in her honour of the minster formerly dedicated to St Peter and St Paul. The cult of Werburg, a Mercian princess of the seventh century, brought great prosperity to this house. It was St John's church which was probably used by Mercian bishops as a quasi-cathedral when they visited the north-west corner of the diocese (*ibid.*: 269).

It was at Chester that King Edgar met six British kings after his coronation in 973, and received promises that they would be his allies. The *Anglo-Saxon Chronicle* records that he sailed with his fleet to the meeting, and a post-Conquest source – Florence of Worcester – says that the British kings rowed him on the Dee from his palace to the church of St John and back again, while he held the boat's rudder (Whitelock 1955: 208). The story of this meeting affirms both the special position of Chester in regard to the politics of the lands round the Irish Sea, and the importance of naval power for a king who wished to retain his sovereignty over north-west England.

Chester was the only pre-Conquest town in our five shires which developed into a major trading centre. Its position on the Dee estuary, at a vital crossing-point of trade-routes connecting York with Ireland, the Isle of Man and Wales, combined with the presence of Viking traders to produce this development.

Before Viking traders made Chester their centre, and indeed after that, there appears to have been a port at Meols, on the north coast of the Wirral. Objects have been found at Meols which suggest that the place had an active role in the trade of the Irish Sea from prehistoric times through to the Middle Ages. Viking connections are established by such objects as a bronze drinking-horn mount which may be as early as the ninth century, and a ring-headed pin with east Scandinavian parallels (Thacker 1987: 257).

Documentary and place-name evidence for Hiberno-Norse settlement near Chester and in the Wirral has already been discussed (above, pp. 128–34). Members of this Hiberno-Norse community must have become involved in coining in the Chester area in the early tenth century. Thacker points to the Norse moneyer called *Irfara*, 'Ireland journeyer', who was operating in the reign of Edward the Elder. Under Æthelstan the Chester moneyers were cosmopolitan, including Germans and Franks as well as Scandinavians and Celts; and Scandinavian influence in the Chester mints was strong throughout the later Saxon period. That the Chester Norsemen were engaged in trade as well as in coining is shown by a significant number of metalwork finds which indicate connections with Dublin and the Isle of Man. Church dedications to St Olave and St Bridget also testify to the importance of the Hiberno-Norse community in the development of the city.

It is the quantity of coins produced there which mainly demonstrates the outstanding commercial importance of Chester. In the tenth century Chester seems often to have had more moneyers at work than London (Metcalf 1982: 131) and the evidence points to an expansion of the overseas trade which flowed through York, Lincoln and Chester. Thacker (1987: 260-1) says that there were 28 moneyers in Chester in the period from 924-39, and that there were probably as many as 20 striking at the same time, as compared with 10 in London and 7 in Winchester. The number of Chester moneyers declined to 17 between 939 and 955, and after the middle of the century the city did not again rival the great centres of London, York, Winchester and Lincoln in this respect. Its prosperity appears to have fluctuated, with a period of decline in the later tenth century followed by a revival in the reign of Cnut. But there is no doubt that from the early tenth century onwards Chester was a commercial centre of a totally different order from the other West Midland towns which fall within the scope of this study. The trade carried on in Chester must have included long-distance commerce in goods of high value which were offered for sale not by producers but by middlemen or merchants. P.H. Sawyer (1977: 146) contrasts that type of commerce with local exchanges at markets and fairs. It is to be assumed that local exchanges formed most, if not all, of the trade carried on in other towns of the West Midlands. This would be the nature of the commercial activities in the market-place at Worcester, for which regulations are set out in the document discussed on p. 139.

In 980 'Cheshire was ravaged by a northern naval force' (Whitelock 1955: 211), and it is possible that this Viking fleet sacked Chester, as there is evidence for a decline in the town's prosperity at about this date. At one of the excavated sites, Lower Bridge Street, occupation comes to an end at this period. There was also a dramatic decline in the number of moneyers (Mason 1985: 36; Thacker 1987: 262). The mint regained some of its former importance in the reign of Cnut, but some of the Irish trade may have been diverted to Bristol.

The account of Chester in Domesday Book is largely concerned with regulations governing the financial penalties for lawbreaking in the borough. There are penalties for the unauthorized docking of boats at the city port, and these are linked to rules governing the import of marten-skins. This reference to furs which could have come from Ireland or Scandinavia is the only notice in Domesday of the city's long-distance trade.

As regards the size of the trading population, inferences have to be drawn from statements about the number of the houses. The Domesday account says that there were 508 houses in 1066. Events in the stormy period after 1066 reduced this number to less than half. The transference of the cathedral from Lichfield in 1075 indicates that the town was still a considerable urban centre, but during the reign of William I its military importance in relation to the Welsh border may have overshadowed its trading activities.

The Estates of Wulfric Spott

There were many great landholdings, some in royal, some in episcopal and some in lay ownership, and the biggest of these would be largely self-sufficient, freeing the aristocracy from the need for regular buying and selling. A glimpse into the workings of the greatest estate of the West Midlands is afforded by the will of Wulfric Spott, the founder of the abbey at Burton-on-Trent, which dates from the earliest years of the eleventh century. His lands were scattered over a vast area, from the Wirral and the region designated 'between Ribble and Mersey', in the north-west, to Gloucestershire, in the south-west, and on the east from Doncaster to south Warwickshire. Eighty separate estates are named. It is clear that in the north-western properties and in Yorkshire fish was an important resource, and that arrangements existed for transporting quantities of it across the Midlands. The bequest to Burton includes a hundred wild horses, which indicates that there were arrangements for the management of herds of animals which were not the ordinary stock of farms. An empire of this sort would produce most of its own requirements, even the more luxurious ones, and would have little need of help from merchants.

Salt

One resource which most estates would have to obtain from outside their boundaries was salt. The West Midlands had two great inland salt-producing centres, in Cheshire and Worcestershire, and these were, in a sense, trading places; but the distribution of salt was carried out on a curiously fixed, almost ritualized, basis, which cannot be classified as commerce and which allowed no scope for development over the centuries.

The Worcestershire salt-trade, centred on Droitwich, is well-documented from the eighth century (Hooke 1981). There are also many references to the trade in the Domesday Survey, and the picture which emerges from these corresponds in some details with the account given by John Leland about the year 1540. Leland (ii, ff. 93–4) comments that wood for the furnaces is brought from Alvechurch and Bromsgrove, and Bromsgrove is one of the manors for which Domesday records an exchange of fixed quantities of wood for salt. It is probable that the 'grove' of Bromsgrove (also referred to in the nearby Grafton) was a large area of coppiced woodland, maintained and managed for this purpose. Many manors in Worcestershire and the surrounding counties had the right to a fixed quantity of salt. Domesday entries combine with evidence from charter boundaries and place-names such as Salford and Saltway to enable a network of saltways to be traced, running into Shropshire, Herefordshire, Gloucestershire, Oxfordshire and Warwickshire, and across Oxfordshire into Buckinghamshire, where Princes Risborough is the most distant manor from source to have salt rights in Droitwich.

Presumably, since the salt convoys would go regularly along these routes, surplus salt could be sold on the road on a casual basis. But the bulk of the output probably went to the manors with an ancient entitlement. It is not clear how or when this system arose. There is Iron Age and Roman occupation at Droitwich, and the distribution network may go back into prehistoric times. The Roman name of both Droitwich and Nantwich (one of the Cheshire centres) was *Salinae*, 'salt-pans'. At both places there was a custom of decorating one of the saltpits on a particular day of the year, and holding festivities round it. The Droitwich ceremony is described by Leland, that at Nantwich is known to have continued into the eighteenth century. These ceremonies were Christianized in their recorded forms, but it is likely that they were of pagan origin (Sawyer 1977: 148).

The Cheshire estates for which salt rights at Nantwich, Northwich and Middlewich are noted in Domesday are less numerous than those connected with Droitwich, and the Cheshire trade may have involved a great deal more supply in response to demand that the Worcestershire one. The selling of the Cheshire salt was, however, ritualized and subject to minute regulation. One-and-a-quarter folios of the Cheshire Domesday are occupied with the tolls and customs which applied to the trade in time of King Edward. The concluding sections state:

> Whoever carted purchased salt from these two Wiches paid 4d in toll if he had four or more oxen to his cart; if two oxen he paid 2d toll, if there were two packloads of salt. A man from another Hundred paid 2d for a packhorse load, but a man from the same Hundred paid only ½d for a packload of salt. Anyone who so overloaded a cart that the axle broke within one league of either Wich paid 2s to the office of the King or the Earl, if he could be caught within the league; similarly, anyone who so overloaded a horse that he broke its back paid 2s if caught within the league; beyond the league, nothing. Anyone who made two packloads of salt out of one paid a fine of 40s, if the officer could catch him; if he were not found he paid no fine through anyone else. Men on foot from another Hundred who bought salt there paid 2d on 8 manloads; men of the same Hundred paid 1d on 8 loads. (DBi, f. 268b)

The names of the inland salt-producing centres of the West Midlands have as generic Old English *wīc*, the earlier senses of which are discussed under Warwick (above p. 155). The use of the term in Droitwich, Nantwich, Middlewich and Northwich is related to that seen in the names of the early trading centres of southern and eastern England, but it is a different concept of trade that is referred to. Maintaining the status quo seems to have been a primary object of the inland salt-makers over many centuries, and this is the opposite of a commercial outlook. At Droitwich production was deliberately limited in the sixteenth century by only working for six months of the year, and by discouraging the digging of more and deeper pits. And the fee paid by the burgesses to the king was the same – £100 – as had been agreed when their ancestors received a charter from King John. Things continued in much the same way until the end of the seventeenth century, when a long struggle began which eventually broke the monopoly held since King John's reign by the burgesses of Droitwich.

10 The Late Anglo-Saxon Landscape

Underlying the aspects of history which are noticed in the main historical sources is the life of the countryside, and there are absorbing questions for the historian about how and where people were living during the centuries when the Welsh language was giving way to English speech and the pagan religions to Christianity, and when the structure of the early English kingdoms was being replaced by the administrative patterns of shire and hundred. Some records survive from the last two centuries of the period which enable historians to reconstruct aspects of the developed landscape of that era, and the last two decades have witnessed major developments in the understanding of Anglo-Saxon land-utilization and settlement forms. Modern work on the landscape of the tenth and eleventh centuries will be considered under the following heads: open-field farming, scattered and nucleated settlement patterns, the provision of churches, and pre-Conquest sculptural remains.

Open-field farming

Open-field farming is now believed by many historians and geographers to be a development of the tenth century, rather than a system brought by the Anglo-Saxons from the Continent - as proposed by H.L. Gray in 1915 - or arising largely in the twelfth-thirteenth centuries - as proposed by Joan Thirsk in 1964. Gray's proposal was developed in 1938 by C.S. and C.S. Orwin in a book called *The Open Fields*. This was an extremely influential work. The model which it offered, of a system of communal land-clearance and exploitation introduced and practised as a matter of expedience by early Anglo-Saxon pioneers, became an orthodoxy; and it was this model which was attacked by Joan Thirsk in 1964. Her startling new proposal that the system developed gradually, and mainly in the centuries after the Norman Conquest, gained a brief acceptance; but in the debate which followed a consensus emerged in favour of the tenth century as the likeliest period for the development of open-field agriculture. Aspects of the debate are covered in the publication of papers from a seminar held at the Oxford University Department for External Studies in 1978 (Rowley 1981).

The history of the subject is set out in a paper by H.S.A. Fox (1981). His conclusions are that the advent of the system should be sought in the later centuries of the Saxon period, that one of the catalysts may have been the disruption caused by Danish settlements in the East Midlands, and that the need to make provision for pasturing of animals within the boundaries of an arable community's land was a crucial factor. This last would be precipitated by the fission of ancient multiple estates, parts of which had been set aside for pasture, into smaller separate properties. Some estates had pasture land at a distance from the main area, and when outlying pastures developed into independent settlements this resource was no longer available to the main estate. Such a relationship between estates and woodland pastures some distance away is found in Warwickshire, and is discussed in Chapter 1 and Chapter 11. The steady encroachment of the plough on heathland and woodland would also contribute to the need for some arable land to be periodically used for pasture, as the fallow land was in an open-field system.

A number of disparate pieces of evidence slot in with the thesis of a tenth-century origin, most notably the testimony of tenth-century charter boundaries in Berkshire and Worcestershire, which refer to furlongs, headlands and intermingled strips. Support can also be adduced from the changing senses of some words. The earliest meaning of the word *feld* (Gelling 1984: 235–45) is 'open country', and when the word is used as the generic in settlement-names this may be an indication that the plough has encroached on land which was previously used mainly for grazing, with the consequent formation of new settlements. Many of the ancient settlements with names in *-feld* are on the edge of forest, but a number relate to the 500-foot contour, and these may represent a movement of arable up to the lower slopes of land too high for cultivation. Huddersfield and Sheffield on the east side of the Pennines are instances of this. The use of the word for large areas of communally cultivated land appears in charters from c.960. Before this the charters use the term *yrthland*, 'ploughland', for arable, and *feld* for common pasture. Latin *agros* is used to gloss OE *yrthland*, but by the time of the Norman Conquest *yrthland* and *ager* have been replaced by *feld* and *campus* in texts referring to arable matters. This semantic change may be due to a rearrangement of arable in some regions which produced areas of uninterrupted ploughland so large as to deserve a term meaning 'open land'.

The agricultural arrangements under discussion are alternatively known as the Midland system, a name coined by H.L. Gray in 1915 because its main manifestation was in a zone running through the centre of the country from mid-Somerset to lowland Northumberland (a misleading use of 'midland' to anyone accustomed to modern terminology). The salient characteristics of the system are:

i Arrangement of a community's arable land in strips within interlocking bundles (*culturae* in Latin, furlongs in English) within two or three great sectors (called *campi* in Latin, fields in English). The strip was the unit of ownership, the furlong the unit of cultivation.

ii Distribution of every peasant farmer's holding in strips which lay in each of the fields.

iii The setting aside each year of one of the fields for common fallow grazing.

iv The communal regulation of all farming activities.

Fox points out that the rotation of crops, though an essential part of the system, is not a defining characteristic, since it could be managed without a twofold or threefold division of the arable.

The detailed implementation of this system varied from manor to manor. More significant for our study of the West Midlands, however, is the enormous variation in the proportion of each community's land which was organized in this way. Geographical situation was a major determining factor in this. Communities were likely to have more or less of their land laid out in open fields depending on whether they were in lowland areas devoid of woodland, in wooded areas, or in hilly country.

In our five counties, only the southern part of Warwickshire is classic 'open-field' country, in which the greater part of each parish was laid out in strips and furlongs in several great fields and subject to the operations of communal cultivation and regular fallowing. The sudden conversion of some estates in this area to grazing land in the later Middle Ages caused the pattern of strips and furlongs which was there at the time of the last season's ploughing to be preserved in the form of ridge and furrow; and whilst the precise pattern to be seen in modern grassland is not likely to date back to pre-Conquest times (since it has been shown that the layout of the furlongs was subject to periodical reorganization), the general effect is a true guide to the nature of land-use in the earlier years of the system. Such patterns of ridge and furrow, uninterrupted by hedges, would cover vast areas of land in this region. South Warwickshire has long been known as the Feldon, and while this name is not recorded until the sixteenth century, it is likely to date from Anglo-Saxon times. It probably derives from Old English *feldum*, literally 'at the open lands', which could be a reference to the contrast with the woodland of the northern part of the shire. Alternatively, if the name arose in the tenth century, it could mean 'at the open fields' referring to the new agricultural system.

In the whole of the Feldon area of Warwickshire a general resemblance in land-use can be assumed between the parishes. Elsewhere in our region a detailed study of each parish is required in order to determine what proportion of the land was in communal cultivation. In the wooded region of north Warwickshire there were miniature field systems, several operating in each parish. Five contiguous Arden parishes - Elmdon, Sheldon, Bickenhill, Yardley and Solihull - have been analysed in detail (Skipp 1981). By 1300 there were probably 16 or 17 individual sets of open fields in these parishes, and at least 10 of these can be regarded as having originated in the Anglo-Saxon period (*ibid.* 180). Skipp's study of medieval Yardley (Skipp 1970) gives an excellent impression of how matters were organized (fig. 63). Miniature field systems were set among great areas of woodland and heath, and the shortage of pasture which was acute in the parishes of south Warwickshire would not have been any problem in the north of the county.

The general characteristic of multiple, relatively small, sets of open fields is found in many areas of the other counties in our study. Detailed information which demonstrates this is now available for some parishes in Shropshire and Staffordshire.[1] In south-west Shropshire many of the larger parishes had multiple sets of open fields, one for each of the townships into which the parish was divided. Alberbury, for instance, contained 12 townships, and the field systems belonging to each of these would be small (fig. 64). In the east-Shropshire parish of Little Wenlock it is estimated that

Figure 63   The eastern half of medieval Yardley (from Skipp 1970).

the arable fields were surrounded by common waste and woodland which covered two-thirds of the area (fig. 65). Similar situations are found in some parishes in south-west Staffordshire. The open fields of Tettenhall Regis lay at Tettenhall village, Wergs, Compton and Wightwick. At Enville 'the number and distribution of open fields ... reflects a gradual process of bringing forest woodland into cultivation. Each of the three manors had its own set of fields ... and there was ... a separate set for Lyndon.' At Bobbington (fig. 66), where much of the parish offered the sort of rough pasture misleadingly known as 'waste', there is no surviving reference to open-field agriculture; and it seems unlikely that the growth of a nucleated settlement at Bobbington with the twelfth-century church at its centre owes anything to a rearrangement of the arable land.

Miniature open-field systems were likely to be enclosed by agreement between the strip owners at a relatively early date, as opposed to the parliamentary enclosure of whole parishes which transformed the landscape of areas like south Warwickshire in the second half of the eighteenth century. Such early enclosures often resulted in the preservation of furlong shapes; in Shropshire an excellent example of this can be seen on the east slope of the ridge on which the village of Wentnor stands. There is a good

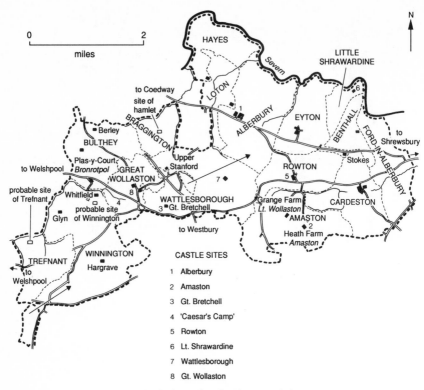

Figure 64 The townships of Alberbury (from *VCH Shropshire VIII*, by permission of the General Editor).

view of it from the Long Mynd (fig. 67).

Staffordshire had some classic open-field parishes, such as Elford north of Tamworth and Barlaston in the Trent valley. The general condition of the county, however, has been well described by Professor David Palliser (1976: 76–7). He points out that while Barlaston is a typical example of the small parish-cum-manor with a nucleated village, such settlements are only common in parts of Staffordshire, particularly the river valleys. Much settlement was of the contrasting type, dispersed among hamlets and isolated farmsteads, especially in the vast moorland parishes of Leek, Alstonefield and Stoke-upon-Trent. Almost all villages and hamlets had some open-field arable in the early Middle Ages, but it was only in the nucleated villages of the lowlands that open-field systems became firmly established. On the upland, such systems often failed to develop fully, and where they did, they frequently disappeared early.

In the greater part of our region much of the cultivated land was probably cleared by individual effort and farmed in severalty (i.e. by farmers who were not bound by communal regulations). Medieval records from Shropshire show the process of forest assarting south of Shrewsbury[2] and heath

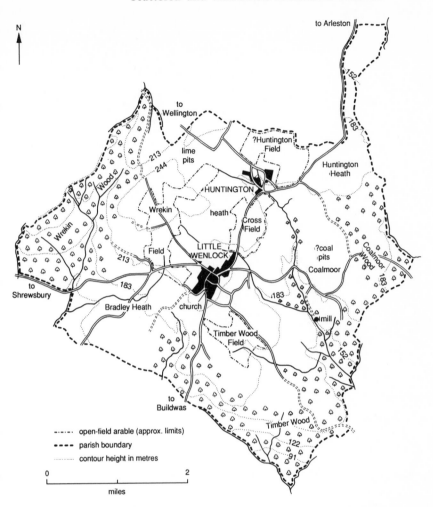

Figure 65 Arable, waste and woodland at Little Wenlock (from *VCH Shropshire IV*, by permission of the General Editor).

reclamation in High Ercall, north-east of Shrewsbury,[3] still proceeding in the twelfth century, so the process was far more complete at the end of our period. There was likely to be a much larger pastoral element in the economy of parishes which had a high proportion of heath and woodland than would be possible in the Warwickshire Feldon.

Scattered and Nucleated Settlement Patterns

There is a general association of open-field farming with nucleated villages, and this type of village is certainly characteristic of areas like the Warwickshire Feldon. In such regions it is the general rule for each parish

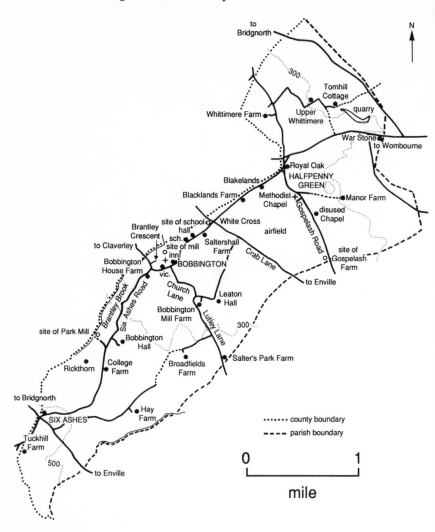

Figure 66   Settlements in Bobbington, 1981 (from *VCH Stafford-shire XX*, by permission of the General Editor).

to contain a single large village. Additional settlements often have names like North Fields Farm or Offchurch Fields, showing that they are the result of parliamentary enclosure, after which some farmers ceased to live in the central village and moved to new farmhouses built on sites formerly incorporated in the field-system. In some parishes there are hamlets in addition to the main village which are obviously ancient foundations, but there are not enough of them to invalidate the general pattern.

There is much debate among historians and geographers concerning the antiquity of large nucleated villages, one suggestion being that it was the organization of the open fields, perhaps in the tenth century, which caused

Figure 67 Wentnor, Shropshire, from the Long Mynd (photograph M. Gelling).

them to be created. There is good archaeological evidence to support the thesis that in some areas settlements were small and scattered in the earlier Anglo-Saxon period. Field-walking and study of pottery recovered by this means show that in some parishes in the East Midlands and in East Anglia there were a number of very small early Saxon hamlets in parishes which now contain a single large village. In the light of this work we should perhaps consider both the discernible settlement pattern and the documented open-field systems of south Warwickshire as characteristic only of the last two centuries of our period.

It is much more difficult, however, to estimate the likely antiquity of settlement patterns in areas which were less dominated by open-field agriculture; and a good deal that is being written at present about the late nucleation and earlier instability of settlements seems less applicable to the counties which adjoin Wales than to those which lie further east. Even if the model were likely to be applicable in the western Midlands, the test of field-walking for pottery could not be applied. There is now sufficient archaeological evidence to permit the conclusion that pottery was not used in the post-Roman centuries in regions which lay to the west of the Gloucestershire and Worcestershire stretches of the River Severn. This evidence is set out in a paper by Alan Vince (1988), which has the title 'Did they use pottery in the Welsh Marches and the West Midlands between the 5th and 12th centuries AD?'. Two of his conclusions (49, 54-5) deserve quotation. These are:

It seems to me that the absence of pottery west of the Severn is a true reflection of the original state of affairs and that, rather than pottery becoming scarcer and scarcer as one travels west there was actually an abrupt break on one side of which people were living a Germanic lifestyle, as shown by their pots, buildings, location of settlements and metalwork, and on the other side of which they weren't.

and

To sum up, it is possible to see a reluctance to use pottery along the Welsh Marches from the end of the Roman period right up to the 12th century. When it was used it was often imported, even if only from the other side of the Severn, and its introduction can be seen to be linked to alien institutions – the *burh* and the Norman castle.

Recent small-scale excavations at Wroxeter church (Moffett 1990) have produced a few sherds of hand-made pottery believed to be of post-Roman date; but this is insufficient to reverse the general conclusion that the area west and north of the Severn was for practical purposes aceramic. It is therefore impossible to prospect for settlement sites dating between the fifth and ninth centuries west of the Severn by field-walking. Some high-status sites, like that at Atcham, may appear on air photographs, but until archaeologists devise an effective means of detecting low-status settlements which used no pottery, we can retain the hypothesis that a great many such settlements were where they are today.

In Shropshire and Herefordshire many settlements are in situations so closely delimited by the topography that it is hardly possible that there should have been a significant change in their position. When the name of the settlement contains a reference to the situation of such places, the chances of the village having been in much the same position at least since the first coming of the English seems very high indeed. In south Shropshire there is a narrow valley called Hope Dale which lies between two parallel ridges. One of these is the famous Wenlock Edge, the other is known to geographers as the Aymestrey Limestone Escarpment (see fig. 68). Streams rise at fairly regular intervals along the valley, and there are funnel-shaped openings at the sources. Each of these openings contains a settlement with a name ending in *hop*, which is the regular Old English term in this area for a particularly secluded situation. The series from north-east to south-west is: Presthope (now overlooking its hollow), Easthope (with a raised circular churchyard), Wilderhope, Millichope, Middlehope, Westhope and Dinchope. There are 12 miles between Presthope and Dinchope. Such names could hardly have arisen in a context where settlement consisted of shifting hamlets. These sites must have been perceived as a unitary phenomenon all deserving the same generic in their names. The settlements may have moved about a bit in their hollows, but the sites would surely be perceived as permanent rather than shifting by the people of the neighbourhood. This applies to many other settlements with *-hop* names in north Herefordshire and south Shropshire.

Figure 68   Hope Dale, Shropshire, from Halford at its south end. Wenlock Edge centre, Aymestrey Limestone Escarpment on the right. Lower Dinchope is just visible, with its stream flowing west, through Wenlock Edge. The other *hop* settlements are at springs from which streams flow through the eastern escarpment. On the left of the picture is a belt of territory which the Anglo-Saxons called *Langanfeld*, 'long open space'. The village of Cheney Longville, bottom left, derives its name from this, and so does Longville-in-the-Dale, nine miles north-east. Also in this strip is Felhampton *'feld* settlement'. The 'long open space' is bounded on the west by the Church Stretton hills. The Wrekin can be seen on the skyline (photograph Arnold Baker).

Other instances can easily be adduced. The Herefordshire village of Eye, north of Leominster, sits firmly on the small 'island' of raised ground to which the name refers. At Whitney ('white island') near the boundary of Herefordshire and Radnorshire, Old Whitney Court occupies a typical 'island' site, and it is known that the village was in the vicinity of the Court until flooding in the eighteenth century caused its removal to the present position, half a mile away. The Shropshire village of Wentnor (Old English *Wentan ofer*) is at the end of a broad, flat ridge of the type regularly referred to in place-names by the generic *ofer* (see fig. 67). Another fine example of this is Tittensor, Staffordshire. At Fitz, north-west of Shrewsbury (Old English *Fitteshōh*), the church and manor-house occupy the tip of a long, low ridge which is the *hōh* (literally 'heel') of the place-name. Edge, south-west of Shrewsbury, is on the eastern tip of a narrow sandstone outcrop. The same conclusion can be drawn about some Welsh names. Ross in Herefordshire has obviously always stood on the 'promontory' to which its name refers, and Doward, south-west of Ross, is likely

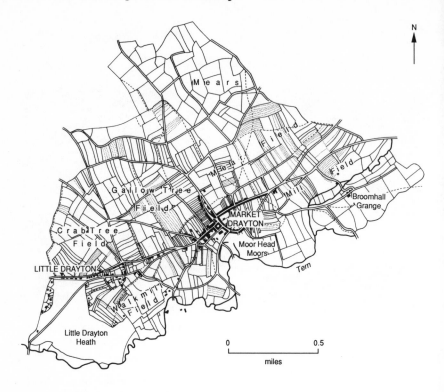

Figure 69   The open fields of Market Drayton (from *VCH Shropshire IV*, by permission of the General Editor).

always to have been situated between the 'two hills' of the name.

Dispersed settlement patterns are commoner than nucleated ones in Shropshire and Herefordshire, but where there are larger settlements it does not seem likely that these owe their special character to late developments such as the introduction of open-field agriculture. Wrockwardine ('enclosed settlement by the Wrekin') is a large village in a commanding situation. The parish includes the seven hamlets of Admaston, Allscot, Bratton, Charlton, Clotley, Leaton and Orleton, and it is clear from field-names and field-shapes on the Tithe Award map that all eight settlements had their own field systems. There is no question of a Feldon-type field system which had Wrockwardine as its focal point. It is a reasonable hypothesis that Wrockwardine, with its partly pre-English name and dominant situation on a raised shelf of land, was a pre-English settlement of more than average size and importance. The same considerations apply *a fortiori* to Leominster in Herefordshire, situated on a slight rise in the centre of the plain over which 15 of its 16 Domesday members were scattered.

Barlaston in Staffordshire, instanced above as a parish in which open-field agriculture was fully established, has a name which means 'Beornwulf's estate'. It is a reasonable supposition that the nucleated village of Barlaston was formed at the same period as the organization of its open fields, and there will be other parishes in our five counties, outside the Warwickshire Feldon, where such considerations apply. One such is Market Drayton in north-east Shropshire (fig. 69), where the field-systems of Market and Little Drayton took up much of the area of the parish in the eighteenth century.[4] But it is likely that in much of our area the model of small early hamlets coalescing into villages in the two centuries before the Norman Conquest is not relevant. There is probably a large inheritance from pre-English settlement patterns, and these may have involved the grouping of a number of hamlets round a central village, an arrangement demonstrated very clearly in the parishes of Wrockwardine and Alberbury.

In the last decade several landscape historians, most notably, perhaps, C.C. Taylor, have developed the model of small, shifting, early Saxon settlements which only coalesced into nucleated villages at the end of the Anglo-Saxon period. But settlement studies are relatively young, and the current synthesis (Taylor 1983), while stimulating, is based on a limited quantity of research, little of which has been carried out in our area.

The Provision of Churches

Churches are a major element in the modern landscape, and they must have been even more conspicuous in late Anglo-Saxon and immediate post-Conquest times, when most other village buildings would be of a humble nature. As part of a consideration of the late Anglo-Saxon countryside it is appropriate to look at what is known or conjectured about the origins of churches.

It is necessary to recognize a major distinction between institutions known as mother churches or minsters and 'local' or 'village' churches. Recent scholarship has established a sequence of English church development, starting with a system of large parishes served by teams of priests operating from important central churches, followed by the rapid proliferation between the tenth and twelfth centuries of local churches each with a resident priest. During the eleventh and twelfth centuries there was a major campaign of stone church building at a local level. The minster parishes were gradually divided among the local churches, and the modern parochial system crystallized between the eleventh century and the end of the thirteenth.[5]

In the Old English language the single word *mynster*, with its Latin equivalent *monasterium*, did duty both for houses of monks which were not necessarily part of a parochial system, and for houses of priests. Modern historians overcome this ambiguity by using *monastery* for the former, and *minster* or *mother church* for the latter. As regards the large areas served by the minsters and the smaller areas served later by local churches, there is again only one word to be deployed. Both are *parishes*, but historians use the Latin word, *parochia*, for the large parishes of the old minsters. The vernacular word *parish* is not recorded till the thirteenth century, and it is not known by what term speakers of Old English designated the districts assigned to churches. Perhaps the necessity seldom arose except among clerics, and they used the Latin word. The Oxford English Dictionary cites

Old English *preost-scīr* and *scrift-scīr* ('priest district' and 'confession district') as the only near-equivalents on record. A minster parish is sometimes *hyrnesse* 'obedience, lordship', but that term applies equally to secular lordships.

A coherent network of *parochiae* may have been established in the seventh and eighth centuries by kings and bishops who made use of ancient monasteries as well as of more recently founded minsters. Churches to which *parochiae* were allotted were required to assist in the process of conversion and to provide the rudiments of pastoral care for their territories.

Since there is no documentary source which lists the minster churches of the West Midlands they have to be identified from traces of their former superior status which survived into the medieval period. A number of historians and historical geographers have attempted this task,[6] using such evidence as the receipt of ecclesiastical dues from subordinate parishes or the mention of more than one priest in the Domesday Survey. Alan Thacker's Cheshire map, here reproduced as fig. 36, uses separate symbols for 'church in Domesday Book with two or more priests' and 'mother church of ancient parish of more than five townships in existence by 12th C but not in Domesday Book'. Whatever combination of criteria are considered to be diagnostic, it is evident that detailed local studies must underlie claims to identification of minster churches, and it would not be possible to compile a definitive list of such foundations for our five counties.

The minster *parochiae* varied considerably in size. In south-east Shropshire, for instance, minster churches appear to have been relatively thick on the ground. None of them can have had a *parochia* comparable in size to that of Leominster in Herefordshire. The foundation of a church at Leominster is accredited to King Merewalh of the Magonsæte, and the place must have been a major centre of Christianity from the seventh century. Brian Kemp's study shows that the mother church retained its primacy till a relatively late date. Leominster was given to Reading Abbey, in Berkshire, by Henry I, and this powerful corporate overlord was able to control the development of chapelries within the great *parochia*. For part of it, a large area close to Leominster, the organization of chapelries was centred on a chapel at Eye, and Kemp traces the evolution of this into an independent church.

Eventually, of course, most of the dependent chapelries of minsters became independent churches with their own parishes. There has been much discussion in recent years about whether this process is likely to have started in the ninth century or somewhat later,[7] but it seems probable that most of it took place between the tenth and twelfth centuries. If a minster church belonged to a powerful abbey, as Leominster belonged to Reading, there would be zealous guardianship of the ecclesiastical rights of the minster in all the estates which made up its *parochia*, and the provision of lesser churches to serve each of these estates would be subject to overall control and planning. In less closely organized *parochiae* the provision might be more haphazard, often depending on the initiative of the thegns who held estates within the area. The close relationship between

Anglo-Saxon estates and lesser churches had the effect - most beneficial for the historian - of confirming and fossilizing the boundaries of land-units which were in most cases of considerable antiquity when the churches were built. It is to this that we owe the frequent correspondence of modern parish boundaries with those in Anglo-Saxon land grants; and the common proximity of church and manor house also often bears witness to the relationship.

The difficulty of estimating the date at which local churches became a widespread phenomenon is not eased by the attitude of the Domesday commissioners, who were notoriously inconsistent in their references to churches. They sometimes note a church and sometimes list one or more priests in the population of a manor, so there is some positive evidence to be obtained from Domesday Book. But some churches known to have been in existence do not appear there, and it is never permissible to argue that a manor had no church in 1086 because there is no trace of it in the Survey.

The various spatial relationships between churches and other settlement features offer scope for research. A comprehensive survey of south-east Somerset has shown that in that area churches are more frequently sited in isolation from, or peripherally to, villages than fully within them, and Dr Richard Morris (1989: 242-3) links this to the theories discussed above about late formation of villages and the migratory tendencies of settlements in earlier times. Morris's fig. 70 (here fig. 70) seems, however, to tell a different story as regards Herefordshire and south Shropshire. It is a distribution map of these areas with symbols for isolated churches, churches which adjoin isolated farms, churches situated in villages, churches in close proximity to mottes, and mottes which are not associated with churches. Much the most frequent symbol is the third one, representing churches in villages. Closer study might show that many of them are on the periphery of the village rather than within the area which is likely to have been its medieval nucleus; but the Tithe Award maps for Shropshire[8] show a great many instances of churches which were centrally placed in nineteenth-century villages. This is certainly the case in Wrockwardine, which has been instanced above as a settlement likely to have been in the same position since the beginning of our period. The Shropshire maps also show many instances of churches which stand beside manor houses with the village at a distance - Bitterley is a good example - and of churches which stand apart from the village with no such obvious reason - Stanton-upon-Hine Heath with its magnificent raised circular churchyard is one of these (see fig. 33). Generalizations from such a mass of material are perhaps premature, as may be the case with generalizations about village sites. But the matter of church-siting has potential for a great deal of study, and it might profitably be taken up for limited areas by local historians.

Surviving Anglo-Saxon masonry in a church seldom represents the earliest structure. Most local churches would be built in timber in the first instance, and pre-Conquest masonry is likely to represent early stages in the 'Great Rebuilding' which took place between 1050 and 1150 (Blair 1988: 9). Some monasteries and minster churches were probably stone-built from the beginning, however. At Much Wenlock Priory there are stone foundations which (despite claims for Roman origin) could well be those of St

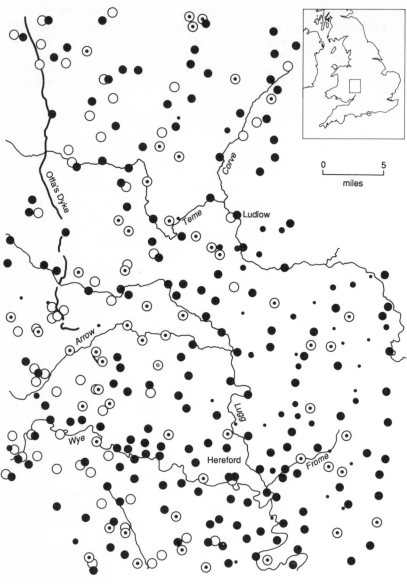

- • isolated church
- ● church and isolated farm or building
- ⬤ church in village
- ○ motte, unassociated with church
- ⊙ church and motte in close topographical association
  ('close' has been taken as c.200 yards [180 metres] or less)

Figure 70　Church sites in the Welsh Marches (from Morris 1989).

Mildburg's late-seventh-century church (Biddle 1988). Part of the north wall of Wroxeter church is possibly seventh or eighth century (Moffett 1990). At the minster church of Wootton Wawen in Warwickshire, the foundation charter of which dates from between A.D.716 and 737, recent work by Dr Steven Bassett has established the presence of more extensive early masonry than was previously recognized. At Tredington in the southern tip of Warwickshire the church structure preserves side-walls of an Anglo-Saxon nave 'of ample size and unusual interest' (Taylor, H.M. and J. 1965); this church is assumed to have been a minster, and it may well have been stone-built in its original form. In other churches, however, surviving pre-Conquest features, such as the large stretches of herringbone walling at Diddlebury in Shropshire and Wigmore in Herefordshire (internal in the former, external in the latter), may belong to a relatively late phase of rebuilding.

Churches whose structure dates from after the Norman Conquest sometimes have pre-Conquest carved stones either built into their walls or standing in the graveyard. This type of evidence as manifested in our five counties remains to be considered.

Pre-Conquest Sculptural Remains

In Cheshire, where no pre-Conquest masonry survives in church buildings, the former presence of pre-Conquest churches is sometimes indicated by the presence of crosses and other sculptural fragments.[9] The earliest and most famous of the surviving Cheshire crosses are the pair in the market-place at Sandbach, where the church was probably an early minster. Scenes from scripture are carved on them, and other ornament includes an inhabited vine-scroll. They are assigned to the ninth century, and certainly predate the Viking period (fig. 71). Other pre-Viking pieces are a fragment from Overchurch, which has a runic inscription as well as typical ninth-century Mercian ornament, and two fragments from Chester.

Sculptural remains from the post-Viking period are relatively frequent in the northern part of our area of study, in Staffordshire as well as in Cheshire. A number of Cheshire monuments belong to a class of circle-headed crosses which occur in areas of Viking settlement along the western seaboard between Anglesey and Cumbria, with especially large concentrations in Cumberland, west Cheshire and Flintshire. Three heavily decorated fragments at Neston are contemporary with and related to this class (White 1988). The crosses are called circle-headed because the cross heads are adorned with a connecting ring which forms a continuous circle superimposed over the cross arms. There are regional subgroups within the class, and some of the monuments have been identified as the products of a workshop at St John's Chester. Crosses closely resembling those at St John's have been found at Hilbre and West Kirby in the Wirral (fig. 72).

Another class of crosses, found in east Cheshire, especially near Macclesfield, and elsewhere in the Peak District, in Staffordshire and Derbyshire, is distinguished by their round shafts. The main portion of the shaft is cylindrical with a smaller four-sided section on top. The cross head seldom survives. Staffordshire crosses of this type stand in churchyards at

Figure 71 One of the Sandbach crosses (photograph M. Gelling).

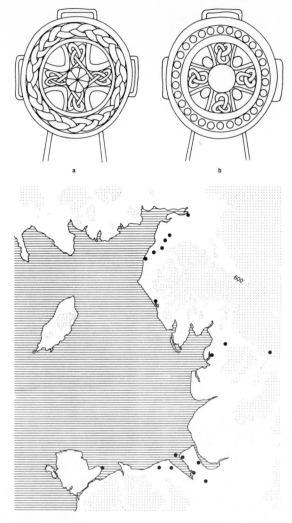

Figure 72   Circle-headed crosses (from Bailey 1990).

Alstonefield, Leek, Ilam, Chebsey and Stoke-on-Trent. In Cheshire, on the other hand, they were erected in open moorland, beside trackways, at crossroads, on boundaries, often in positions of considerable prominence. The site of Cleulow cross in Wincle is at the crossing of the Congleton-Buxton and Macclesfield–Wincle roads, near a township boundary. It stood on a mound and formed a notable landmark at the head of a valley. The site of Greenway cross in Oakenclough is on the edge of the deep valley of Wildboarclough. Crosses of this type sometimes occur in pairs. Their precise function is uncertain, but it is obviously possible that the Cheshire moorland sites are original, and that the Staffordshire monuments have been moved from similar positions to be placed in churchyards.

The most famous Staffordshire sculpture of the pre-Norman period is the

cylindrical column which stands in St Peter's churchyard, Wolverhampton
(Cramp 1975: 187–9). It is considered originally to have carried a cross head.
It is elaborately carved with bands of ornament combining the acanthus-
leaf decoration which is characteristic of the late tenth century with friezes
of birds and beasts pecking fruit in plant scrolls which resemble much
earlier Anglian friezes, particularly those at Breedon in Leicestershire. Some
commentators have dated it to the mid-ninth century, but Professor
Rosemary Cramp prefers to see it as a later work. The choice of interpretation lies between considering it to represent a revival of antique motifs (i.e.
the pecking birds and beasts) in the tenth century, or to be a precocious
ninth-century copy of Carolingian work (which would account for the acan-
thus). If the later date be accepted it is possible to associate the cross with
the founding of a religious house at Wolverhampton by the Lady Wulfrun,
the mother of Wulfric Spott, in the last decade of the tenth century.

Surviving pre-Norman sculpture is rare in Herefordshire and Shropshire,
though there is a piece of a Mercian cross of the eighth or early-ninth
century built into a late wall of the church at Wroxeter. Paradoxically, the
most striking manifestations of Anglo-Saxon, Celtic and Viking art in this
part of the West Midlands date from after 1066, when a school of stone
carving arose in Herefordshire which owes at least as much to pre-Conquest
as to Norman influences. The most famous example is the wonderful
decoration of the Norman church at Kilpeck. In other churches, where the
main fabric is of later date, tympana and fonts survive which are carved in
this style. The font at Chaddesley Corbet in Worcestershire, further east
than most examples, is perhaps the most clearly Anglo-Saxon in inspira-
tion. The dragons, with their gnashing teeth and raised forepaws, are
reminiscent of much earlier animal ornament (fig. 73).[10]

Figure 73   Chaddesley Corbet font (photograph M. Gelling).

11 The Domesday Survey

Domesday Book provides a wealth of information about our region at the end of the Anglo-Saxon period. It has been noted, however, that the Survey does not give a comprehensive list of churches, and this caveat applies also to settlements. Absence of mention in Domesday Book never constitutes evidence that a settlement was not flourishing in 1086. The taxable resources of places of subsidiary status were sometimes reckoned along with those of a central manor, and a total was given for the whole unit without the component parts being named. It is likely, however, that most of what was taxable was accounted for in the Survey in one way or another, and the series of maps which accompany this chapter has been prepared on the basis of that hypothesis.

The potential of Domesday Book for reconstructing the pre- and post-Conquest landscape has been extensively explored, the most systematic studies being those in the Domesday Geography series published between 1952 and 1977 under the general editorship of H.C. Darby. Four of the counties which make up the area of this study are treated in the second volume, *The Domesday Geography of Midland England*, 1954. Cheshire, however, is in the fourth volume, *Northern England*, 1962. In this series the Domesday statistics for plough lands and plough teams, population, areas of woodland and meadow, fisheries and special local resources such as salt are shown on county maps. Some of these items are marked precisely with symbols located at the places named in the Survey, and these include the woodland figures which have been discussed in Chapter 1. The population and plough statistics, however, are shown as densities to the square mile either within hundreds or within arbitrarily drawn divisions of the counties. Although no Domesday statistics can be taken as absolute, they have great value for comparative purposes, enabling major distinctions to be observed, e.g. between areas of more or less woodland and greater or lesser agricultural exploitation.

The first statistic noted for a manor in Domesday Book is regularly the hidage. This is the key to the sum which would be demanded from the estate if a national tax was levied. Figs 74–8 are an attempt to present the hidage figures for our five counties cartographically, on the assumption that there is likely to be some relationship between hidage assessment, area, and quality of land. In order to show such a relationship it is necessary to have areas to match with the statistics of hidage. We cannot put boundary lines round all the manors named in Domesday Book, but parish outlines preserve boundaries which are likely to be of comparable antiquity. The maps in figs 74–8 show ecclesiastical parishes, as mapped by the Institute of Heraldic and Genealogical Studies, and the figures are the total of hidage assessments for all places named in Domesday Book which lie within those parishes. Some parishes (such as Cheadle and Wilmslow in Cheshire) contain no settlement which is named in Domesday, and in these outlines no figure is shown. The taxable resources of such areas can sometimes be assumed to be accounted for in the figures given for neighbouring places. It is important to note, however, that this does not apply to the districts of Ewias and Archenfield in Herefordshire, for which the Domesday returns are incomplete.

Domesday regularly gives the hidage at the date of the survey, in 1086, and as it was 20 years earlier, in the time of King Edward. Where these differ, the pre-Conquest hidage has been used, as it is the late Anglo-Saxon landscape which is under consideration. For non-Scandinavianized parts of the country Domesday reckons mostly in hides and virgates (which are quarter-hides), but some Staffordshire and Cheshire entries give assessments in carucates or bovates, and carucates are also used in some parts of Herefordshire which had not long been under English rule. Domesday arithmetic is notoriously tricky, and it is likely that another reckoner would arrive at totals different in some cases from mine, but it is hoped that the figures given here are sufficiently accurate to convey a valid general picture. Where the Survey mentions a fraction of a hide which is not obviously translatable in terms of virgates a plus or minus sign has been added to the total for that parish. Carucates have been counted as hides. Little attempt has been made to assess errors in the text of the Survey though these may not be infrequent. A possible instance occurs in the account of Barston, Warwickshire, which has three entries. These describe holdings of 10, 9, and half a hide respectively, but commentators think that the 10-hide estate is an accidental duplication, and a query has accordingly been shown against the total on the Warwickshire map.

The parish outlines shown on figs 74-8 are of absorbing interest in their own right, without the correlation with hidage assessments. There is a great variety of size. A parish may be exceptionally large for two contrasting reasons: it may be the area belonging to an outstandingly important settlement, or it may be an area of outstandingly poor land. Leaving aside the parishes which are larger than their neighbours for the first reason (e.g. Stratford and Brailes in Warwickshire, Stottesdon in Shropshire, Leominster in Herefordshire), there is a very marked tendency for parishes to be small in more fertile areas and large in regions of heath, marsh and forest. It is a corollary of this that many small parishes contain settlements for which Domesday Book records a relatively large hidage.

The two halves of Warwickshire provide the expected contrast (fig. 74), with small parishes and large hidages in the south (the Feldon) and the centre (the Avon Valley), and larger, more lightly assessed parishes in the north-west. A number of the north-western parishes, such as Tanworth, Sheldon, Maxstoke and Polesworth, contain no places named in Domesday Book. In some cases the resources of these blank areas were reckoned, not with neighbouring manors, but with places in the Feldon which had outlying wood pastures in Arden. The hidage of the parent manor would, however, only be marginally increased by the woodland. This is clearly demonstrated in the documented relationship between Long Itchington and Arley. There is a surviving charter of 1001, by which Æthelred the Unready grants 25 hides of land at Itchington to a thegn (S 898). There are two sets

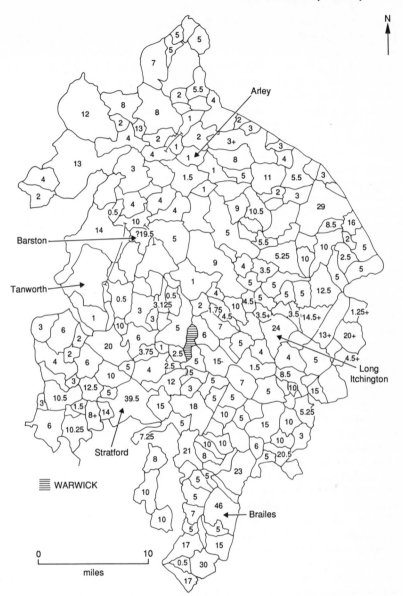

Figure 74 Parishes and Domesday hidages in Warwickshire. (The parish maps in Figs 74-8 are reproduced with permission of the Trustees of the Institute of Heraldic and Genealogical Studies.)

of boundaries, the first of which describes the area of the modern parish of Long Itchington. The second set, introduced by the statement 'and the hide at Arley belongs to Itchington', describes the modern parish of Arley, a land-unit which obviously originated as an outlying woodland pasture. Domesday Book gives a hidage of 24 for Long Itchington and one for Arley, though the area of Arley is about half that of the Feldon parish. This single-hide assessment for a relatively large area contrasts with the ratings in the centre of the county, where the minute parish of Norton Lindsey rates one hide, and the fractionally smaller one of Milverton is assessed at one and three-quarters. Brailes, in the southern tip of the county, is credited with a large quantity of woodland in the Domesday account, without any indication that this is not in the area of the main estate. It is known from later evidence that this woodland was in Tanworth, but although Tanworth is a larger parish than Brailes it is likely that the hidage of the woodland area only amounted to a very small proportion of the 46 hides which is the assessment of Brailes. The low taxation-rating of woodland would not, of course, diminish its value to the farmer as a resource for pasture, building materials and fuel.

Hidages in Staffordshire (fig. 75) are lower than in other West Midland counties. They were so even in the tenth century, and they were drastically lowered between then and 1066. There are only a few surviving Anglo-Saxon charters for the county, and not all of them give estate hidages, but most of the ones which do so name a figure considerably higher than the Domesday one. Madeley, on the Shropshire border, was granted to the Bishop of Winchester in 975 as a three-hide estate (S 801), but in Domesday the two estates in the parish only total one hide and half a virgate. In 985 the Lady Wulfrun was given nine hides at Wolverhampton with one hide at Trescott (in Tettenhall parish), and this looks like an estate with an adjoining piece of pasture land (S 860). Domesday rates Wolverhampton at four-and-a-half hides, Trescott at one virgate. In 966 Wulfric was given three hides at Abbot's Bromley, and a clear boundary clause describes the area of the modern parish (S 878). Three is a small hidage for such an area, but in Domesday Book it is only rated at half a hide. In the same part of the county, however, is Rolleston, which was granted at two-and-a-half hides in 1008 (S 920), and had the same assessment in 1086. Rolleston's rating presumably included the areas of some neighbouring parishes which have no settlements named in Domesday.

The highest Domesday assessment in Staffordshire is for the large parish of Penkridge, where the 14 estates named total 18 hides and one virgate. Adjoining parishes of similar size, such as Brewood (eight) and Cannock (two) have much lower assessments, as do the large areas of Eccleshall (seven) and Stone (seven-and-a-quarter). These low assessments may in some cases be accounted for by the woodland, moorland or heathland nature of the areas. This consideration accounts for Cannock, but Stone and Eccleshall are not obviously disadvantaged as compared with Penkridge; and Barlaston, which adjoins Stone and has been noted above as a typical open-field parish, is only rated at half a hide. The low hidation of Stafford-shire, the ancient heartland of Mercia, is an as yet unexplained phenomenon. For the great moorland parishes of the northern tip the

Figure 75 Parishes and Domesday hidages in Staffordshire.

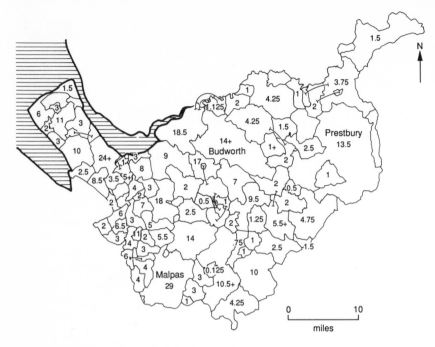

Figure 76   Parishes and Domesday hidages in Cheshire.

assessments - mostly in fractions of hides - are appropriate, but many places in the county are very lightly assessed compared with similar estates elsewhere. A large number of Staffordshire manors are recorded as 'waste' in 1086, but this devastation, which was mostly due to post-Conquest events, does not affect the hidage.

The low hidages of the eastern part of Cheshire (fig. 76) are explicable in terms of landscape: the Pennines and the Pennine slopes were largely moorland and woodland. In north-central Cheshire there was a good deal of marsh and heath. In this area the enormous parish of Budworth, with its relatively low assessment of 14 hides, is dotted with -heath and -moss names on the modern map, and must also have contained a good deal of woodland, attested by names in -ley. Arley in Budworth (like its Warwickshire namesake) may fairly be translated 'clearing on the edge of which eagles nest', and this suggests an undeveloped countryside at the time of the change to English speech. In the western parts of Cheshire hidages are larger in relation to area. The Wirral is the most highly assessed region of the county, apart from its northern tip where the Scandinavian names are concentrated. Small parishes with high assessments are found in the area round Chester.

Small parishes rated at between one and five hides are particularly characteristic of Shropshire (fig. 77), and it is likely that in many cases these small units were once parts of large multiple estates. Places which were nuclei of such estates can sometimes be distinguished by their central positions - Stottesdon and Diddlebury, for instance, both surrounded by

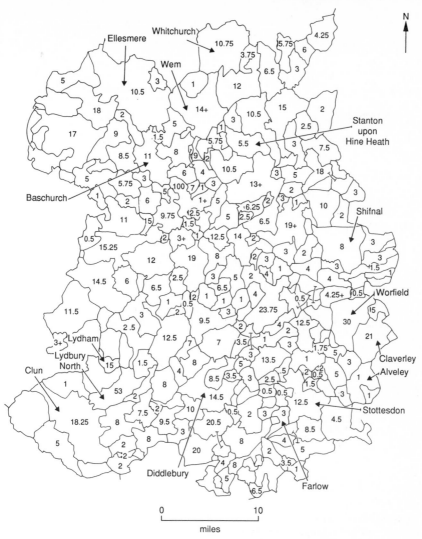

Figure 77 Parishes and Domesday hidages in Shropshire.

smaller parishes which are contiguous with them. Some large parishes, however, such as Worfield and Claverley in the east of the county, look like multiple estates which were not broken up. Both parishes contain numerous subsidiary settlements, and the hidages (30 and 21) are exceptions to the usual rule that woodland areas were lightly assessed.

Even in the least fertile parts of Shropshire there are no instances of large areas with the minute assessments characteristic of the Staffordshire moorlands. Baschurch, Ellesmere, Wem and Whitchurch are large parishes in sandy and marshy land, but they are all rated at more than 10 hides. Stanton-upon-Hine Heath, with 5½ hides, presents a contrast to Cannock in Staffordshire, which is a much larger heathland parish assessed at only

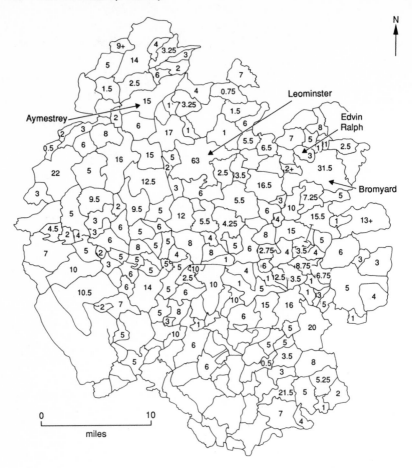

Figure 78   Parishes and Domesday hidages in Herefordshire.

2 hides. Marsh (as in the Weald Moor parishes), mountains (as in Clun), and sometimes woodland (as in Alveley and Shifnal), have caused a relatively low hidage/area ratio, but it is noteworthy that the 18¼-hide assessment for Clun is the same as that for Penkridge, a much better situated Staffordshire parish of similar size. There are fewer blank spaces on the Shropshire map than on the Staffordshire one.

The 100 hides which are stated to be 'accounted in the City's tax' in an entry relating to Shrewsbury cannot be seen as an assessment based on agricultural resources. Leaving that aside, the largest Shropshire assessment is for Lydbury North, where the Bishop of Hereford's 53-hide manor was the subject of a single entry. As noted above (p. 159) this place is a possible candidate for the original site of the bishopric. It must certainly have been a prosperous estate. In 1086 32½ of the hides were waste, but at some time before the Conquest the manor must have been able to bear this heavy burden of taxation. Some surrounding land-units are not named in

Domesday Book, and Lydbury North certainly included Bishop's Castle, but even so the hidage/area ratio is very high. The nearby small unit of Lydham was rated at 15 hides, which is also surprisingly high.

Leominster (fig. 78), with its dominating position in the area of Herefordshire which the *Domesday Geography* calls the Central Plain, is an excellent example of a large land-unit surrounded by smaller units which were obviously split off from the original area. The Domesday description of the pre- and post-Conquest manors reads:

LEOMINSTER. Queen Edith held it, with 16 members: LUSTON, YARPOLE, AYMESTREY, BRIMFIELD, ASHTON, STOCKTON, STOKE (Prior), MARSTON (Stannett), UPTON, (Miles) HOPE, BRIERLEY, IVINGTON, CHOLSTREY, LEINTHALL, EDWYN (Ralph) and FARLOW.

In this manor, with these members, were 80 hides. In lordship 30 ploughs.

There were 8 reeves, 8 beadles, 8 riding men, 238 villagers, 75 smallholders and 82 slaves, male and female; altogether they had 230 ploughs.

The villagers ploughed 140 acres of the lord's land and sowed it with their own wheat seed. They gave £11 and 52d in customary dues. The riding men gave 14s 4d and 3 sesters of honey.

There were 8 mills at 73s and 30 sticks of eels; the woodland paid 24s and pasture dues.

In this manor the King now has in lordship 60 hides, 29 ploughs and 6 priests, 6 riders, 7 reeves, 7 beadles, 224 villagers, 81 smallholders and 25 slaves, male and female; between them they have 201 ploughs. These men plough and sow 125 acres with their own wheat.

In customary dues they give £7 14s 8½d, 17s for fish, 8s for salt and 65s from honey.

8 mills at 108s and 100 sticks of eels, less 10; woodland 6 leagues long and 3 leagues wide which pays 22s. From these, 5s are given for buying timber in Droitwich, and 30 measures of salt are had from there. Each villager who has 10 pigs gives 1 pig in pasture dues.

From cleared woodland comes 17s 4d. A hawk's eyrie there.

To this manor Hugh Donkey pays 5s; Roger of Lacy 6s 8d; Ralph of Mortimer 15s; Bernard Beard 5s; Ilbert 5s; Osbern 6s 8d; Godmund 5s; Godwin 40d; Alfward 40d; Saemar 40d; Widard 3s; Alfward 30d; Brictmer 20d; Alfward 20d.

In all these payments £23 2s are reckoned, besides the eels.

This manor is at a revenue of £60, besides the supplies of the nuns. The County states that if it were (properly) valued this manor could be assessed at six times £20, that is £120.

Of the 80 hides of this manor Urso of Abetot holds 3 hides in EDWYN (Ralph); Roger of Lacy 3½ hides in HUMBER and 1½ hides in BROCKMANTON; Ralph of Mortimer 1 hide in AYMESTREY and 8 hides in LEINTHALL which pay tax; William

son of Norman ½ hide in LYE and 1 hide in EYTON. In these, 3 ploughs in lordship; 11 villagers, 22 smallholders and 2 priests; between them they have 10 ploughs; 16 slaves.
2 mills at 24s. At Leinthall woodland 1 league long and 1 league wide.
In total, value of these lands £12 11s.
Leofwin Latimer holds as much land in Leominster as is worth 25s.
St. Peter's has 15s from Ralph of Mortimer's land in Aymestrey.
Before 1066 two manors, Stanford and (Much) Marcle, belonged to this manor; they now pay £30 to the King, as stated above.[1]

Two of the places named as 'members' of this great manor are outliers. These are Farlow, which is in Shropshire some 16 miles north-east of Leominster, and Edvin (or Edwyn) Ralph, which is 9 miles east. Farlow is on the edge of the massif of Clee Hill, and land there would provide hill pasture. Edvin means 'Gedda's fen', and land there would be outlying meadow. Stanford and Much Marcle, which had belonged to the manor before the Conquest, lie in heavily wooded country east and south of Edvin.

The woodland retained by Leominster in 1086 is likely to have lain in the western and southern extremities of the area of the manor. It is possible that the simplex name Lye means 'the wood', constituting a name for an area of woodland which served a number of manors. Upper and Lower Lye are hamlets, a mile apart, in the parish of Aymestrey. They are seven-and-a-half miles north-west of Leominster. There are six entries for Lye in Domesday, one of which (quoted above) is for a half-hide holding which has been split off from Leominster. There were two other half-hide holdings in 1086, also one of three hides and one of one hide. An entry repeated after two of the holdings says that Ralph Mortimer holds '57 acres and all the woodland in Gruffydd's manor of Lye'. The wood was presumably being broken up for arable use in the late eleventh century. This is still a well-wooded area, and there are some other woodland names, but it should be noted that some names which now end in -ley do not contain *lēah*. Wapley and Shirley (both near Lye) are *hlith* names, this being a term for a concave hillside. Gatley in Leinthall Earls is another *hlith* name.

Leominster is a magnificent example of a multiple estate still surviving in 1066. Most modern historians would probably consider it likely to have been a pre-English entity, taken over by the Mercian-backed rulers of the Magonsæte in the mid-seventh century, but perhaps having its origins in the Iron Age, before the Roman period. In the terms in which early medieval historians are thinking at the present time it could be considered large enough to have once been a kingdom in its own right in the post-Roman period. There is, however, nothing comparable to Leominster in the rest of the Herefordshire Domesday. Bromyard has the next highest assessment, 31½ hides. Bromyard certainly contained a number of subsidiary settlements, but these are not named, and the account gives little indication of the complex organization necessary to the management of such an estate, though there was a reeve among the inhabitants. Two priests are mentioned, appropriate to the minster church, which is named in a surviving charter of 840–52 (S 1270).

Epilogue

The preceding chapters have considered the origins of western Mercia and charted the additions to its post-Roman landscape through the centuries up to the coming of Norman rule. The transformation of the place-names which caused Welsh toponyms to be replaced by English is perhaps the most dramatic of all. Over much of the region, however, the population must have been mainly of Welsh stock, irrespective of whether they were speaking English or continuing to use Welsh as they did in Archenfield.

The union of the western part of the area (apart from Archenfield) with the greater Mercian kingdom took place in the first half of the seventh century, under the last pagan king of Mercia. Because it became part of Mercia, permanent Christianity there was established in the Roman, rather than the Celtic tradition, though it is likely that British Christian traditions lingered on to influence the physical nature of churchyards.

Patterns of settlement may have remained largely as they were in pre-English times, except in the southern half of Warwickshire, where there was a wholesale landscape reorganization, probably in the tenth century.

The building of Offa's Dyke could only have been achieved with the active consent of the people living along its course. This implies that whatever their ethnic origins people in the west of our region wished to have their cattle protected from raids by Welshmen of other political allegiances. The people of Archenfield, though more unequivocally Welsh, were probably of the same mind about this, and they may have undertaken to keep non-Mercian Welshmen out of the area south of Hereford where the Dyke appears not to have been built.

The major catastrophe of the Danish invasion in the second half of the ninth century is not likely to have had a radical effect on settlement patterns in the West Midlands, except in so far as the coming of open-field farming and nucleated villages in south Warwickshire can be considered partly due to the stimulus of heavy Danish infiltration into the East Midlands. In the West Midlands, place-names only attest the presence of a few Danish farmers in north Staffordshire and east Warwickshire. There were Norwegian settlers, perhaps colonists, in the Wirral at a slightly later date, but their presence was not widespread in Cheshire. The main effect of the Danish wars on the region was to bring about a total transformation of its administrative geography. Military centres were selected, some of which became shire towns, and the shire outlines were probably drawn at this time.

Despite the administrative importance of the new shire centres, Chester was the only town to achieve major economic significance as the hub of a network of long-distance trade routes. Otherwise the economy of the West Midlands was probably largely self-sufficient except for salt. The salt trade of the inland centres in Worcestershire and Cheshire was organized on curiously archaic and static lines.

The Norman Conquest was to bring a new aristocracy, but there was probably little change in the life of the people until the castles were built. Castles were indeed major additions to the landscape. Sometimes, as at Oswestry, they caused a shift in the settlement pattern of an estate. When they were built in shire towns they did considerable violence to the late Anglo-Saxon street layout. The building, upkeep and provisioning of these castles must have affected the lives of many people. The next major change was to be the plantation of numerous new trading-centres, which began at the end of the eleventh century and continued throughout the twelfth and thirteenth. Castles and the post-Norman-Conquest boroughs were the major medieval additions to the landscape which lie beyond the scope of the present study.

Much remains obscure and mysterious in the history of the early Middle Ages, but by constant sifting and re-examination of the available evidence progress continues to be made on the elucidation of the main outlines. It is hoped that the synthesis offered here is both a fair representation of recent work in this part of England, and an advance, particularly in its analysis of local toponymy, on earlier accounts.

Abbreviations

Sources

AC	*Annales Cambriae*, in J. Morris, *Nennius: British History and the Welsh Annals*, London and Chichester 1980.
ASC	*Anglo-Saxon Chronicle*, tr. and ed. D. Whitelock with D.C. Douglas and S.I. Tucker, London 1961.
DB	Domesday Book, see p. 200n.
HB	*Historia Brittonum*, tr. and ed. J. Morris, *Nennius* 1980.
HE	*Bede's Ecclesiastical History of the English People*, ed. B. Colgrave and R.A.B. Mynors, Oxford 1969.
Leland	*Leland's Itinerary in England and Wales*, ed. Lucy Toulmin Smith, London 1907-19, reprinted 1964.
S	P.H. Sawyer, *Anglo-Saxon Charters: An Annotated List and Bibliography*, London 1968.

Journals and Series

AntiqJ	*Antiquaries Journal*
ArchJ	*Archaeological Journal*
ASE	*Anglo-Saxon England*
BAR	British Archaeological Reports, British Series
BBCS	*Bulletin of the Board of Celtic Studies*
BNJ	*British Numismatic Journal*
CBA	Council for British Archaeology
EHR	*English Historical Review*
EPNS	English Place-Name Society
JBAA	*Journal of the British Archaeological Association*
JEPNS	*Journal of the English Place-Name Society*
MedArch	*Medieval Archaeology*
N.S.	New Series
TBWAS	*Transactions of the Birmingham and Warwickshire Archaeological Society*
TLCAS	*Transactions of the Lancashire and Cheshire Antiquarian Society*
TRHS	*Transactions of the Royal Historical Society*
TSAS	*Transactions of the Shropshire Archaeological Society*
TSSAHS	*Transactions of the South Staffordshire Archaeological and Historical Society*
VCH	Victoria County History

Notes

3 Anglo-Saxon Archaeology

1. Some information about the Wasperton cemetery is now available in *Current Archaeology* 126 (October 1991), pp. 256-9.

5 The Reign of Penda in Welsh Literature and English History

1. Cf. e.g. Hooke 1986: 13-15, postulating a quick change of alliance by Cynddylan after 642, and Kirby 1977: 35-8, ascribing the Mercian conquest to Penda's successor.
2. N. Brooks (1989: 163-4) discusses the recurrence in West Midland place-names of personal names which appear in the Mercian royal genealogy. He concludes that references to *Creoda* (Credenhill, Herefs. and Wilts., Curbridge, Oxon., Curdworth, Warwicks., Kersoe and *Creodan ac*, Worcs.), and *Penda* (Penley, Flints., Pinbury, Gloucs., Peddimore, Warwicks. and Pinvin and *Pendiford*, Worcs.) show that these personal names had a unique popularity in this area and that these place-names probably commemorate members of the Mercian dynasty indirectly.
3. Detailed documentation about the Shropshire place-names is now available in Gelling 1990.

6 Church and State in the Second Half of the Seventh Century

1. This occurs in an account of a vision seen by the monk. A recent examination of the story (Sims-Williams 1990: ch. 9) concludes that the vision happened in 715 or 716, and Boniface's letter about it must have been written before the spring of 719.

8 The Danish Wars and the Formation of the Shires

1. *Cwat-* in *Cwatbrycg* is a district-name of obscure etymology from which Quatt and Quatford are also derived. The name became simply *Brycg* before the end of the Anglo-Saxon period, and the affix *-north* was added in the thirteenth century, probably to distinguish this place from several others called 'Bridge' further south. See Gelling 1990: 56-9.
2. The *regiones* of part of the West Midland region are discussed in detail in Gelling 1982b: 67-71.
3. The class of names in which *trēow* is combined with a dithematic personal name is discussed in Gelling 1984: 211-18.

9 Towns and Trade

1. A convenient summary of the evidence for these trading settlements can be found in Tatton-Brown 1986: 24.
2. The principal excavators were F.T. Wainwright, J. Gould, K. Sheridan and P. Rahtz. The reports were published in the *Transactions of the Lichfield and South Staffs. Historical and Archaeological Society*. Papers which are especially relevant to the origins of Tamworth are to be found in vols IX (1967-8), X (1968-9), XIV

(1972-3) and XVI (1974-5). Vol. XIII (1971-2) contains the account of the pre-Conquest mill from which fig. 56 is taken.

3. Old English *hȳth* is the term used in place-names for inland ports, v. Gelling 1984: 76-8.
4. In a lecture at Oxford in December 1984.
5. There was a tradition of a previous burial at Lichfield, in a ceremony performed by the contemporary archbishop, Hygeberht. This was followed by the disappearance of the body and its miraculous discovery, after which it was transferred to Hereford (Matthew Paris, *Historia Major*, ed. W. Wats, 1684, p. 982).
6. Blunt (1974: 99) says this is 'an unexpectedly large number'.
7. M. Beresford discusses *Francheville* Isle of Wight in *Medieval Archaeology* 3 (1959) pp. 202ff. It was founded in 1256. The Shropshire 'free town' must have been earlier, since it is referred to in the early thirteenth century.
8. D.J.P. Mason's excavation report on the Bridge Street site includes a full discussion of the ways in which the rather sparse evidence for the Æthelflædan defences might be interpreted (Mason 1985: 36-9).

10 The Late Anglo-Saxon Landscape

1. Information in this paragraph is taken from *The Victoria History of Shropshire*, vol. VIII (Condover and Ford Hundreds), 1968, and *The Victoria History of the County of Stafford*, vol. XX (part of Seisdon Hundred), 1984.
2. *The Cartulary of Haughmond Abbey*, ed. U. Rees (Cardiff 1985), contains deeds relating to Leebotwood in the second half of the twelfth century. These reveal a vigorous policy of assarting (i.e. making clearings in woodland for the purpose of cultivation).
3. M.C. Hill in *The Demesne and the Waste* (*TSAS* 62, 1984) gives a detailed account of the expansion of arable in High Ercall.
4. *The Victoria History of Shropshire*, vol. IV (Agriculture), 1989, p. 170.
5. This development is set out by J. Blair (1988: 1). He says that it is widely accepted in its main lines.
6. Kemp 1968 is an early, probably unsurpassed, essay. T. Slater's claim for All Saints, Warwick is noted in Chapter 9. A collection of recent studies is to be found in *Minsters and Parish Churches: The Local Church in Transition*, ed. J. Blair, Oxford 1988. This includes a paper on minsters in south-east Shropshire by J. Croom and one on Leominster by B. Kemp.
7. R. Morris (1989: 149) considers that the origins of local church-building go back to the second half of the ninth century, and that such churches had become common by the second half of the tenth century.
8. The late H.D.G. Foxall produced a series of maps on which the Shropshire Tithe Maps were redrawn to a uniform scale of 6" to the mile, with the field-names from the schedules written on the fields. These were prepared for the *Victoria History of Shropshire*, but copies are available without restriction. I had the privilege of acquiring each one as it was produced.
9. This material is described and discussed in Thacker 1987: 275-81, and the following account is based on that discussion.
10. There is a list of churches in the Welsh Marches where examples of the Herefordshire school of carving can be seen, and a discussion of the style, in Taylor, H.M. and J., 1963: 235-45.

11 The Domesday Survey

1. The translation quoted here is that in the edition of Domesday Book published by Messrs Phillimore under the general editorship of J. Morris. The volumes of the five counties of this study are: Warwickshire 23 (1976), Staffordshire 24 (1976), Cheshire 26 (1978), Shropshire 25 (1986), Herefordshire 17 (1983).

References

Adkins, R.A. and Petchey, M.R. (1984) 'Secklow hundred mound and other meeting place mounds in England', *ArchJ* 141, 243-51.

Alcock, L. (1971) *Arthur's Britain*, London.

Bailey, R.N. (1980) *Viking Age Sculpture*, London.

Barker, P. (ed.) (1981) *Wroxeter Roman City Excavations 1966-1980*, London.

Bassett, S. (ed.) (1989) *The Origins of Anglo-Saxon Kingdoms*, Leicester.

Bateson, Mary (1899) 'Origin and early history of double monasteries', *TRHS* N.S. 13, 137-98.

Biddle, M. and Kjølbye-Biddle, Birthe (1988) 'The churches of Much Wenlock', *JBAA* 141, 179-81.

Birch, W. de Gray (ed.) (1892) *Liber Vitae: Register and Martyrology of New Minster and Hyde Abbey*, Hampshire Record Society.

Blair, J. (1985) 'Secular minster churches in Domesday Book', in *Domesday-Book: A Reassessment*, ed. P. Sawyer, London, 104-42.

⸺ (1988) 'Introduction: from minster to parish church', in *Minsters and Parish Churches: The Local Church in Transition 950-1200*, ed. J. Blair, Oxford, 1-19.

Blunt, C. (1974) 'The coinage of Athelstan, 924-939: a survey', *BNJ* 42, 61-155.

Bonney, D.J. (1972) 'Early boundaries in Wessex', in *Archaeology and the Landscape: Essays for L.V. Grinsell*, ed. P.J. Fowler, London, 168-86.

Brooks, N. (1984) *The Early History of the Church of Canterbury: Christ Church from 597 to 1066*, Leicester.

⸺ (1989) 'The formation of the Mercian kingdom', in Bassett 1989, 159-70.

Brooks, N., Gelling, M. and Johnson, D. (1984) 'A new charter of King Edgar', *ASE* 13, 137-55.

Bullough, D. and Rahtz, P. (1977) 'The parts of an Anglo-Saxon mill', *ASE* 6, 15-37.

Cameron, K. (1965) *Scandinavian Settlement in the Territory of the Five Boroughs: The Place-name Evidence*, Nottingham. Reprinted in *Place-name Evidence for the Anglo-Saxon Invasion and Scandinavian Settlements*, EPNS 1975, 115-38.

⸺ (1968) 'Eccles in English place-names', in *Christianity in Britain 300-700*, ed. M.W. Barley and R.P.C. Hanson, Leicester, 87-92.

⸺ (1976) *The Significance of English Place-names*, Sir Israel Gollancz Memorial Lecture, British Academy, printed separately and in *Proceedings of the British Academy* 62, 135-55.

⸺ (1980) 'The meaning and significance of Old English *walh* in English place-names', *JEPNS* 12, 1-53.

Campbell, J. (1979) 'Bede's words for places', in *Names, Words and Graves; Early Medieval Settlement*, ed. P.H. Sawyer, Leeds, 34-51.

⸺ (1979b) 'The church in Anglo-Saxon towns', in *The Church in Town and Countryside*, ed. D. Baker, Oxford, 119-35.

⸺ (ed.) (1982) *The Anglo-Saxons*, Oxford.

Carver, M. (1978) 'Early Shrewsbury: an archaeological definition in 1975', *TSAS* 59, Part 3 (1973/4), 225-63.

Chadwick, Nora (1953) 'The conversion of Northumbria', in N. Chadwick *et al.*, *Celt and Saxon*, Cambridge, 138-66.

Charles, B.G. (1938) *Non-Celtic Place-names in Wales*, London.

Clark, Cecily (ed.) (1970) *The Peterborough Chronicle* (2nd edn), Oxford.

Coates, R. (1988) *Toponymic Topics: Essays on the Early Toponymy of the British Isles*, Brighton.

Cole, Ann (1985) 'Topography, hydrology and place-names in the chalklands of southern England: *funta*, *æwiell* and *æwielm*', *Nomina* 9, 3-19.

Colgrave, B. and Mynors, R.A.B. (eds) (1969) *Bede's Ecclesiastical History of the*

English People, Oxford.
Coplestone-Crow, B. (1989) *Herefordshire Place-Names*, BAR 214.
Cox, B. (1976) 'The place-names of the earliest English records', *JEPNS* 8, 12-66.
Cramp, Rosemary (1975) 'Anglo-Saxon sculpture of the reform period', in *Tenth-Century Studies*, ed. D. Parsons, Chichester, 184-200.
Crawford, Barbara E. (1987) *Scandinavian Scotland*, Leicester.
Croom, Jane (1988) 'The fragmentation of the minster *parochiae* of south-east Shropshire', in *Minsters and Parish Churches*, ed. J. Blair, Oxford, 67-83.
Darby, H.C. and Terrett, L.B. (eds) (1954) *The Domesday Geography of Midland England*, Cambridge.
Darby, H.C. and Maxwell, I.S. (eds) (1962) *The Domesday Geography of Northern England*, Cambridge.
Davies, Wendy (1977) 'Annals and the origin of Mercia', in Dornier 1977, 17-29.
—— (1979) *The Llandaff Charters*, Aberystwyth.
—— (1982) *Wales in the Early Middle Ages*, Leicester.
Davis, R.H.C. (1976) *The Early History of Coventry*, Dugdale Society Occasional Papers no. 24.
—— (1982) 'Alfred and Guthrum's frontier', *EHR* 97, 803-10.
Dodgson, J. McN. (1970) *The Place-names of Cheshire*, Part 1, EPNS 44.
—— (1971) *The Place-names of Cheshire*, Part 3, EPNS 46.
—— (1981) *The Place-names of Cheshire*, Part 5(i), EPNS 48.
Dornier, Ann (ed.) (1977) *Mercian Studies*, Leicester.
—— (1987) 'Place-names in (-)wich: a preliminary linguistic survey', *Nomina* 11, 87-98.
Dudley Stamp, L. (1946) *Britain's Structure and Scenery*, London.
Dumville, D. (1977) 'Palaeographical considerations in the dating of early Welsh verse', *BBCS* 27, Part 2, 246-51.
—— (1977b) 'Kingship, genealogies and regnal lists', in *Early Medieval Kingship*, ed. P.H. Sawyer and I.N. Wood, Leeds, 72-104.
—— (1989) 'The Tribal Hidage: an introduction to its texts and their history', in Bassett 1989, 225-30.
Dyer, C. (1980) *Lords and Peasants in a changing Society: The Estates of the Bishopric of Worcester, 650-1540*, Cambridge
—— (1985) 'Towns and cottages in eleventh-century England', in *Studies in Medieval History presented to R.H.C. Davis*, ed. H. Mayr-Harting and R.I. Moore, London, 91-106.
Ekwall, E. (1922) *The Place-names of Lancashire*, Manchester.
—— (1928) *English-River-names*, Oxford.
—— (1960) *The Concise Oxford Dictionary of English Place-names* (4th edn), Oxford.
Esmonde Cleary, A.S. (1989) *The Ending of Roman Britain*, London.
Faull, Margaret (1975) 'The semantic development of Old English *wealh*', *Leeds Studies in English* 8, 20-44.
Fellows-Jensen, Gillian (1978) *Scandinavian Settlement Names in the East Midlands*, Copenhagen.
—— (1985) *Scandinavian Settlement Names in the North West*, Copenhagen.
Finberg, H.P.R. (1964) *Lucerna*, London.
—— (1972) *The Early Charters of the West Midlands*, Leicester.
Ford, W.J. (1976) 'Some settlement patterns in the central region of the Warwickshire Avon', in *Medieval Settlement*, ed. P.H. Sawyer, London, 274-94.
Fox, C. (1955) *Offa's Dyke*, London.
Fox, H.S.A. (1981) 'Approaches to the adoption of the Midland system', in Rowley 1981, 64-111.
Gelling, Margaret (1961) 'Place-names and Anglo-Saxon paganism', *Univ. of Birmingham Historical Journal* 8(i), 7-25.
—— (1970) English entries in M. Gelling, W.H.F. Nicolaisen and M. Richards, *The Names of Towns and Cities in Britain*, London.
—— (1974) 'Some notes on Warwickshire place-names', *TBWAS* 86, 59-79.
—— (1976) *The Place Names of Berkshire*, Part 3, EPNS 51.

────── (1978) *Signposts to the Past: Place-names and the History of England*, London.
────── (1982) 'The -*inghope* names of the Welsh Marches', *Nomina* 6, 31-6.
────── (1982b) 'The place-name volumes for Worcestershire and Warwickshire: a new look', in *Field and Forest*, ed. T.R. Slater and P.J. Jarvis, Norwich.
────── (1982c) 'Some meanings of *stōw*', in *The Early Church in Western Britain and Ireland*, ed. S.M. Pearce, BAR 102, 187-96.
────── (1984) *Place-names in the Landscape*, London.
────── (1987) 'Anglo-Saxon eagles', *Leeds Studies in English* 18, 173-81.
────── (1988) *Signposts to the Past* ... (2nd edn), Chichester.
────── (1989) 'The place-name Burton and variants', in *Weapons and Warfare in Anglo-Saxon England*, ed. S.C. Hawkes, Oxford, 145-53.
────── (1990) *The Place-names of Shropshire*, Part 1, EPNS 62/3.
Gould, J. (1969) 'Third report of the excavations at Tamworth, Staffs. 1968 ...', *TSSAHS* 10, 32-42.
────── (1973) 'Letocetum, Christianity and Lichfield (Staffs.)', *TSSAHS* 14, 30-1.
Gray, H.L. (1915) *English Field Systems*, Harvard.
Hill, D. (1974) 'Offa's and Wat's Dykes - some exploratory work on the frontier between Celt and Saxon', in *Anglo-Saxon Settlement and Landscape*, ed. T. Rowley, BAR 6, 102-7.
────── (1977) 'Offa's and Wat's Dykes: some aspects of recent work', *TLCAS* 79, 21-33.
Hines, J. (1984) *The Scandinavian Character of Anglian England in the pre-Viking Period*, BAR 124.
Holt, R. (1988) *The Mills of Medieval England*, Oxford.
Hooke, Della (1980-1) 'Burial features in West Midland charters', *JEPNS* 13, 1-40.
────── (1981) 'The Droitwich salt industry: an examination of the West Midland charter evidence', *Anglo-Saxon Studies in Archaeology and History* 2 (BAR 92), 123-69.
────── (1985) *The Anglo-Saxon Landscape: The Kingdom of the Hwicce*, Manchester.
────── (1986) *Anglo-Saxon Territorial Organisation: The Western Margins of Mercia*, Univ. of Birmingham Dept. of Geography Occasional Publ. 22.
Insley, J. (1985) 'Some Scandinavian personal names in south-west England from post-Conquest records', *Studia Anthroponymica Scandinavica* 3, 23-58.
Jackson, K.H. (1953) *Language and History in Early Britain*, Edinburgh.
Kemp, B.R. (1968) 'The mother church of Thatcham', *Berkshire Archaeological Journal* 63, 15-22.
────── (1988) 'Some aspects of the parochia of Leominster in the 12th century', in *Minsters and Parish Churches*, ed. J. Blair, 83-97.
Keynes, S. and Lapidge, M. (1983) *Alfred the Great*, Harmondsworth.
Kirby, D.P. (1977) 'Welsh bards and the border', in *Dornier 1977*, 31-42.
Leeds, E.T. (1936) *Early Anglo-Saxon Art and Archaeology*, Oxford.
────── (1945) 'The distribution of the Angles and Saxons archaeologically considered', *Archaeologia* 91.
────── (1949) *A Corpus of Early Anglo-Saxon Great Square-Headed Brooches*, Oxford.
Lloyd-Jones, J. (1927) 'Rhai geiriau benthyg o'r Lladin', *BBCS* 2, 297-8.
Losco-Bradley, S. (1977) 'Catholme', *Current Archaeology* 5, no. 59, 358-64.
Mason, D.J.P. (1985) *Excavations at Chester, 26-42 Lower Bridge Street 1974-6, The Dark Age and Saxon Periods*, Chester.
Metcalf, D.M. (1978) 'The ranking of boroughs: numismatic evidence from the reign of Æthelred II', in *Ethelred the Unready: Papers from the Millenary Conference*, ed. D. Hill, BAR 59, 159-201.
────── (1982) 'Anglo-Saxon coins 2: Alfred to Edgar', in *Campbell 1982*, 130-1.
Moffett, C. (1990) 'The Anglo-Saxon church of St Andrew at Wroxeter', in *From Roman Viroconium to Medieval Wroxeter*, ed. P. Barker, Worcester, 8-9.
Morris, R. (1989) *Churches in the Landscape*, London.
Musson, C.R. and Spurgeon, C.J. (1988) 'Cwrt Llechrhyd, Llanelwedd: an unusual moated site in central Powys', *MedArch* 32, 97-109.

Myres, J.N.L. (1986) *The English Settlements*, Oxford.
Nash-Williams, V.E. (1950) *The Early Christian Monuments of Wales*, Cardiff.
Noble, F. (1983) *Offa's Dyke Reviewed*, BAR 114.
Orwin, C.S. and Orwin, C.S. (1938) *The Open Fields*, Oxford (3rd edn 1967).
O'Sullivan, Deirdre (1980) 'Curvilinear churchyards in Cumbria', *Bulletin of the CBA Churches Committee* 13, 3-5.
—— (1985) 'Cumbria before the Vikings: a review of some "Dark Age" problems in north-west England', in *The Scandinavian in Cumbria*, ed. J.R. Baldwin and I.D. Whyte, Edinburgh, 17-35.
Palliser, D.M. (1976) *The Staffordshire Landscape*, London.
Pearce, Susan M. (1978) *The Kingdom of Dumnonia: Studies in History and Tradition in South-Western Britain AD 350-1150*, Padstow.
Pierce, G.O. (1968) *The Place-names of Dinas Powys Hundred*, Cardiff.
Pretty, Kate (1989) 'Defining the Magonsæte', in Bassett 1989, 171-83.
Rees, Una (1975) *The Cartulary of Shrewsbury Abbey*, ed. Una Rees, 2 vols, Aberystwyth.
Rivet, A.L.F. and Smith, C. (1979) *The Place-names of Roman Britain*, London.
Robertson, A.J. (1939) *Anglo-Saxon-Charters*, Cambridge.
Rollason, D. (1982) *The Mildrith Legend: A Study in Medieval Hagiography in England*, Leicester.
Rowland, Jenny (1990) *Early Welsh Saga Poetry: Study and Edition of the Englynion*, Woodbridge.
Rowley, T. (ed.) (1981) *The Origins of Open Field Agriculture*, London.
Rylatt, Margaret and Gooder, A. and E. (1977) *Coventry Archaeology and Redevelopment*, Coventry.
Salin, B. (1904) *Die Altgermanische Thierornamentik*, Stockholm.
Salway, P. (1981) *Roman Britain*, Oxford.
Sawyer, P.H. (1974) 'Anglo-Saxon settlement: the documentary evidence', in *Anglo-Saxon Settlement and Landscape*, ed. T. Rowley, BAR 6, 108-19.
—— (1977) 'Kings and merchants', in *Early Medieval Kingship*, ed. P.H. Sawyer and I.N. Woods, Leeds, 139-58.
Shoesmith, R. (1982) *Hereford City Excavations Vol. 2*, CBA Research Report 46.
Sims-Williams, P. (1990) *Religion and Literature in Western England 600-800*, Cambridge.
Skipp, V. (1970) *Medieval Yardley*, Chichester.
—— (1982) 'The evolution of settlement and open-field topography in north Arden down to 1300', in Rowley 1981, 162-83.
Slater, T.R. (1983) 'The origins of Warwick', *Midland History* 8, 1-13.
—— (1985) 'The topography and planning of medieval Lichfield: a critique', *TSSAHS* 26, 11-35.
Smith, A.H. (1964) *The Place-names of Gloucestershire*, Part 3, EPNS 40.
Smith, R.A. (1908) 'Anglo-Saxon remains', VCH Staffordshire I, 199-215.
Stafford, Pauline (1985) *The East Midlands in the Early Middle Ages*, Leicester.
Stanford, S.C. (1980) *The Archaeology of the Welsh Marches*, London.
Stenton, F.M. (1943) *Anglo-Saxon England*, Oxford.
—— (1955) 'Foreword' in Fox, C., 1955.
—— (1970) *Preparatory to Anglo-Saxon England, Being the Collected Papers of Frank Merry Stenton*, ed. Doris Mary Stenton, Oxford.
—— (1971) Third edition of Stenton 1943.
Tatton-Brown, T. (1986) 'The topography of Anglo-Saxon London', *Antiquity* 60, 21-7.
Taylor, C.C. (1969) 'The origins of Lichfield, Staffs', *TSSAHS* 10, 43-52.
—— (1983) *Village and Farmstead. A History of Rural Settlement in England*, London.
Taylor, C.S. (1957) 'The origin of the Mercian shires', in *Gloucestershire Studies*, ed. H.P.R. Finberg, Leicester, 17-51.
Taylor, H.M. and Taylor, J. (1963) 'Pre-Norman churches of the Border', in N. Chadwick *et al.*, *Celt and Saxon*, Cambridge, 210-50.
—— (1965) *Anglo-Saxon Architecture*, Cambridge.

Thacker, A.T. (1985) 'Kings, saints, and monasteries in pre-Viking Mercia', *Midland History* 10, 1-25.
—— (1987) 'Anglo-Saxon Cheshire', VCH Cheshire I, 237-85.
Thirsk, Joan (1964) 'The common fields', *Past and Present* 29, 3-25.
Thomas, C. (1971) *The Early Christian Archaeology of North Britain*, Oxford.
—— (1981) *Christianity in Roman Britain to A.D.500*, London.
Todd, M. (1981) *Roman Britain 55 BC-AD 400*, Glasgow.
Vince, A. (1988) 'Did they use pottery in the Welsh Marches and the West Midlands between the 5th and 12th centuries AD?', in *From Roman Town to Norman Castle: Essays in Honour of Philip Barker*, ed. A. Burl, Birmingham, 40-55.
Vincent, A. (1937) *Toponymie de la France*, Brussels.
Wacher, J. (1975) *The Towns of Roman Britain*, London.
Wainwright, F.T. (1948) 'Ingimund's Invasion', *EHR* April 1948, 147-69.
Watson, W.J. (1926) *The History of the Celtic Place-names of Scotland*, Edinburgh.
Webster, G. (1975) *The Cornovii*, London.
White, R.H. (1988) 'Viking-period sculpture at Neston, Cheshire', *Chester Archaeological Society Journal* 69 (1986), 45-58.
Whitehead, D.A. (1980) *Hereford City Excavations* Vol. 1, CBA Research Report 36.
—— (1982) 'The historical background to the city defences', in Shoesmith 1982, 13-24.
Whitelock, D. (1955) *English Historical Documents I c.500-1042*, London.
Whybra, J. (1990) *A Lost English County: Winchcombshire in the Tenth and Eleventh-Centuries*, Woodbridge.
Williams, Ann (1982) '*Princeps Merciorum gentis*: the family, career and connections of Ælfhere, ealdorman of Mercia, 956-83', *ASE* 10, 143-72.
—— (1986) '"Cockles amongst the wheat": Danes and English in the western midlands in the first half of the eleventh century', *Midland History* 11, 1-22.
Williams, I. (1932) 'The Poems of Llywarch Hen', *Proceedings of the British Academy* 18, 269-302.
Wilson, D. (1985) 'A note on *hearg* and *wēoh* as place-name elements representing different types of pagan Saxon worship sites', *Anglo-Saxon Studies in Archaeology and History* 4, 179-83.
Wormald, P. (1982) 'Offa's Dyke', in Campbell 1982, 120-1.
Wrander, N. (1983) *English Place Names in the Dative Plural*, Lund Studies in English 65.
Wright, R.P. and Jackson, K.H. (1968) 'A late inscription from Wroxeter', *AntiqJ* 48, 269-300.
Yalden, D.W. (1987) 'The natural history of Domesday Cheshire', *The Naturalist* Vol. 112, no. 983, 125-31.

Index

Counties, which are the pre-1974 units, are designated by the following abbreviations.

p.n. el. = place-name element. Occurrences of place-names on maps have not been indexed.